To Jean,
    Best wishes,
        Sadie Penzato

Growing up Sicilian & female

In America, in a Small town, in the Thirties.

by Sadie Penzato

Bedford Graphics, Inc.,
Publisher, New York

For

Paula Stellefson, my daughter,
and in memory of John Paul,
my son.

Acknowledgments

*F*or helping me to bring this book to fruition my greatest thanks and appreciation go to my daughter Paula and to Louis Roban, both of whom gave me those most precious gifts, time and freedom. Thanks: to Caroline, Joey and Frankie for their encouragement, memories and feedback about our family life; to Mildred Starin, Mary Pagano, Tom Porfidio and Toni Ambasciani, dear friends, for their undying faith and patience; to my editor Rose Kernan, who was midwife for this book; to my close friend Silvia Flynn for her work on the design of the cover; to yet more friends, Rosemary Lyons, and Rita Perretta who listened, read and encouraged me with their praise, and to Earl C. Joslen, a true entrepreneur, for being there when I needed help in publishing. My last thanks go to all others, Sicilian and otherwise, who gave unconditional support and affection.

Introduction

*T*his book was a story waiting to be written. When I sat down and began, it was as though someone else was dictating to me. (Someone else was! The child in me. Every one of us has a valid story to tell.) While putting down, in black and white, that which has lain dormant within me for so many years, I made many insightful discoveries. At the start, the most vivid memories were those concerning prejudice and name calling. My hatred for my father was also a vivid memory. I had planned those themes as a major part of this story. However, the prejudice became less important, almost minor, as other memories began flooding my mind. And, like him or not, to my surprise, my father became the central character.

Writing is a form of catharsis and it helped me to learn about myself, my family and what it means to be of Sicilian-American extraction and to grow up in America. It helped me understand my father.

We humans are such complex organisms that there is never any clear, precise answer to "why?" Genes or environment? Many things have much to do with how we cope, find joy, and achieve goals. My wish is that as you read this book, glimmers of memories, more good than bad, rush back and help you re-live them. Childhood is universal. Thus, non-Sicilians too, will see themselves in this book.

The use of cliches and proverbs at the end of some of the chapters is not accidental. They sum up what I want to convey. Some believe cliches are an excuse for not thinking. Perhaps, for they are corny, but "Corn is another word for truth." Professor G. Scott Wright said that to me many years ago, and I have never forgotten it.

My spelling of the Sicilian dialogue may distress some. My writing of this foreign language is self-taught. I was grateful for help in editing from Josephine Marsiglio, a fellow Sicilian female. Her father and my father lived in adjoining villages in the central mountains of Sicily. Unfortunately, each town and village has its own tongue and as such, uniformity in spelling is impossible. In some instances I wrote words the way I remember them being spoken. I also referred to *Arba Sicula*, a literary Sicilian journal, printed semi-annually, filled with various Sicilian dialects and edited by Dr. Gaetano Cipolla of St. John's University in Jamaica. It was of great help.

Table of Contents

1. *The First Day*   1

2. *The House*   21

3. *Miss Loselle*   29

4. *Suzy's House*   43

5. *Mamma's Tree*   63

6. *Tanti Cosi*   85

7. *Educashe' and Food*   99

8. *The City*   113

9. *Spring Flowers and
     Memorial Day*   117

10. *Jello and
     The Summer Kitchen*   127

11. *The Movies*   133

12. *Campfires and Camaraderie*   159

13. *The Bennetts and Dolls*   165

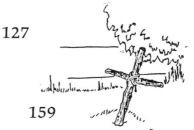

Table of Contents

14. Roots, Winter and Hygiene   171

15. Storms and Prayers   179

16. Frankie and Cold Hands   189

17. Beauty and Virginity   197

18. Guilt and Conscience   211

19. Caroline   225

20. Papa   235

21. The Twenty Cent Career   251

22. The Red Haurachies   263

23. Worlds Fair and
    Bowery Bums   275

24. The Prom   287

25. War and Leaving   297

26. The Last Summer   309

Mama's Sicilian Receipes   315

1939

chapter 1

The First Day

*M*emories. From an early point in life, until its end, memories enrich us, teach us, and, if we let them, sometimes destroy us. They can serve to recreate a time and place, a human "time machine", if you will. Carried with us, they fill our hearts and minds and transport us to wherever we choose to go. Sometimes they intrude and give us no choice. Whether good or bad, memories are voyages the heart takes. As such, I think back to my early years spent growing up on a magnificent farm in upstate New York. Some experiences stand out in contrast to others. For me, one day in particular was one of those special times.

It began on an unusually hot September morning as I waited, impatient, for the bus to arrive. I was sweaty from excitement. Across the street my house stood–serene, elegant, and beautiful, at least on the outside. Gazing up at it, I was filled with warm comfortable feelings. They calmed me a little. Since I was only six years old, the arrival of the bus seemed an eternity away. It was actually due to arrive in a few minutes. To pass the time, I began to hop about, first on one foot and then the other. Doing so felt good and helped me get rid of the kind of creepy feelings I was starting to get as I thought about getting on that bus. Never having been on one before, well, it was scary! Standing there, peering anxiously far off towards Forest Glenn Road where the highway curved, I knew I would be the first to see the bus as it approached. Suddenly, there it was, far off in the distance. "It's coming, it's coming!" I screeched and started jumping up and down. Waves of anticipation and excitement washed over me.

"Cut that out or I'll smack you!" my fifteen-year-old brother Benny growled. Although gentle by nature, being the eldest he often tried to imitate Papa. Doing so sometimes made him seem bossy and intimidating, especially at those times when he gruffly ordered the rest of us around or cuffed those of us who did not move quickly enough to suit him. As the first-born male in the family he got away with murder. "It's only a school bus. You act like you're going to heaven, for Chris'sake. It's only school!"

From a safe distance, I made a face at him and then kept jumping up and down. Suddenly, I felt a hand clamp firmly but gently on my shoulder. Without even looking I knew that firm hand belonged to my sister Caroline. You just didn't fool around with her. Caroline was tough and sometimes mean, but only if you got her mad. Even though she was only fourteen, she wasn't afraid of anybody, not even Papa. Caroline got hit a lot.

After she grabbed my shoulder in that way, I, just as nice as you please, walked slowly toward the road and waited quietly. As the bus came closer and closer, I could feel my self getting almost sick to my stomach! I wondered why? The bus lumbered toward me and slowed down as it prepared to stop. All at once I could feel my heart pounding loudly against my ribs. In fact, it sounded so loud to me that I glanced about to see if others could hear it. I was surprised that they couldn't.

They all stood quietly, almost stoically, waiting for the bus to stop. Suddenly, a weird idea filled me with such anticipation that I forgot the funny pain in the pit of my stomach. Standing a bit closer to the road than the others, I squeezed my eyes shut and willed the bus driver to stop directly in front of me. When I heard the bus get close enough so that I could see the driver, opening my eyes I concentrated and gazed directly at him. He gazed back. The bus stopped and the door opened precisely in front of where I was standing. "My God, it worked!" All at once I could feel my face get hot and flushed. It felt almost worse than the waiting and made me dread having to mount the steps. Holding back, I wanted the others to get on before me. Angrily I thought to myself, "It worked! It sure did! But what a dumb thing to do, stupid! Now you'll be the first one on and everybody will stare at you."

I hesitated a moment longer. Then reaching up and grabbing the chrome handrail, hoisted myself onto the high first step of the big gray bus, with the number eleven on its side. Boarding the school bus marked a very special point in time in my life; one I had looked forward to and dreamed about for almost as long as I could remember. It was the start of my first day of school.

School! It was a magical word, filled with exciting promises. School! It was a place where you could learn to read, to discover the meaning of all those tiny black marks that filled pages next to and below the exciting pictures in books and comics. School! It was a place to play where there were lots of other kids. Most of all it was a place where, in order to go there, you had to wash and get dressed in your best clothes.

It seemed to me that I had been waiting forever to "go to school." Each morning when my brothers and sister got up, prepared for, and then went off to classes, I often wanted to cry because they always left me behind. It was lonely being the baby of the family by five years. Living on the farm, far from the village, I rarely had playmates my age. Of course, there was always Mama, but she wasn't some kid with whom I could play Tag or Hide 'n Seek.

Mama was an excellent seamstress. Before school started, many days had been spent sewing on the old Singer treadle sewing machine in order to get me ready for school. For what seemed like hours, my mother fitted homemade cut out newspaper patterns on me. From them, she then cut the cloth for the dresses. I had never had the "luxury"of a store-bought dress. Store-bought clothes were considered too expensive and not that well made! Because of this, she sewed most of the family clothes.

3

Standing there, being fitted for those pesky patterns, I started to think about the last time she had taken me to the city and I started to fidget. This annoyed her. *"Serina! Sta'ti piu cuiatu, masenno, t'aya pungidi c'un punzoni."* (Sadie, hold still, otherwise I may stick you with one of these pins.) The slight prick of a pin and Mama's sharp reprimand made me hold absolutely still so she could finish pinning the newspaper pattern on my body and make adjustments. I guess fitting a pattern on the body of a fidgety little kid without sticking her with a pin is no mean feat. It seems, when asked to hold still for more than ten seconds, I always developed a really urgent itch! Yet, no matter how bad, I endured the discomfort of not scratching. Mama was known for her saintly patience except for when it came time to fit her homemade patterns on someone. Then she would brook no interference; no twitching, no sneezing, and no movement at all on the part of the person being fitted.

It was boring. Having to stand motionless more than two minutes was pure torture. And being forced to stay in the sewing room for all those hours that it took to make a dress! I had to be constantly available. First, so Mama could try the dress on me as it was being sewn together to be sure of proper fit and second, so I could thread the sewing machine needle whenever the thread broke. Mama couldn't see the eye of the needle and eye glasses were expensive.

Finally, Mama finished my school wardrobe. So there I was, weeks later, climbing aboard the bus, wearing my favorite dress. It was red and white flowered rayon, shiny and trimmed with lace and bows. A very large, matching red ribbon sat atop my short black hair which was combed in a bowl cut with bangs. Somewhere on Orchard Street, for a few cents, Mama had purchased a huge box filled with round paper spools, each of which was partially filled with a different colored ribbon. From such a wide assortment, she was assured of colored ribbons to match what ever outfit I might be wearing. I believe Mama had some sort of fixation about ribbons since she rarely let me out of the house without one tied round my head. She, of course, thought they made me look prettier. That was debatable. Anyway, I was a tomboy and really hated those ribbons!

4

On that first day of school, Mama and Caroline fussed and fussed, tied and retied the ribbon until it suited them. Grimacing and fidgeting as the two of them clucked and fussed over me, I felt like a Christmas present. The bangs of my black hair formed little "J's" on my forehead where Mama had wet them and then slid the teeth of the comb gently along their bottom, in one direction. I was crazy about the look of those curved bangs. My greatest wish was to have curly hair since mine was straight as a nail. Those funny curved bangs were the closest I came, at that time, to curly or wavy hair. Of course, by the time I got to school, the bangs would have dried and would hang down poker straight again to my eyebrows. Mama had not learned that one could add sugar to the water and make hair stiff for hours. I always envied Caroline, who had such a head of curls that her nickname was "bushel-head," a name she loathed. Oddly enough, and nature being what it is, Caroline longed for hair as straight as mine. I learned early that we often want what we do not or cannot have.

Back to the bus. After hoisting myself up, upon reaching the top step, I started down the aisle, eyes searching for an empty place to sit. By now, painfully self conscious, I was aware of everyone staring at me and at what I was wearing. My heart had been pounding from the moment that the bus had approached and then stopped. As I proceeded down the aisle it was still dancing wildly inside my chest. My throat felt dry. I gulped a bit.

All at once, above the hum of regular conversation, I heard some snickers and assumed that they were directed at me. My face reddened. Blood began pounding in my temples. It made me almost giddy. I wanted to turn and run off the bus but knew that was impossible. Head and eyes down, to avoid looking at those who were staring at me, I continued toward the rear of the bus. As I passed a seat near the middle, I heard a loud whisper that seemed directed toward me.

"WOP!"

Startled, I turned my head toward where the sound had come from and saw the person right away. Perplexed, I stared, thinking, "Is she talking to me? What did she say? 'WOP'?

She said 'WOP'? What a funny word and from such a funny looking little girl!"

There on an aisle seat, scowling and staring back at me was a red-haired, freckle-faced girl, about ten years old who had a wide mouth, thin lips, and slightly bulgy, pale blue eyes. Baffled, I continued to stare intently at the girl who had whispered. Noting her funny face, I started to smile and continued down the aisle. Putting my hand up to my mouth I tried to stifle a giggle, but couldn't. It wasn't a kind thought, but the moment I saw her, that bulgy-eyed girl reminded me of the bulgy-eyed bullfrogs that sat croaking on rocks in the pond in the meadow. Still giggling I shook my head slightly in disbelief thinking, "Well, she looks like a frog and frogs make funny sounds. Heck, she probably wasn't talking to me anyway."

Unabashed, wishing to find a seat and never having heard the word "WOP" before, I continued down the aisle. My sister and brothers followed a short way behind. Obviously, they had not heard what she said. At the rear of the bus, we found empty seats and sat down. I sat next to a window, bouncing and sliding all over the seat. The bus rattled and creaked on protesting its heavy load all the way to school. "Gee whiz, this isn't at all what I expected," I thought to myself.

Soon I found myself staring out the window fascinated by each house each time the bus stopped to pick up students. Some of the homes were mere hovels and the kids waiting in front of them were so poorly dressed that I really felt sorry for them. I suddenly realized that maybe I should be glad Mama could sew such pretty clothes. At the same time, it made me extra glad that I lived in a nice looking house. One I didn't have to be ashamed of.

Each time the bus pulled up to where students stood waiting, I wondered if they too were feeling what I had felt as I waited for the bus. As each child came on board, I looked pointedly at them to see if they were short or fat, pretty or ugly. I was also curious as to what they were wearing. One by one they came nervously down the isle, aware of being scrutinized by everyone. Toward the end of the run, a few students had to stand.

Probably because it was the first day of school, the kids on the bus were relatively quiet and did not seem very friendly. I had eagerly looked forward, that first day, to meeting lots of kids. I imagined they would have smiling faces and there would be much talking and laughing. Similar, maybe, to the kind of loud talk and laughter such as when the "boarders" came to stay at our house at the beginning of the summer season. The "boarders" consisted of carloads of Italian and Sicilian families from Manhattan, Brooklyn, Queens, and the Bronx. For a few dollars a week they could vacation at the big house Papa had purchased a few years earlier at the height of the depression. Some of my happiest times and memories derive from those summers when the boarders filled our house. Growing up on a farm was such an extraordinary and wonderful time. Sharing it with others made it that much better.

It was like a party that lasted all summer long. There was continuous conversation, there was laughter, there was singing, there was dancing, and joke playing. The warmth, fun, and noise of those times permeated the house. It overflowed with happy, boisterous people. This made me feel that it truly was the "best of times." In retrospect, to live in a house filled with joy and laughter was certainly a positive experience. Those positive feelings helped alleviate the painful ones.

As the bus entered the town limits I was totally absorbed and fascinated by the number and variety of houses now so close together. It was hard to imagine living that close to other people. I reasoned that the neighbors could probably hear everything that was going on next door. Shuddering at the thought, I knew how embarrassing it would feel, having other people listening in on those times when Papa went into a rage. Often he would become infuriated over some seemingly minor thing. When he did so, he would shout and loudly curse, sometimes beating us. Just thinking about it gave me a sinking feeling and I shook my head slowly from side to side. Rolling my eyes upward I thanked God I did not live that close to other people. It was bad enough when he acted that way around the boarders!

7

At the corner, the bus slowly turned to the right and started slowly up a hill, past the rectory of the Catholic church. Certain we were getting closer and closer to school, I was so excited I could hardly sit still! Then I saw it! There it was in the distance, at the top of the incline. Even from far away it looked enormous. It was made of red brick and was three stories high. I can remember staring in awe. It looked even bigger than the cow barn, the largest building on the farm which I always thought was the biggest building in the world (that is, until Mama took me to New York City for the first time).

As we approached, other buses were lined up discharging students. Soon my bus pulled into line, slowed down and then stopped in its designated place. The doors swung open and everyone rushed to get off. Some children were carrying lunch boxes, others, brown paper bags. Almost everybody toted a new pencil box or some kind of school bag.

Like many others, I, too, carried a lunch bag in one hand and with the other, clutched my most prized possession to my chest. My new, red pencil box. For the first time in my life, I had art supplies, real stuff to draw with. That red box held all of the items with which I could make pictures–colored pencils and pencils with erasers. It also had a small, red, rectangular, hand-held pencil sharpener, a ruler, and a few other things that puzzled me. I didn't know what to do with them. One item was an odd looking half-circle of thin, flat shaped metal with numbers on it. Another puzzlement was a narrow tubular, silver-colored object that was hinged at its V-shaped middle. One side ended in a really sharp point and the other side had a round small pencil clipped to it. I never used those oddly shaped items. It was quite a while later that I finally learned what they were. Early on, I just wasn't curious.

What I enjoyed most of all was that for the first time in my life I had long pencils. Ones that had never even been sharpened. That came as a surprise because up until then I had only seen pencils that already had points. I thought that is how they all came. In the past, any pencils I had been given were mere stubs with flat, worn down erasers. I would bite the end of the metal casings at the base of the pencil, crushing it so that the eraser would protrude and be used to its fullest.

I reveled in the luxury of using new pencils and especially appreciated the small pencil sharpener. Now I no longer had to use one of Mama's kitchen knives to sharpen pencil points. Even more fun were the colored pencils which I used on the drawings that I made of all sorts of things - especially horses and people. Everything that caught my attention or stimulated my imagination was captured on paper. Drawing was my escape, my joy, and eventually my salvation.

Holding tight to my possessions, I was the last one off the bus. Caroline turned, and taking the big brown bag in one hand and my small hand in the other, helped me hop off the high last step. Together we marched up the broad front steps and to the main entrance of the school. Here and there a teacher stood, pointing or giving directions. Surrounded by the swirling hordes of children streaming into the building, I felt overwhelmed. It all made me feel very small and very unimportant.

Entering the large, double, wide-open front doors of the school, we found ourselves in the lobby. Its walls, visible above the heads of the crowd were faced with black marble. The floor of white marble extended to the right and to the left forming long corridors that led to classrooms. Still holding my hand, Caroline turned right, following other children, some with parents. The two of us continued down what seemed an endless hallway. It was lined with metal locker doors, broken at intervals by doorways to class rooms.

Just before the very end of the corridor we turned left into an open doorway and entered. There was a sign on the door, *Kindergarten, Miss Tomkins.* Caroline paused just inside, waiting for the teacher to acknowledge her. Meanwhile I peered out from behind the safety of my sister's skirt. I could not believe what I saw and remember thinking to myself, "This must be what Heaven is like!" I felt I was quite familiar with Heaven since Mama was always talking about it, and telling me how beautiful and wonderful it was. Before now, however, I had never been able to really picture it in my head.

I stood and stared. The kindergarten room had tall, graceful windows that rose to the ceiling from a bay area. At its base were built-in window seats padded in a cheerful chintz print.

9

Small tables with little matching chairs filled half the room. The other half of the room was a large empty area for play. Boxes with partly open lids, overflowing with toys, lined one whole wall.

From a desk in the back of the room, a very pretty, petite woman in a lovely print dress and wearing black, open-toed shoes approached us, smiling. Looking at her I found myself staring at her feet! Never before had I seen shoes with holes in their toes. Then, glancing up at her face, I thought it really odd that this lady had red, red lips and cheeks. Lipstick or rouge were foreign to me and I was surprised at her brightly colored face. The contrast made her skin appear even whiter than it really was. Her hair was dark and curled.

In a firm, friendly voice she said, "Hello Caroline, this must be Sadie!" I winced and felt my body stiffen, like when you get ready when you know you are going to get a good slap or whack. Then I thought to myself, "Oh, how I hate my name. It is so ugly, 'Sadie', I hate it, I hate it! It sounds ugly!" As far as I was concerned, nobody else I knew was named Sadie. There were lots of Maries, Anns, Pattys, Janes, Josephines, and Margies. It had always seemed to me that my name was something in my life that made me somewhat different from others and added to my misery over the difference.

Because of my name, I hated to meet people. They would always say, "And what is *your* name?" Invariably I expected them to laugh, and invariably they did. Crimson with embarrassment I heard them say each time, "Sadie? Your name is Sadie? How did a little Sicilian girl get a funny Jewish name like Sadie?" Many years later I learned how and it became one of my favorite stories.

By now, Miss Tompkins had squatted down and was at eye level with me. We stared at each other for what seemed a long time. Her face was very close to my face and I wondered why she smelled like flowers. Uncomfortable in being stared at, I pulled back a little, against my sister's skirt. I felt my face flush and grow warm. Fidgeting, I wanted to look away, but feared the teacher might take it as a sign of disrespect.

My father had admonished me often in the weeks and days before school started. "Iffa you no be gooda in'a school, 'n you getta hit by the teach', whena you geta home, you getta real good licken. *Ti rhumbu le coshi,* (I'll break your legs) ifa you no lissen to you teach'. She be lika me o' you Mama ana you do whata she say. 'N neva', neva' tell a lie, ana you watcha you good name. You loosa you good name, you no canna buy it back *capice?* (understand?)"

My father often spoke to me partly in broken English and partly in Sicilian. Perhaps he believed I could understand more fully if he interjected some English words occasionally. Listening to him, I had nodded respectfully and silently. Papa often referred to honor and especially to respect for one's elders. To be a person of honor, a person who kept his or her word despite all odds, a person who would never cheat or lie or steal, that was the ideal. Papa stressed that a good name, once lost, could not be purchased, that it was your most valuable possession. Anyone with a "bad name" was considered an outcast, probably never again to be respected by the family. No one could honor someone who brought disgrace upon the family. Like a sponge, I soaked up whatever was told to me. I had been totally indoctrinated and taught to unquestioningly believe all of Papa's and Mama's opinions and beliefs. Their beliefs were to guide my actions and my life for a long time. Those actions sometimes caused me to suffer pain and frustration.

During my twenties, I led a sheltered, mundane life. Surrounded by people who shared my views, not until I started college at the age of thirty-one, did I learn that not everyone had been brought up with my stringent ideas of right and wrong, good and bad. As I became enlightened, I was, in turn, shocked, dismayed, and greatly surprised. Despite doubts, I still clung to many of those deeply ingrained beliefs. My behavior led some to believe me naive or ignorant. To my chagrin there were many times when I was. It took me many, many years to finally understand that reality, in truth, falls far short of the ideal. That human beings can err, can break all the "rules" and the world does not come to an immediate end.

Miss Tomkins stood, took my hand and led me to where some children were playing. She turned, smiled, and waved to Caroline, dismissing her. Caroline stood and waited for me to look back and wave goodby. Engrossed and curious about my surroundings I completely forgot her. Disappointed, Caroline turned, shrugged her shoulders and walked out of the Kindergarten door, heading for her own class room, two flights up.

At school, the days passed by and every day seemed more wonderful and exciting than the one before. As each morning dawned, I could not wait to get up, get dressed, and go off to Kindergarten. Even at that early age, clothes suddenly became much more important than merely to cover of one's body. Soon, as with many other children in my class, I became unduly aware of who wore what. It started to become a sort of measure of "success" to be dressed nicely so that others noticed.

What with dressing up in proper clothes each day, with learning to read, write, paint, and draw, with having stories read aloud, with eating cookies and milk at snack time and with having friends and toys to play with, it did seem to me that I had indeed "died and gone to heaven". I discovered that I enjoyed going to school far more than anything else I had done in my short life.

Each day in class seemed to be a marvelous new adventure. I had made many friends and was quite happy about that. Usually, I hated to see the school day end for I knew as I rode back to the farm on the school bus, that I would have to change into ugly old work clothes and get to work on my hated chores. Although I loved my family very much, life outside of school seemed dreary and colorless.

In life, there is always good and bad. Although no one had made any nasty ethnic remarks to me since that first day of school, my sister and brothers were not so lucky. During those early years at school, we were aware of the animosity of many of the town's people. It came in the form of dirty looks, mumbled insults, and sometimes outright physical abuse. These "looks" and attacks occurred sometimes on the bus and often on the school grounds. A few times a month, my brothers and often my sister came home, bruised and occasionally bleeding from fights that had ensued over having been called "guineas," "wops," "dagos," and "spaghetti benders." Despite, or possibly because of, her tough veneer, Caroline especially, seemed to have been picked on even more than the others. Often, two, sometimes three, girls ganged up on her in the bathroom and had "beaten her up" for being "Eyetalian."

For some reason, I experienced much less of the kind of pain my siblings endured. However, in due time I did have a few encounters with prejudice. My most memorable encounter of that nature came about a few years after I entered Kindergarten, when I was around eight years old. That unexpected incident marred my love of school and helped shape my viewpoint of the "other" world for quite a long time. The "other" was composed of those native villagers whom my family referred to as "Yankees." (In later years, in college, I learned about WASP, an acronym for white Anglo-Saxon Protestants. Sadly, we do have our share of pejorative terms with which to address one another.) "Other" also encompassed those with different ethnic roots–Poles, Irish, Dutch, but not counting Italians, of course. There seems to be some controversy over whether or not Sicilians are Italians. What is the difference between Italians and Sicilians? Is an Irishman British? Is a Corsican French? A Sicilian is a Sicilian!

Unfortunately, for many years, and to some degree even today, as an ethnic group, Sicilians were looked down upon by many Italians who live north of them (starting with Calabria). This behavior seems especially true of many northern Italians, who, it seems, "look down" upon all of those who reside south of Rome. (I speak from experience!) Even some Romans probably feel the brunt of this provincial form of prejudice. This patronizing attitude tends to make those from the south, especially the Sicilians, more than a little defensive, positively feisty, and inordinately proud. Thus, meeting with the prejudice of a small American town came as no real surprise to my Sicilian family.

It was the last day of apple picking season and Papa had decreed that everyone was needed at home to work that day. Mortified at missing school, I cried as if my heart was breaking. (The tears came more at the thought of the physical labor involved in staying home rather than missing school.) My father, who was usually inured to tears pretended to be convinced of my love of learning. Grudgingly, he let me go to school and off I went, all by myself.

That morning, as I stood waiting for the bus to approach from Forest Glenn Road, I felt a small shiver of apprehension. I couldn't understand why or explain it. There seemed to be a small voice somewhere deep inside warning me to be aware and to be very careful. About what, I did not know. It occurred to me that this would be one of those few times that I would be boarding the bus all by myself. Perhaps that was the reason for the strange feelings of uneasiness flooding my senses. I thought to myself, "Sure, that's what it is. Heck, I hardly ever get on the bus alone. Somebody's always with me. Yea, that's why I feel funny, 'cause I'll be all by myself today." Comforted by my rationalization I soon felt better.

Far off in the distance, near Forest Glenn Road, I could see "old number 11" rounding the curve and approaching. It drew closer and closer. As I waited for the bus to pull up to where I stood, I played my little game of staring at the driver and willing him to stop where I wanted. It always seemed to work and I was waiting for the time it wouldn't. This was it! To my chagrin, the bus skidded to a halt just a bit past where I was standing. I had to take a few steps before reaching the door. It seemed an ominous sign. I could feel my heart begin to beat faster as feelings of apprehension washed over me. The door creaked open and I quickly mounted the bus steps.

When I reached the top, I looked down the aisle for a place to sit and spied a seat halfway to the rear of the bus. I strode toward it and just as I reached it, the bus started up with a lurch. I lost my balance and unceremoniously plopped down so hard onto the seat that I almost bounced off again. As I settled back on the seat, I warily noted that the person seated next to me was a squat, plump sixth grader named Wilda. Wilda was the older sister of the "frog-faced" girl who had whispered that strange word to me on that first day of school. That memorable day now seemed so long ago that I had just about forgotten the incident. I do however, remember asking at home and learning that "WOP" was not a very nice thing to call someone.

14

Wilda was a rather solitary, unfriendly girl who rarely smiled or said hello. I seriously considered changing my seat. But no, Wilda might wonder why and feel bad if I did that. I did not want to offend her so I just stayed where I was. That little voice I had discovered just that morning was telling me to merely murmur hello, look straight ahead, and mind my own business.

The bus was picking up speed. As it did, my small, skinny, frame was jounced about. Suddenly, I felt Wilda's hip whack against mine. It was a strong deliberate move on her part and it sent me flying off the seat and onto the floor with a loud thump. I felt my body hit the floor at the same time that the side of my head struck the metal leg frame of the opposite seat. It all really hurt and I let out a howl of pain. Looking up, puzzled and angry I asked, "Hey! What'ja do that for?"

Seeing my pain and bewilderment, Wilda's broad, mean face broke into a wide smile. Her rather large teeth were coated with a yellowish film and her cruel eyes were screwed up and looking like tiny slits. Throwing back her head, she let go an ugly laugh and then glared down at me, ignominiously sprawled in the aisle, still in pain, looking surprised and helpless.

Triumphantly she said, "That'll fix you, you little Wop, spaghetti bender! You think you're so hot, well, you ain't nuthin' but a dumb dago! You and yer stupid black guinea famb'ly. Yea, we don't want yer kind around. Go back to New York, where you belong!" Licking her lips and relishing her moment of victory, she looked exultantly around at everyone on the bus. Not all, but a few children clapped. Someone whistled. Looking up at her, I was astonished at the intensity of hatred in her eyes, aglow with victory.

I was aware that many of the kids on the bus were laughing. Worse yet, they were not only laughing but pointing at me as well. Some were still clapping their hands in glee. There were no big brothers or a big sister to defend me. All at once, I felt completely alone and vulnerable. Tears welled and spilled; tears not simply from the pain of my head hitting the metal leg. Wilda's cruel words had bitten deeply. My heart felt numb. My dignity was shattered! It was my first experience of being humiliated in public in that particular way. Suddenly, from out of nowhere, I remembered my father's words. I realized that my "honor" had been challenged. I could lose my "good name" and be considered a coward. The thought was devastating. I could not allow that to happen to me. For a moment more I lay there and pondered that thought as I tried to pull myself together.

The bus driver looked straight ahead and said nothing. The bus rattled on with the children on board still laughing and pointing to my prone figure sprawled in the isle. Perhaps many were glad to see me, a foreigner among them, put down in this way. Perhaps some of them thought that maybe now those "dagos" and "guineas" wouldn't act so "uppity." Perhaps some of them felt sorry for me. Perhaps some didn't care one way or another.

For the few short moments that I lay there, many thoughts rushed through my head. Before I could even begin to sort them out, from somewhere deep within my gut I felt a surge of fury rise. It was hard and cold as a blade of steel. Strangely enough it was the same kind of anger and frustration I felt when my father, sister, or brothers punished me if I did not immediately obey their commands. Because of those sometimes actual and sometimes imagined injustices, frustration and anger had probably been building inside of me for a long time.

It was unthinkable to strike back at those in the family who angered me. Besides, I was unable to, since I was the smallest and least powerful. But I knew full well that I could strike back at this, this mean, ugly person who had purposely hurt and humiliated me in front of everyone. Although small and thin, I was strong and quick. From wrestling with my brothers at play I had become adept at wriggling out of almost any hold they could devise. Only my oldest brother, Benny, could really hold me down without hurting me and make me "give up."

Wilda's laugh turned to a shriek as I "flew" up from the floor and pounced on her. Straddling her solid, thick figure, I quickly grabbed both of her ears and holding on to them firmly, angrily began to pound the surprised girl's head against the back of the seat. To protect herself and to fight back,

Wilda quickly reached out, her fingers groping on my face, seeking to gouge or scratch my eyes. As her searching fingers clawed at my face, I suddenly felt Wilda's thumb on my cheek. Turning my head toward it, I opened my mouth and quickly bit down as hard as I could. CRUNCH! I could taste warm blood as my teeth clamped firmly on Wilda's errant thumb. I held on tightly! In my anger, I would probably have bitten it right down to the bone had not two husky boys rushed to pry me off the gyrating body of the screaming girl. As they tried to pull me off, I refused to let go, hissing at Wilda through bloody, clenched teeth, "You give up, you give up?"

"Yes, yes!" screamed Wilda. Amazingly, the bus driver drove calmly on. He had learned long ago that unless death seemed imminent, it was best to let kids fight their own battles. As the boys finally dragged me away, kicking and screaming, eyes wild, teeth bloody, I spat out, "You call me dirty names; "wop," "spaghetti-bender," "guinea!" I'm more of an American than you are! I'm no damn Yankee, hating everybody except damn Yankees, 'n pickin' on little kids. I'm not mean and rotten like you. You're not a REAL American. A *REAL AMERICAN* wouldn't do that. You STINK! An' I was born here in America, just like you! If you ever call me anything like that again I'll kill you! Or my brothers will, you hear me? I'll kill you... you... you damn Yankee you!!"

In my rage and frustration, I was just repeating, in part, what I had heard my parents say when my brothers and sister had come home from school or other places disheartened and furious over ethnic slurs. Often they were bruised, sometimes beaten by fellow classmates. At times, the insults came covertly from teachers, overtly from other adults. Helpless and ignorant in the face of intolerance, my parents tried as best they could to lessen their children's pain and rage at being the victims of taunts, cruelty and injustice.

I am convinced that research would prove, in no uncertain terms, that some of the most bitter, frustrating and vexing feelings of hatred, futility, inferiority, and inadequacy can emerge from the experience of having to cope with rejection and derision directed toward one's self because of the accident of birth. The feelings of injustice are especially painful since race is a factor over which one has absolutely no control. Because of my family's encounters with discrimination and bias, the pain suffered in those formative years left its mark on us. For a long time thereafter, our relationships with some adults and some fellow classmates and students on the bus evolved into an "us-verses-them" mentality.

That evening around the supper table when I described in great detail my "battle"and victory over an older and larger adversary, my family was delighted and congratulated me on my brave actions. Vengeance and prowess at fighting were a great part of the mentality of growing up Sicilian, male or female. As children we were taught that we should never start a fight, but if challenged or insulted, we had to fight and strive to win at any cost! The deeply ingrained belief that your "honor" was a most precious commodity and to have it sullied in even a minor way and not defend it was the behavior of a coward. You defended yourself, regardless of the size of your antagonist. Better to fight and be beaten bloody, than to turn away like a "sissy."

Fighting was considered an honorable activity and a way to develop cunning, show superiority, and power. Whenever possible, you *never* let anyone get the better of you, whether in an argument or in a fight. On the other hand, you revered age and wisdom. If an older person said or did anything insulting or mean, you would not reply. You would withdraw as respectfully and as gracefully as possible, avoiding offense to the older person, no matter how much you wished to retaliate. Only a clod would answer back, strike, or attack an elder NO MATTER WHAT! There was a whole litany of unwritten laws concerning the ages of those involved in confrontation. Your peers were to be dealt with severely if they started a fight. However, anyone wearing a uniform or badge of authority was to be treated with deference and respect–that meant a policeman, a teacher, a priest or nun, a principal or anyone "in charge." Respect was highly revered and not to be taken lightly.

The problems my family encountered with name calling and discrimination slowly diminished over the years, but never really disappeared. (Does it ever?) Eventually, at least on the surface, things seemed better. Each year, by the end of the school term, there were fewer overt actions, probably because we had learned to defend ourselves so well. From time to time during many of those early years in New Paltz, various "incidents" continued. We felt that although prejudice was no longer as visible at "the table" it was still there in a "pot" at the back of the stove, simmering and waiting to spill out again. My family resigned itself to the fact that there would always be a few people who would dislike us and would always consider us foreigners. Being Sicilian was something we could not escape, nor did we try. We learned early in life that no matter how we strove to win the approval of "certain" people, because we were "different," we would always be on the outside looking in. In time, we also learned that such an attitude was confined not only to New Paltz, it could be found everywhere, in *any* town or city.

Therefore, despite those early, unpleasant, and hurtful experiences, my memories of New Paltz and its people are good. I learned to love the town in which I grew up. I also learned to love many of the people in it. It was a place rich in things that help form roots, strong relationships, and loyalty. Maybe at first some ignorant people were cruel and insensitive, but in time, there were so many more who were kind, helpful, and caring.

I still think of it as "my home town."

chapter 2

The House

*O*ur house was magnificent, huge and glorious, painted pure white with dark green shutters. The paint was peeling a little, here and there, but basically the structure was in very good condition. It wasn't until many years later at college, during a course in American architecture, that I realized and appreciated the fact that I had grown up in an exquisite and classic example of a Greek Revival house. It had been built early in the nineteenth-century. If you can recall what classic southern mansions look like, you can envision the house. An unusual feature however, was the fact that it had a Dutch roof line as did the barn roofs.

The huge front porch, facing east, had been modeled after the Parthenon. The Greek-styled pediment was held up by four, tall, graceful Doric columns. Set in the peak of the pediment was a large, fan-shaped window. A smaller, similar style porch was situated on the north side of the house. On each porch a set of wide, beautifully proportioned steps went from ground level, six steps up to the porch landings. Neither porch had handrails.

In the southeast corner of the house was my "summer" room. (When more boarders arrived than we had room for, some members of my family would have to give up their rooms and find other places to sleep.) I was assigned a cot in a small "sun" room, about six by eight feet, with enormous six-foot high windows, filling the entire east and south walls. On the narrow, west wall was a door leading to my parent's room. Two sliding pocket doors, each three feet wide, comprised the north wall. They led to a spacious room. This room (that we called the living room) must have been an office or library at one time, for on one wall, there was a floor to ceiling glass-doored bookcase with large drawers on the bottom. From this room, which was at least eighteen feet wide and sixteen feet long, another door opened to a twelve foot wide hallway. The doorways and windows had ornate trim, with low relief sculpture decorating the upper corners.

The hallway, with an arch at its halfway point, stretched about forty feet down the center of the house. It was twelve feet wide. On the left side of the hall, a long stairway with a lovely cherry-wood bannister led up to a generous landing between floors. I get positively ill when I remember how we all used to slide down that bannister and let our heels click, click, click on the beautifully turned cherry spindles as we whizzed down to the bottom. The wall of the landing, facing west, had an oval-shaped, red glass window beautifully etched with white and set in a rectangular window frame. It was probably about two by three feet in size. Looking out the window, one could get an exquisite, mono-chromatic pink-colored view of the valley. Sunsets were especially glorious. When I was still a very small child, upon reaching the landing, if accompanied by an adult, I would always ask that person to lift me up so I could look out of the rose-colored window. I distinctly remember that no matter how long they held me up to look, I never seemed to get my fill of the gorgeous pink view of the valley. It looked gloriously magical and unreal. One of my happiest memories occurred on the day that I was finally tall enough, standing on tip toe, to look out and see the view unaided. Thereafter, whenever I reached the landing I spent a great deal of time just staring out of the window at the varying shades of pink landscape and sky. It never ceased to fascinate me. Many years later, when Professor Bolotowsky, my painting professor, told me to paint a sky any color but blue, I chose pink. As I think about it now, I am certain that the rose window is the reason so many of my paintings of landscapes often have totally pink skies of many shades and hues. The heart remembers, even when the head forgets.

From this rose-window landing, steps only four inches high, and a continuation of the cherry-wood bannister led up a very short flight to the hallway on the second floor. This hallway had an enclosed stairwell leading up to the attic–huge, mysterious looking, and dimly lit by one small window at each end of the room. In contrast to the spookiness of the cellar, the attic was a benign, friendly place and I would retreat to its solitude those times when I wanted to be totally alone. It was here, under loose floor boards, where I hid my most treasured possessions. In fact, I sorted out my school papers, saving only those which were marked with "A"s. Here, I stored them for posterity. Many years later, the current owner met me. She said her little boy had found my school papers. He had come to her, papers in hand, in awe. I chuckled with delight over that, since not all my school grades had been "A"s, especially the ones in arithmetic!

There were six more bedrooms located on the second floor; four were very large, two were quite small, and each of those contained a fan-shaped window which opened out. In the summer, the entire second floor was rented, thus eliminating the bedrooms that my sister and I used during the rest of the year. After a few summers, when the boarders started coming in droves, Papa had a large bathroom installed at the end of the second floor hallway in a space that formed the pediment over the front porch.

The front door was very wide, solid wood and paneled. Narrow leaded glass windows framed the top and upper half of each side. This lovely entrance was flanked by two beautiful antique coach lamps. Originally the front door had a large shutter door attached to it, in the way that storm doors are used on houses today. Inside the house, the window sills were a foot deep. Each bedroom had a fireplace, all of which had been sealed up by the time the house had been sold to my father. The first floor consisted of many rooms–a front parlor, a back parlor, and a dining room. Across the hall from what was the library, were what could only be called "drawing rooms." Large pocket doors separated two huge and gracefully proportioned rooms. Both had wood-mantled fireplaces, both also sealed. In addition, there was the sun room, two large extra bedrooms, and a generously proportioned, ancient kitchen. In all, aside from two enormous hallways, the house had fourteen rooms.

There was neither indoor plumbing nor central heating in the house when Papa purchased it. On the counter next to the kitchen sink was a black hand pump connected to a cistern in the basement. This "plumbing" supplied all the water for "general usage." To get water for drinking and cooking, we had to go to an outside pump. It was located at the end of a thirty-foot long path, leading away from the kitchen door. Sometimes the pump had to be primed, (water was poured down an opening in its top from a reserve bucket kept nearby), after which we had to use much muscle to hand-pump the water. The harder you pumped, the faster it gushed, quickly filling one or two buckets. They were then quite heavy and carrying them back to the house was a difficult chore. In winter, if the water splashed on one's foot, it would feel almost frozen by the time one reached the kitchen door. I can still recall the icy cold, sweet taste of that water. It was especially delicious on a hot summer's day when sipped from the tin dipper that hung from a hook on the pump.

An outhouse was attached to the rear of a huge woodshed which had been added onto the main house at some earlier, unknown time. (The woodshed later became the summer kitchen under my father's stewardship of the farm.) Inside the outhouse, were not only two of the customary oval-shaped openings cut into a wide wooden ledge, but also a smaller, opening for little children. Each time I would use the outhouse, I got enormous satisfaction, a feeling that I was special since the small opening was one that only I could use. Everyone else's "butt" was too big for it. Thus, it was my "special" toilet upon which no one else in the family sat. You may think this an odd sort of satisfaction, but when few things in your surroundings ever make you feel superior in some way, any little thing that does is a milestone. An old Sears catalog was often the source of bathroom paper and lasted quite a while. When that ran out, wide strips of newspaper were piled neatly next to each seat opening. Talk about recycling! But we recycled out of economic necessity, not out of concern for the environment.

After we moved to the farm, as soon as Papa could afford it, one of the first things he did was to have a family bathroom installed downstairs. For this, he partitioned off the northeast corner of the large kitchen. I can still remember the excitement. It was like electricity and filled the air as we all watched as an honest-to-goodness bathtub was installed. In our city tenement my family had had to share a toilet with others on the same floor. The kitchen had only a large, two- bowled sink, one side much deeper than the other, designed to be used with a washboard for laundry. This deeper side had an enamel, removable top. Two sturdy legs supported the sink. The deeper sink is where I remember being bathed as a child and the rest of the family used it in that way too. Never having had a real bathroom, the installation of this shiny new bathtub, toilet and sink seemed the epitome of luxury. It made us feel grand!

Papa neither knew nor cared that he had purchased one of the finest mansions in the area. He only knew that he had gotten what he considered an excellent deal; having acquired a farm of two hundred and twelve acres for $25,000 at the height of the depression. With the land came the mansion, various barns, coops, cows, pigs, chickens, orchards, rolling meadows, ponds, and a very wide creek running through the eastern edge of the property. A smaller stream bounded the western border.

My family was blissfully unaware of the fact that many in the village felt a great deal of animosity toward us. Some of the villagers were irritated, to say the least, by our arrival. How did this alien looking foreigner, with his wife and five children "dare" to come in, (and from their point of view) "take advantage" of the widow Van Orden by buying her lovely estate. It was apparent, however, that because of bad times, the widow Van Orden could not handle the farm by herself.

Certainly, like so many others at that time, she was experiencing financial difficulties.

In 1934, which was close to, if not the height of, the depression, $25,000 was considered a fortune. My frugal Sicilian father had obtained a mortgage from Mrs. Van Orden. He had also used a local (WASP) lawyer, who was also the bank's lawyer. I believe there were others in the area, but growing up, Peter Harp's name was the only lawyer I ever heard mentioned. (An Italian lawyer in that part of the country in those days was as scarce as a Pizza parlor!) The real estate agent, Mr. Shaw was also a WASP. However, there was an Italian real estate man. An unusual one. A Mr. Delay. His father was a linguist who spoke seven languages. Well-educated and well-spoken, Mr. Delay came from Rosendale, a smaller village about seven miles north of New Paltz. Perhaps he was a northern Italian, I don't know. Neither do I know how common or uncommon illiteracy was in the sparsely populated Italian community. I only know that neither of my parents could read, in any language! I also believe that, few Italians and even fewer Sicilian immigrants were literate, even in their own tongue, at that particular niche in time. This could prove a real detriment insofar as signing contracts or mortgages. Papa brought Caroline along to read the "fine print."

Many in the village knew that doctors had told my father that if he did not move out of the city and go to live in the country he would not live very long. His bankers were aware that he was in less than excellent health. They worked out a mortgage with Mrs. Van Orden that called for a $15,000 down payment with the remaining $10,000 to be paid off in ten years. Those terms, combined with his poor health, his lack of knowledge about farming and his illiteracy, made certain people feel that he would soon be unable to make the mortgage payments. Thus, they derived comfort in the belief that eventually the bank would foreclose and he would lose the farm.

As I sit writing these words, I wonder now, from this distance in time, where my father got the courage to do what he did. Being illiterate was enough of a disadvantage, but in addition, he knew nothing about farming apples or raising vegetables. He knew even less about caring for dairy cows, pigs, and hundreds of chickens. Yet, he risked the entire amount of what he had hoarded over the years, pennies, nickles and dimes, earned from the moment he had disembarked and started work in the new world. Papa's entire life's savings were used to purchase that farm. In his fruit and vegetable store on Scamel Street in New York City my father, called *Pipino*, (Sicilian for *Giuseppi*, Joseph in English) had labored long, hard hours and saved every penny he could. When others urged him to invest in the stock market during the booming twenties, my father smiled and said no, he would double his money by folding it once and putting it in his pocket. He emerged from the great crash in excellent financial shape.

The closing for the farm was held in the dead of winter and the money for it was delivered to New Paltz by my mother. One cold December day, she and her brood of four boarded a bus in New York City, bound for the small upstate village where my father awaited her arrival. Caroline had accompanied him, to read and translate any necessary documents.

Contemplating what I am about to write, I sit in amused disbelief realizing that my mother, who was also illiterate, casually carried, *in cash*, the $15,000 down payment tucked into a big, brown paper shopping bag; the kind that had round wooden dowels attached to the paper handles. Bravely, she had carefully covered the enormous sum of money with a sweater and a dozen oranges. During the trip, she peeled a few and handed them out to her children as the bus brought them all closer and closer to the farm. She reasoned, and rightly so, that no one would ever suspect that a plump, obviously foreign and modestly dressed woman would carry such a great amount of cash in a mere brown paper shopping bag. Especially when accompanied by four children, who could be a great distraction.

From the moment Papa had arrived in America, he had a dream. He wanted some day to be very rich. Therefore, money was spent on only the barest necessities. He was an unremittingly frugal man which made him appear to be miserly. This trait became a family joke and my middle brother,

Frankie, kidded about it when Papa was out of earshot. Frankie laughingly declared "If you ask the 'old man' for a dollar it's like cutting off his left hand. Ask him for a fin, and it's like asking for his right arm." He would then chuckle and say "Jeez, ask him for more 'n he's likely to have a heart attack." We would all laugh and nod in agreement whenever Frankie made the remarks, which he did, often.

Despite his frugality, on Saturday night when I would approach and nervously ask for money to go to the movies, papa would reach into his pocket and unhesitatingly give me 15 cents, the price of admission. And even though I never asked, after a moment he would wink at me and hand me an extra 5 cents for a candy bar. He gave all of us movie and pocket money, but he had to give more to the older ones who worked much harder. He sometimes seemed to give it grudgingly. Probably, because he had to part with much more than the amount he doled out to me. Despite his frugality, we never experienced want and we certainly did not consider ourselves poor.

chapter 3

Miss Losell

Genes form us, but society adds much to our final shape. After the episode on the bus and my victory over Wilda, I changed. A new, if debatable source of strength was now at my command. Sad to say, I became a sort of a bully. The play wrestling with my brothers helped me develop real prowess and I soon discovered that it was relatively easy to knock down almost anyone in my class.

There were two exceptions–a boy of Italian decent and a very tall, blonde, blue-eyed child, the son of Papa's lawyer. His name was Edwin and for me it was love at first sight, no fooling. This love had developed sometime in the first half of my Kindergarten year, a few years prior to my bout with Wilda. I first noticed him as he stood apart from everyone, shyly watching the rest of us at play. He was much taller than any of the other children. His hair, the color of pale, polished gold, shone bright and clean as it hung down in straight bangs which framed remarkable blue eyes. Eyes fringed with incredibly long, golden lashes.

Surrounded all of my life by predominantly dark-eyed, dark haired people, blue-eyed people were a novelty. I had never seen eyes the clear, cool, almost aquamarine color my classmate possessed and I was thoroughly enchanted by them.

When my feelings of "love" first arose for him, I could not understand the strange acrobatics my heart performed–it seemed to swell with happiness whenever I glanced at him and noticed how very handsome he looked. His cheeks were softly full, round, and rosy. His tiny little nose was turned up only slightly and his rosebud-shaped, shell pink lips were full and sweetly curved. In my eyes, he was indeed the most beautiful person I had ever seen!

My feelings for him were a complete mystery to me! I could not understand why I felt this way. I only knew that what I wanted most of all was to get very close to him and stay near him as long as possible. However, sensing that this behavior was something Mamma would not approve of, I tried hard to ignore him. I could not and soon found I had no control over the lovely, pleasant feelings I experienced just being near him and just *looking* at him!

When I really thought about it, I found it odd that my feelings for him were the same pleasant feelings I experienced when eating a chocolate ice cream cone, or looking at my Shirley Temple doll, or the exhilaration I felt when riding a horse. Believe me, trying to sort out these feelings about a boy, as apposed to the other feelings of pleasure was a new and puzzling sensation.

Curious and overwhelmed, I wondered where all these peculiar feelings were coming from. Perhaps I could ask Caroline about it sometime? Maybe there were times when Caroline had funny feelings too and maybe she would be able to explain them to me. The only thing I was really certain about was that I wished that Edwin would want to be near me as much as I wanted to be near him.

However, try as I might to entice him or interest him, it was never to be! He did not appear to know I even existed and even after I offered to draw pictures for him (many pictures of anything), he would only smile faintly and walk away from me. His rejection was devastating and each time he ignored my overtures I felt pain, a kind of numbness of the heart, an empty feeling in my stomach.

Soon a sadness enveloped me. I was not quite sure what I was feeling but I knew it was the opposite of the joy I had felt previously whenever I looked at him. By now, he had reached the point where he would not even talk to me, let alone allow me near him. After a while, I found myself moping around and I did not seem to find as much fun in play and talk as before. I was, of course, too young to realize that I was feeling my first broken heart. Only a small one of course, but the first of many more to come. At that time, however, I only knew that I felt very sad when he walked away from me and ignored my attempts to be friendly.

From watching movies and listening to adult conversations, I surmised that what I had been feeling previously had been "love." "Love" was supposed to be some wonderful, joyous feeling you felt about some special person in your life. Certainly those first feelings had indeed been joyous, overwhelmingly so. I had no idea that love could also feel like this, this sort of dullness and sorrow. It had never occurred to me that sometimes you would not be loved back and that it could be hurtful. I thought hard about it. But when I tried to figure it out, I got more and more confused. Then I began to feel anger.

Well, if he didn't love me back I would "fix his wagon." We would have to fight! Yet, when I challenged him, to my chagrin, I found he was so strong that none of the special tripping tricks my brothers had taught me would make him fall down.

Besides, he was much too gentle and after our first encounter, which I, of course, had instigated, he refused to fight. He would say "Heck, I ain't gonna fight with some dumb girl!" After that he would frown or scowl and walk away whenever he saw me coming. Thoroughly frustrated, I finally learned to get over my anger and soon he again was just another one of my classmates. Such is the power of love and the value of experience.

We have a tendency to think of little children as asexual, when in fact some of the first and strongest feelings of love, emotion, and even sexual arousal can often come in the primary years of one's life. Movies and songs play an enormous part in shaping our perceptions. Since "love," "being in love," and "being loved" by another was, and of course, still is so much a part of the popular culture, any aware child could be influenced and then be convinced of being "in love."

Somehow, after failure with Edwin, the days seemed less exciting since there was no one with whom I could fantasize about being "in love with." Therefore, I quickly cast about for another to be my enamored and quickly discovered Peter, the only other Italian in my class. I admired him because he was handsome, strong, and very smart. He could also beat up *anybody* else in class, including Edwin. This would never happen since Edwin was his best pal.

During the school day, my girlfriends and I would whisper to one another about our "love" for this one or that one. Giggling and self-conscious, we would spend much time discussing some imagined "boyfriend" of the moment. Much time and effort went into "being in love" even in Kindergarten. This effort became more intense as the grade levels went up. Each year, Valentine's Day was a day of great sadness for many and great joy for a few chosen others. I can still recall the pain of being one of the girls who got the fewest number of Valentine cards. Year after year, it seemed that Patty, Peggy, and Betty Lou always got the most.

I now recall a kind-hearted teacher in fourth grade who gave me a dozen Valentines and a list of students. Secretly, she asked me to sign "guess who" on the cards and then drop them in the large Valentine box in the front of the room. When the cards were handed out, those particular students received only one Valentine each on that special, yet sad day. Smiling, they would look around the room expectantly searching for their secret admirer. Some of those children were so unattractive that I'm sure lots of the other kids in class wondered who on earth would ever send them a Valentine card. I am not sure the teacher was so kind, after all. It was almost sad.

Be that as it may, soon I was "mooning" over Peter, but alas, again my love went unreciprocated. It so happened that dark-eyed, dark-haired Peter was attracted to only blonde, blue eyed girls. However, despite his neglect, I persisted and still daydreamed about him, referring to him as my boyfriend when discussing such things with my friends.

An incident in a Christmas play soon brought my love to the brink of ending. What brought this first disenchantment with Peter was when the teacher cast us as twin Indian dolls for the Christmas play. I was ecstatic at first over the thought of being cooped up in a box close to him during rehearsals. At the same time, I was quite unhappy over being cast as an Indian since I coveted the leading role of the "Christmas Doll." The part went to Ann Van Winkle, a blonde, fair-skinned, blue-eyed girl of Dutch descent. I was mystified when the part did not go to Patty since she was so much prettier than Ann. But Ann was a very studious and obedient student and the implied message was that good grades were rewarded accordingly by the teacher.

Being an Indian was not my idea of anything glamorous or desirable but I had to agree that Peter and I with our straight, jet black hair and dark-brown eyes, would be very convincing as such. Since we were supposed to be Christmas presents under the tree, for at least half of rehearsal time we had to remain together inside of a large cardboard box, the front of which was covered with thin craft paper. At a certain signal, we were to burst forth from the box and do an Indian rain dance, center stage, for a few minutes.

During rehearsals, we were enclosed in the box for what seemed forever! As boredom set in, Peter, maybe just to stay awake, would tickle me in "taboo" places and at first I would only squirm uncomfortably. When his tickling continued, I, in angry, whispered hisses, would command him to stop. Delighted over my anger and discomfort, he would tickle and poke me even more. During rehearsals the "box" we were in was always quivering and shaking, at risk of falling over so that the teacher would admonish us and shout, "Hold still in there! You won't be in the play if you misbehave!"

Angry and frustrated, I was tempted to punch Peter squarely on the nose for being so fresh. Yet, so deeply inculcated was my Sicilian training as a female in a male-dominated world that I restrained myself. Neither did I complain to the teacher about it since I somehow felt responsible for his behavior.

After all, I was a girl. If I were a boy, he wouldn't have those places on me to tickle.

It was this boorish behavior that made me begin to like him less and less. Anyway, he had eyes only for Patty. Patty Millham, with the golden-brown banana curls, sparkling blue eyes, deep dimples, and perfect smile. Oh how I longed to look like her. Yet Patty, for all her delicate prettiness, was as much of, if not more of a tomboy than I was. We respected each other, but we were not close friends, at least not in the lower grades.

It was another later incident with Peter that brought my love to an absolute finish. In fact, it made me actually dislike and resent him for quite a while. It came about in this way. One Saturday afternoon my sister Caroline had taken me to see Walt Disney's "Snow White and the Seven Dwarfs." The following Monday, during play time, I suggested to a group of fellow playmates that we re-enact "Snow White." It would be fun to pretend and they all agreed enthusiastically. With ulterior motives in mind, I then decreed that Peter would be the prince and I, of course, being the only girl with black hair would be "Snow White." Then, since I was one of the few who had seen the movie, I gave instructions that after I bit into a make-believe apple and lay down, pretending to be dead, that Peter would ride up on a make believe horse, dismount, and kiss me to break the spell and wake me up.

Upon hearing this part, Peter made loud, disgusting sounds like someone throwing- up and announced, in a loud voice "YYukk! Are you crazy? Kiss YOU? I ain't never gonna kiss you or anybody else! Yuk! Go find some other dopey kid to kiss you. Anyhow, who would want to kiss you, yer so ugly!"

Surprised at his grossly unfavorable reaction, I realized at this point that it was obvious that there was no way Peter was going to kiss anyone, especially me and that I would have to find some other "dopey kid" to be the prince.

Noting Peter's reaction, the children within earshot broke into gales of laughter, pointed toward me and said,"Yeah, an yer ugly too! OK 'Snow White' what'cha gonna do now?"

I turned crimson with embarrassment and rage. It was an incident I never really forgot. Unfortunately, perhaps that little episode accounts for the fact that when I started dating in my teens, I always avoided dating Italian boys and vehemently expressed disdain for them. Many, many years later, upon dating Italian and Sicilian men, I heartily regretted my early avoidance of them.

One school year led into the next and sorry to say, all during my primary grades, I was quite bossy and aggressive. Being at the very bottom of the pecking order at home, I found that fighting and defeating kids in school gave me a sense of power and helped make me feel better about myself.

Due to my father's admonitions about not starting a fight, during the course of many a school day, I would subtly needle some poor unsuspecting student to the point where *they* would then instigate one. Once it started, I would always be victorious and arrive at the point where I usually made my victim "give up." Afterwards, I would march off triumphantly with a small cadre of children who admired my fighting prowess. Others followed me because of my ability to draw, a fact which both pleased and puzzled me.

My aggressive and negative behavior continued sporadically until I reached the fifth grade. I had built up a reputation for being tough and was quite proud of myself. My belligerence had been strongly encouraged at home, mostly by my brothers, who did not want to see me getting "picked" on because I was so small and scrawny.

My "Waterloo" came on a warm spring day during lunch time. For some reason that eludes me now, my best friend Suzy and I had a disagreement. I recall quite clearly that we were near the baseball diamond on the playing field across from the school. Voices raised in anger, we soon began to fight. A crowd gathered. Suddenly, I found myself with my back on the ground and Suzy sitting on my stomach, fist poised to punch me in the face. Lying on the ground, my knees up in the air, I was suddenly aware that all the boys in the crowd that surrounded us could see my panties. Mama had always admonished me to keep my knees together and *never* let *anyone* see my panties. Indeed, to let a boy get even a glimpse of your panties was a sin and I would probably roast in hell if I allowed it.

As the thought flashed through my mind I flushed with fear and apprehension. It was at that precise moment that I felt Suzy's fist connect with my nose. The warm blood spilled out of my nostrils. I could taste it on my lips and also as it trickled down the back of my throat. Mortified and angered at the fact that Suzy had knocked me down *and* bloodied my nose in public and, worse yet, that my panties had been exposed to everyone, I found a reserve of strength. Quickly pivoting my body to one side, I flipped her off and she went sprawling. Jumping up quickly and holding my nostrils together with forefinger and thumb, I ran swiftly into the school and directly to the girl's room for paper to stuff up and stop the bleeding nose.

Suzy and I were never again close. Now it was Suzy who got the attention and adulation of that small cadre of students who used to follow me around. She too could draw very well. Her parents were commercial artists and her very apparent artistic abilities were probably greatly appreciated at home.

That incident with the bloody nose, however, helped me realize, despite what my family said, that fighting other children really was a detriment and endeared me to no one. Worst of all, it made me unattractive and less desirable to boys, a fact I was to rue a few years later, in seventh grade.

Soon I discovered that excellence in reading and reasoning in scholastic areas was a much better way to gain attention, especially from teachers. Thus, I quickly learned to apply myself diligently and to excel in the subjects I loved most–art, reading, and science.

At the end of that year in fifth grade, I was totally astonished to learn that I had obtained a score of 100% on a *State Achievement Test* in science. My teacher told me that this indicated that even though I was a fifth grader, in science, I had scored at a ninth-grade level. I could hardly believe it. Her explanation brought me the most profound sense of elation and good feelings about myself. She was delighted and made it very clear how proud she was of my accomplishment. My test performance also brought much admiration from the class supervisor, Miss Wicks, who proudly announced this achievement to the whole school. I can still recall how after she came into my classroom and announced the results, many of my classmates turned and looked at me with surprise and admiration. So rewarding was this feeling that thereafter I applied myself and went on to excel in science. My subconscious must have stored that memory and perhaps that is why, years later as a teacher, my philosophy was, "Nothing succeeds like success."

As I progressed though school, I found that there were other areas of study in which I could excel. But no matter what subject matter came up, I had only one real love–drawing. "Art" was everything to me even though I loved to sing almost as much as I loved to draw. I had a strong, clear, second soprano voice and one day in sixth grade my music teacher, Miss Harding said,

"Sadie, did you ever consider being a singer."

"Me? A singer? No. I do like to sing, but I never thought about becoming a singer."

"Well, you should give it some thought, you really have a lovely voice."

I felt my face flush pink with pleasure since I was greatly surprised and highly flattered. Although happy over what Miss Harding said, I answered "Thank you Miss Harding, it's really nice of you to say that, but I love art and I couldn't ever be anything but an artist. Miss Loselle would just die if I told her I was going to be a singer instead of an artist. And much as I love to sing, I don't think it's as hard to do as art. And, well, I just never thought of ever being anything else but an artist someday." Miss Harding shook her head in exasperation.

My art teacher, Miss Loselle, was a lovely, softly curved, sweet, and gentle woman. She had very long chestnut-colored hair which she always wore on the top of her head, sometimes in braids and sometimes in a bun. Her eyes sparkled warmly and were the same color as her hair. I thought my art teacher was the most beautiful woman in the whole school. I simply adored her. Best of all, she seemed quite fond of me. Miss Loselle admired just about everything that I did in art class. So much so, that she took home just about every piece of art work I completed. Rarely did I get to take my art work home.

Years later, when I became an art teacher, it was easy to understand why she wanted to keep my work. It was a real temptation to keep the superior works my students produced. When I did want to keep a piece, I would always ask first, as did, Miss Loselle. At the same time, because I remembered the warm satisfying times of my childhood in the art room, I strove to instill in my students the same supporting and nurturing feelings that I had gotten all those long years ago from my art teacher. What is that saying? "What goes around, comes around."

Miss Loselle encouraged me a great deal and would allow me to use special art materials. Once, she gave me a stretched linen canvas, a wax pen, and small jars filled with inks of many colors. It was the only wax pen in the classroom. I felt honored to be chosen as the one to use it. She instructed me in its use and soon I was at work on a flower painting; flowers that existed only in my imagination. First I had to use hot wax to outline each flower before coloring it in otherwise the paint would bleed into surrounding areas. Although there were times when I found it tedious, my joy in creating the work overcame the impatience that sometimes overtook me. I labored over that canvas for weeks. When I finished it, Miss Loselle quickly took it home.

I was flattered by the fact that my teacher liked my flower piece so much that she wanted to keep it for herself. That painting brought me incredible joy and satisfaction. In fact, I loved doing that wax and dye painting so much that I actually used to dream about it at night. Never did I give a thought to the fact that my mother never got to see the painting that had taken me weeks to complete. I saw no need to take the work home, since our walls were bare of pictures, save two. One was hung over Mama's and Papa's bed. It was of the Virgin Mary standing on a globe of the world which was entwined with snakes. She seemed to be floating in space since there were clouds around her. The other was a reproduction of *The Last Supper* which Mama said was by da Vinci.

Early on, I found that art class was the one place where I truly excelled. Suzy and I were considered the "class artists". We both were exceptional for our age, not only in drawing, but in other areas of art. It took no time at all for me to discover that there was absolutely nothing in the whole world that I would rather do than draw, paint, and sculpt. What made me still love school even after the initial joy wore off and despite homework and some boring teachers was art class and all the wondrous materials at my disposal.

Although I was certain that Miss Loselle was truly fond of me, at the same time, I was convinced that my fifth-grade classroom teacher, Miss MacFarland, disliked me intensely. Miss McFarland seemed to do everything she could to embarrass me. Me, with my long, straight black hair, big dark eyes, and funny homemade "Italian" clothes. Intuitively, and correctly, I might add, I sensed the fact that my classroom teacher took delight in degrading or insulting me. I puzzled over this and wondered why? I rarely misbehaved or gave her any problems. None of us would dare to!

"Huh," I thought to myself, "Miss MacFarland's probably like those dumb kids on the bus, always picking on somebody 'cause they're dif'rent.... She probably doesn't like me 'cause she thinks I'm Italian. Mean, just mean, that's what people like that are."

Along with other subjects, Miss McFarland taught arithmetic. I do believe math was her "major." She seemed to spend an inordinate amount of time teaching arithmetic. Need I tell you, at this point, that arithmetic was *not* one of my best subjects. In truth, it was my worst and I hated it! Although I had tried hard, somehow I had never been able to memorize my multiplication tables and always felt humiliated when called upon to answer in class. I was especially embarrassed when teams were formed to play against each other, one on each side of the room. Each student would have to answer a multiplication question and would have to sit down if he or she gave a wrong answer. The team with the most students standing at the end of the game was the winner. Whenever the game was played I always knew I would be headed for a chair as soon as Miss MacFarland reached the "seven" tables.

Since I never had trouble in other scholastic areas, I felt absolutely degraded and stupid when I couldn't remember how much 7 x 9 was. Even worse was 8 x 9 and, worst of all,

9 x 9. As hard as I tried, I just couldn't get certain figures to work in my head. It never occurred to me that the way math was being taught had anything to do with my "stupidity." Twenty-two years later in a college math class, with a little effort, I learned algebra and Russian multiplication and wondered why math had always been such a difficult subject for me in the lower grades.

But for now, in fifth grade and despite my tender years, I was well aware of Miss McFarland's dislike of me. I also surmised that it was not just because I was "Italian." No, I felt it transcended that, since the woman seemed to seize every chance to do everything she could to hurt or embarrass me. Often she would pick on me and not others, even when others were doing the same thing. Once, in front of the whole class, she even accused me of stealing someone's pencil. I was absolutely mortified and felt that my honor was being maligned. So much so, that I burst into tears in front of the entire class and cried and carried on so hysterically that Miss MacFarland was probably sorry she ever brought it up.

The woman was obviously not aware of how much my Sicilian sense of "honor" had been disgraced by such an accusation. (On second thought, perhaps she was extraordinarily aware of it.) In fairness, I must say, she had no way of knowing that my father had instilled in me the fact that he considered stealing the lowest of the low, even worse than lying and punishable by the worst sort of beating. It took a really long time for me to get over the hurt and shame of her unfounded accusation.

On trips to the cafeteria or gym, when the children had to get in line, Miss MacFarland would always put me at the very end of the line and make me hold hands with the only black child in the classroom, Sammy. Sammy was indeed black– a rich deep, silky, ebony color. Although black people worked for my father, never had I seen anyone quite so dark as Sammy. I became anxious each time we held hands, worried that his color might come off on mine and never wash off. You see, whenever we held hands, Sammy's hand always seemed to sweat. This made me especially fearful. I reasoned that the wetness would definitely enable the color of his hand to come off and stick to my hand. Through trial and error, I had learned early on in art class that when you put a wet brush in paint, the color always came off quite easily and stayed on the brush. On the other hand, the color didn't come off at all if you put a dry brush in the paint.

However, not wanting to hurt Sammy's feelings, I would nervously and dutifully hold his hand all the way up to the door of either the cafeteria or the gym, whichever our destination. When we arrived, I would casually let go and then surreptitiously peek at my hand to see if it was still white. I would breath a sigh of relief and always felt guilty when I found myself reacting to Sammy in this way. In fact, we were friends. I had no prejudice concerning race and was used to being around negroes, a discriptive term used then. In those days, "black" was considered a pejorative term and only the word "negro" was acceptable. Our regular hired hand, Carl, was negro and was like a member of the family. For many years he sat at our dinner table and shared our food.

No, I did not feel any prejudice toward Sammy, in fact I often came to his aid whenever I saw other kids gang up on him or pick on him because of his color. I knew full well how painful it was to be picked on because of being different or even for having coloring different from the rest.Regardless of all that, for reasons beyond my comprehension I did get funny twinges as I noted the "funny" looks from teachers and other students who saw me marching through the halls, holding hands with the only black child in my class.

Miss MacFarland had steel gray hair worn in a very short, almost mannish cut. Never, never did she wear lipstick or makeup like many of the other teachers. Her mode of dress consisted of suits and very ugly "sensible" shoes, either black or brown. She was as cold and mean as Miss Loselle was warm and loving. They were the opposite of one another and hardly ever spoke to each other in school.

Many years later, at the age of thirty-two, I was crossing my college campus on my way to start classes. It was the same college that in earlier years had been known as a "normal school" (today called a teacher's college) for which my elementary school, The Van den Burgh School of Practice, was the "training school." It was a glorious fall day. On the walk ahead of me I saw coming toward me, my former elementary school music teacher, Miss Harding. By now Miss Harding, who had seemed positively ancient when I was ten, strangely enough, now seemed merely old. She remembered me immediately and we were both delighted to see one another again. After exchanging pleasantries I asked "Is Miss Loselle still around? I would love to see her and tell her that I am now studying to become an art teacher." Miss Harding smiled sweetly and the creased laugh lines around her eyes got deeper. She looked at me with faded, but twinkling, blue-gray eyes. Eyes that I remembered had once been a deep, clear, strong blue. Looking pointedly at me and still smiling she said,

"Oh, no, she and Miss McFarland retired some years ago and they both moved to Arizona. You know, they lived together all those years that they were teaching." After a rather lengthy pause, "Oh!" was all I could say.

We both stood and gazed at one another for what seemed a long time. I was not sure whether or not I had detected a minuscule tone of devilish delight in Miss Harding's voice. Neither of us blinked nor looked away, and after a few more smiles and simple exchanges, we shook hands, bid one another farewell and good luck and then parted.

All the way back to my next class, I couldn't get Miss Loselle and Miss McFarland out of my mind. So much seemed so much clearer now.

chapter 4

Suzy's House

I had remained unbeaten and belligerent before the fight with Suzy in fifth grade. After that, we were never really close again. That was too bad, because Suzy and I were inseparable before that fight. Often, after school, she would come home on the bus with me to the farm. After helping with my chores, we would climb cherry trees in springtime and eat our fill, visit the baby calves, and do lots of other neat things around the farm.

One warm day in mid-June when Suzy's mother came to pick her up she asked me if I would like to go home with them and spend the night. Although delighted at being asked, I had mixed feelings.

"I really don't think I can go, I'd have to ask my father."

"So? Let's go ask him," replied Suzy's mother, who was a rather attractive, relatively young woman. Young that is, compared to my parents who, when I was born, were in their forties–Papa was forty-nine and Mama was forty-two. Thus, it seemed to me that I had the oldest set of parents of any kid in school. As such, I had learned early on that my parents did not think the way other parents thought. Not only because they were Sicilian, but because they were "old-fashioned", a term I heard often during childhood.

My brothers and sister never ceased to complain and bemoan the fact that our parents would not allow them to do the things that other kids did. This, they insisted was because Mama and Papa were so very, very "old-fashioned." My brothers and sister were thoroughly frustrated about this and often there was much conflict. Papa had his hands full, trying to make my three brothers and my cousin Chico, who lived with us, obey his rules. They found it difficult to abide by the mores and beliefs of the "old country" when imposed upon them in the "new country", America. Papa, much more than Mama, was especially adamant about what was acceptable behavior and what was not. He still reasoned exactly as they did in the "old country", meaning, to him of course, Sicily.

Fully aware of Papa's beliefs, I broke out in a cold sweat at the suggestion by Suzy's mother that we ask my father's permission for me to leave the farm, stay overnight, and sleep at someone else's house. I was positive that among Papa's old fashioned ideas was the belief that one should always sleep in one's own bed. What foolishness to even think of sleeping in someone else's house!

I was sweating because I could imagine my father cursing and shouting at Suzy's mother in broken English. I could even picture him running them off the property with a pitchfork, which I had seen him do to salesmen and others who annoyed him. "Uh, I, uh, don't think my father would let me go, so uh, let's just not ask him."

"Why darling? I'm sure your Daddy would be delighted to have you come stay the night with us. Why wouldn't he? I mean, what possible reason could he have for not letting you come?"

I thought to myself, "Huh, you don"t know my father!" "Come," Mrs. Marks announced firmly. "We'll go find your Daddy and ask him." Now, an even stronger twinge of fear twitched at my insides and I thought, "She doesn't even know she's not supposed to call my father "Daddy!" How is she ever going to talk to him? He'll probably even end up smacking her for bothering him while he's working."

The word "Daddy" brought back an incident from a few summers before. I remembered overhearing one of the boarders call her father "Daddy." I thought to myself, "Daddy, what a nice sound" and thinking it a term of endearment, I tried it out on my father that evening when he came home. Instead of "Hello Papa, bona sera!," I greeted him with, "Hello Daddy!" Papa stopped dead in his tracks. He stared at me in surprise. Eyes narrowed in annoyance, he quickly approached me. When he was directly in front of me, he drew back his hand and with a swift, firm swing, gave me a backhanded smack. I can still remember the stinging sensation on my cheek as I went reeling. Walking over to where I lay cowering, he looked down at me darkly and said, "I'ma you *Papa*, what'sa thissa 'Daddy?' I no '*Daddy*'. I you Papa, *capi'ce*? You no calla me stuppi names!" Then he stalked off leaving me, his "favorite", crying and rubbing the red welt on the side of my face and wondering why he would consider "Daddy" a stupid name.

Seeing Suzy's mother striding off toward the field where Papa could not only be seen but even heard took me out of my reverie. Papa was plowing in the vineyard and was singing "O Solo Mio" at the top of his lungs. All hope that I had of Mrs. Marks *not* meeting my father was dashed as she and the two of us following closely behind her drew closer to him.

Seeing us approach, he reined his horse to a stop and watched guardedly as we drew near. Papa was covered with fine dust and sweating profusely from guiding the plow. He was wearing a T-shirt beneath a set of loose fitting, faded denim, strap-style overalls. His eyes were shaded by a slightly tattered, straw, cowboy-style hat. For the first time in my life, as I looked at him, I saw him in a different light.

Although covered with sweat and grime, he stood with quiet dignity, tall and straight, waiting for us to reach him and hear what we had to say. Gazing at him I was totally puzzled and surprised to find that suddenly, somehow, my father looked handsome, even stately. I told myself that maybe when I got closer he would again look like he always did.

As Mrs. Marks approached him, picking her way on clumps of overturned grass so that she avoided stepping into the freshly plowed earth, I noticed my father smile in a way that I had never before seen. His eyes took on a gentle quality and the squint lines around them grew deeper, making his eyes look softer. I tried hard to figure out why the look on his face inexplicably somehow made him look even better. Now I worried just a little, since even closeup, he still looked different to me.

Mrs. Marks, looking up, smiled back at him and strangely, almost magically I thought I suddenly saw him through her eyes. I had never really noted before, his deeply tanned skin which made his teeth look extraordinarily white. His eyes, shaded beneath the brim of the hat, looked coal black and seemed to have a magnetic quality of which I had never before been aware. Two wavy swirls of black hair had escaped from beneath the brim of his hat and were plastered against his forehead. The curly hair at his sideburns shone a deep, rich silver as small rivulets of sweat coursed down the sides of his face.

Papa graciously removed his hat when Mrs. Marks finally reached him. Then she stepped off to the side of him, next to the horse, but not too close. For a fleeting moment they both just stood there staring at one another. Watching all of this, it occurred to me that it was strange that my father should remove his hat for this woman he did not even know. Stranger still that he removed his hat for an "American" woman. He never spoke very highly of American woman. They smoked, wore lipstick, and drove cars. Things only "bad" women did. Never had I seen him remove his hat for Mama or for any other woman on the farm. I strained my memory to try to remember when I had seen him remove his hat for *anyone* else, but could not. It seemed almost ominous to me. I was apprehensive.

By now, Suzy's mother, smiling sweetly and tilting her head slightly to one side, while peering up at Papa from beneath long, dark lashes, said in a voice subtley different from the voice I was used to hearing, "Oh, Mr. Penzato, would you let Sadie come to our house and stay overnight? The girls do have such fun together and I promise I'll take really good care of her, oh please, please, she is such a delightful child

46

and I'll bring her back first thing tomorrow night. Since it will be Saturday and there's no school, they can spend the day together."

My eyes were squeezed tightly shut and I prayed as never before. First I prayed that Papa would not embarrass me in front of Suzy and her mother. Second I prayed that by some unheard of miracle, he might say "yes." I wanted very much to go to Suzy's house and stay overnight. Once I had been there for a birthday party and it was like nothing I had ever before seen except at the movies. Waiting for his answer, I held my breath, eyes still shut, speedily reciting a "Hail Mary" to myself, waiting to hear Papa's reply. There was such a long pause that I started another "Hail Mary." Half way through, I heard him answer jovially, "Fa sure, why not? Si, si. *Bene,* (good) yessa', she canna go wi' you. You bringa her backa tomorrow night, early! She gotta lotta work to do. Yeah, OK."

My eyes snapped open in surprise. Papa was grinning broadly and Suzy and I both let out a shriek and started jumping up and down. Overcome with joy and gratitude, I ran up to my father, hugged him really hard around the waist and then said, *"Grazia, Papa, grazia!"* ("Thank you Papa, thank you!") I started to run off, but stopped abruptly. Turning to look at him I said, *"T'sa bene dica."* Smiling and holding out his hand, palm down he replied, *"Santa 'e ricca."* I dashed back to where he was standing. On tiptoe, I reached up and kissed him quickly on the cheek and then ran off joyfully with Suzy who had been watching impatiently.

Mrs. Marks smiled at Papa, mouthed a thank you and carefully picked her way back to the road where her car was parked. When she got to it we were inside and waiting. Peering at me through the open window she said, "Sadie, go get your toothbrush and pajamas. We'll wait here for you." I looked blankly at her. I thought to myself, "Toothbrush? Pajamas?" I had neither. Biting my lip I looked down, turning so red with embarrassment that she could see me flush, even through my deeply tanned skin. Sensing my discomfort and my reason for it, Suzy's mother kindly said, "Oh, never mind Sadie, we have extra toothbrushes at home. And extra pajamas, too! You don't have to go and get yours. Just be sure to tell your

Mom where you are going, ok? Here, we'll even come with you."

Soon, the car pulled out of the huge circular driveway and on to the highway. Never before had I felt such joy and exhilaration. I thought the top of my head was going to fly off. Even though I had never been on one, I thought to myself, "So, this is what it must feel like to go on vacation." All the people who came up to the farm were on vacation, so I knew what it meant. Now I knew how it felt...wonderful! The boarders always seemed to be having a great time. They were away from their work and enjoyed being at play all the time. Now I too was at play and was especially pleased over the fact that I wouldn't have to set the table that night, wash the dishes, or clear off the table and sweep the floor. No going down to the creepy cellar for wine. No, none of that for the rest of the afternoon! With a whole night and a whole day off, I suddenly felt a sense of freedom that overwhelmed me. Never before having experienced this, I felt intoxicated!. Giddy with joy, Suzy and I laughed and giggled all the way to her house.

Suzy's mom and dad were both commercial artists. When her mother handed us paper, pencils, and crayons and told us to go draw until supper time, I was in heaven. While we sat in her room and drew, it seemed very strange to me that Suzy had no chores. She was just expected to spend her time playing. I thought about it as I continued to draw and decided it was because she didn't live on a big farm. The thinking distracted me from my drawing so I quickly put that thought out of my mind and fully enjoyed the pleasure of making lines turn into things.

We drew and colored for a while, but eager to explore my new surroundings I soon grew restless. I wondered why, since at home I relished every moment that I could spend drawing. Here, in strange and different surroundings, drawing did not hold its usual magic spell. Oddly enough, years later when I sought to draw when visiting foreign countries or other places, my drawings did not "work" as well as when I drew only the things I was familiar with or loved. Our minds travel, but often the heart stays home.

"Gee, Suzy, can't we go look at the lake, or walk around the house and barns. I'm tired of drawing."

"Sure, Sadie, its just that I know how much you love to draw so I thought that's what you would want to do. Heck, yes! We can go down to the lake. We can do anything you want."

Soon we headed down the long, sloping hill to a huge lake. Suzy's house was built on the crest of a hill. It was a large house, but compared to mine, it seemed modest in size. Colonial in style, constructed of quarry stone, it was a splendid, newly built house, as beautiful on the inside as it was on the outside. Lovely chintz-flowered furniture filled a living room that had a real, working fireplace. Suzy's bedroom was a picture of what a young girl's room should look like. It was filled with pretty white furniture and decorated with matching curtains and bedspread. There were toys and dolls everywhere, on shelves and on chairs.

Everything looked just like it did in the movies. Having visited only apartments in tenements on the lower east side of New York City or the homes of other Sicilians and Italians, I had nothing but the movies to use as a model of how "Americans" lived.

Mrs. Marks' kitchen was a place of fascination. In comparison the kitchen in my house seemed quite ugly and old fashioned. I was even ashamed of it. In front of a large bricked up fireplace wall in the old farm kitchen in my house was an enormous black coal stove. It had nickel trim and a large warming oven on top that had sliding doors. Set in the brick wall behind the stove was a bin for wood and an old wall oven that was never used. The floor was of dark wood, shiny from years of wear. The sink was made of some kind of grey-colored metal and there was a black and rusty looking hand pump set into a counter on one side of it. No one used the pump any more, but it had been left in place for a long time, even after running water had finally been installed.

My family ate supper seated on ten-foot long benches at an equally long, oil-cloth covered harvest table. Seated at each end, in chairs that did not match, were my parents. Papa sat at the head and Mama sat at the foot.

The six over six, small-paned glass windows were hung with simple cream-colored, coarsely woven cotton curtains. Yes, as I thought about it, Mama's kitchen did seem ugly and old-fashioned compared to Suzy's mother's kitchen. (What I would give to have Mama's old kitchen in my own house today!)

Mrs. Marks' kitchen had shiny natural pine cabinets, a modern gas range, a refrigerator (not an icebox), linoleum on the floor, a nice white kitchen sink, and a highly polished pine table with four matching pine chairs. The windows had pretty ruffled curtains that matched the pads on the chairs. When we sat down at mid-afternoon to have a snack, Suzy's mother placed odd rectangular pieces of padded material on the table top in front of each of us.

"Mrs. Marks, what are these things?"

"My goodness Sadie, they're placemats."

"Placemats? What are they for?"

"They are used to protect the table top."

"Oh."

Thoughts and questions crowded my head. "Why did Mrs. Marks have to protect the top of her table? Did she expect someone to beat on it? And how come she didn't use a table cloth or oil cloth like everybody else did?" So many new experiences were popping up all over the place that soon I stopped questioning and wondering and just enjoyed myself.

During my short stay at Suzy's house, three memorable incidents occurred. They were the kind of incidents that are universal. As children we all experience many of the same things, in different ways, of course, but they never cease to make us aware of new dimensions. These experiences often are the gateways that lead to the myriad beginnings of the process we call "growing up." Universality aside, these particular three incidents were a bit out of the ordinary, and I have never forgotten them.

The first one happened after Suzy and I decided to go down to the lake. It was a while before supper time and unusually hot. That was when Suzy and her brothers suggested it would be a perfect time to go swimming and also show me the rowboat and the other side of the lake. We changed into swim suits and grabbed some towels. They all took off, gleefully barefoot, toward the lake. I was not so gleeful! You see, the others were used to running everywhere barefoot, since much of their property consisted of paved walks and manicured lawns.

"Barefoot, huh," I thought, "Just imagine all of 'em runnin' barefoot through the cow barn or horse barn orespecially the barnyard, full of fresh, squashy manure and mud. Or let's see 'em out pickin' brush, hah, they'd have no feet left."

However, eager to conform, I gave in to peer pressure. I left my shoes behind with theirs. Barefoot, tender feet hurting, I picked my way gingerly down the shale path and through the grass. Finally, I arrived at the small dock at the edge of the lake where the others were waiting impatiently.

I stood awe struck on the dock as I gazed across the water to the other side of the lake. Compared to the pond in the meadow and the old swimming hole in the creek, the lake looked like an ocean. Positively enormous! It also looked ominously deep. Much, much deeper than the familiar old swimming hole. Beckoning to me, Carl the oldest said,"C'mon, get in the boat, we're going to row you across the lake."

I hesitated, never having been in a boat of any kind before, nor in such deep water. Anxiously, I wondered how I could go about avoiding what seemed to be inevitable. However, at the same time I was also excited by the prospect of riding in a real, honest-to-goodness boat like the ones in the movies. I held back only momentarily, since I certainly did not want to be viewed as afraid.

"Ok, Ok, great! Just remember, I can't swim, so you better take care. You promise?"

"Sure, sure, we promise," they all chorused as one voice. Reaching up, many hands grabbed me and swung me down into the rowboat. They helped me to sit, which I found difficult to do, but soon, awkwardly, did so. Almost immediately we took off across the lake at a great speed. Suzy's two older brothers skillfully pulled on the oars. Hair blowing in the wind, I clung to the sides of the boat with all my might.

When we reached the middle of the lake we stopped and then Carl said, "Listen, just listen." All of us were very quiet.

Somewhere, near by, a beaver could be heard gnawing at a tree, mourning doves hooted gently, and a fish splashed and broke the surface of the water, sending out ripples. Swallows flitted over the glistening, pulsating veneer of the calm lake, gorging on flying insects. An iridescent darning needle hummed and paused for a moment on the edge of the rowboat. Weeping cherry and dogwood trees rimmed the near edge of the lake. Their blossoms were reflected in the clear sparkling water. Off in the distance, on the far side, the beautiful stone house sat imperiously atop its cairn.

Because I was accustomed to the farm–the woods and wild underbrush, apple orchards, cow fields, and huge meadows of hay–to me, the attractively manicured grounds were lovely beyond belief. It all seemed so immaculate and so beautiful that I held my breath for a long moment. Then I expelled it in a deep sigh. I was filled with a sense of inner peace. Never having seen anything so entrancing in my whole short life I found myself sitting perfectly still, totally absorbed and spellbound.

"So you can't swim, hey?"

Still engrossed in the placid majesty of the lake, I did not hear Carl. "Din'cha hear 'im Sadie? He asked if you really can't swim," Suzy said. Her voice, close to my ear jarred me from my reverie. Distracted I replied, "What? Swim? Me? No, no, I didn't ever learn."

"Well then, can you float?"

"Float? Oh, you mean like Ivory Soap? No, silly, I can't float. Only soap can float."

Suzy and her brothers laughed out loud. Then they looked at each other, grinning fiendishly with a strange look in their eyes. Carl said, "You think you're pretty funny, huh? Well, they say the best way to learn to swim is when you have to. You know, 'sink or swim?' "

One look at their faces and all at once my palms felt wet and sticky. Suddenly, I could feel my heart pounding fiercely as I saw the three of them reaching toward me. Abruptly, I felt myself lifted high into the air. Quickly and instinctively, I took a deep, deep breath just before I hit the water.

Like a rock! I sank like a rock! Horrified, all three instantly jumped in after me. Diving into the clear water of the lake, they immediately found me and brought me to the surface. All this in almost less than a heartbeat. Tugging and pushing, they finally got me, coughing and choking, back into the boat.

It had all happened so quickly that, if I had not had to spit out a mouthful of lake water or felt my wet hair plastered against my eyes and water streaming down my face, I could almost think that I had imagined it.

Incredulous, Carl said, "M'God, you dummy, you really can't swim. Why dint'cha tell us?"

Still sputtering and choking from the lake water, I retorted, "I did, you big dope, (cough, cough). I did, didn't you believe me? Why would I lie (cough) about a thing like that?"

"Heck, everyone we know that's your age can swim. Gee, I'm real sorry, we thought you were fakin' it so that we wouldn't throw you in. Boy-o-boy, we could've lost you out there and then there would've been hell to pay. Whew, we really came close!"

Chagrined and still coughing, I looked almost with pity at Carl as I pondered what he said. Obviously, he had no idea of how close he himself had come to real danger. He had no way of knowing that had any harm come to me in any way, especially a fatality, one way or another, my father, in order to placate Sicilian vengeance, would probably have seen to it that Carl would somehow have an accident or that some unlucky event would befall some member of his family.

However, as I write these words, it occurs to me that at that time I probably put too much faith in what I believed my father would have done. He was, after all, a law-abiding American citizen. However, at that age, from conversations I had overheard, I was secure in the belief that my father would have had to avenge any harm that would ever come to me, or to any of his family.

Vengeance was, and perhaps still is, a deeply ingrained Sicilian trait. One not only got angry, one also got justifiably "even." Vengeance was considered the only real form of justice. It had always been "an eye for an eye" since time out of mind, therefore, there could be no other way. Male or female, no Sicilian of my father's generation could settle for less than total satisfaction of any hurt, either real or imagined. Not

53

to avenge your own blood was especially unthinkable. Vengeance had to be appeased, no matter the price.

That evening, at the supper table, nothing was said of the near drowning. Suzy's parents never knew how close I believed all of us had come to tragedy that day.

The second memorable event occurred that evening around bedtime. Suzy and I were listening to the radio and her mother reminded us that soon it would be bath time. Surprised, I asked, "Why? Are we going some place special this hour of the night?"Her mother laughed and said, "No, silly, you always take a bath before you go to bed". Puzzled, I answered "You do?" Suzy snorted with impatience since she thought I was joking. "Sure! Don't you?"

I felt my face redden. Then I shrugged my shoulders and peered down at the floor. Sighing to myself, I felt a warm rush of embarrassment and hung my head. Real or imagined, it seemed to me that whenever I was away from home, a great deal of my time was taken up with feelings of shame, ignorance, and inadequacy.

The way Suzy lived was so foreign to me that I realized, in a not very small way, the difference between me and many of the other kids in school was not merely that I was Sicilian and they were not. It was not just a simple difference of skin, hair, and eye color. It transcended mere race. It went much, much deeper. I began to realize that the very way we *lived* was different. Theirs seemed a so much more pleasant, more civilized, less harsh way to live. A way that seemed totally alien to the way I was being brought up. My family had to struggle through life, while others it seemed, danced through.

For the first time that I could remember, I felt ashamed of my heritage, ashamed of my ignorance, ashamed that I washed only when I was dirty while other people seemed to wash–just to be clean–all the time, not just on special occasions.

Why wash a body that does not look dirty? Why not? At that age, I was not even aware that perspiration was offensive. It seemed such a normal thing to me. When you worked hard, you sweated, then it dried. You worked hard again and you sweated again. It never occurred to me to wash because I would other wise "smell!" Everyone in my family had some sort of

54

"smell." Papa didn't smell like Mama. My brothers did not smell like my sister. (She must have known something I didn't, since she always smelled of talcum powder.) The hired hands all had their own particular "smells." The various smells did not seem *that* unpleasant and no one seemed to mind. I always assumed that when I saw my father or my brothers wash themselves off at the water pump after a hard day of work on a hot summer day, that they were washing off the dirt that stuck to the sweat, not the sweat itself.

New experiences brought so many questions. Did anyone have the answers? Would I ever find them? Would I ever learn "American" ways? Who could I ask, without appearing really stupid?

Meanwhile, Suzy's mother had filled the tub with warm water and told us it was time for our baths and bedtime. The tub had been filled almost to the top with hot water. Believe me, I was impressed. In my house, when Saturday night came and we all finally did take a bath, only about six inches of water was allowed in the tub since my father felt that water was not to be wasted. Besides, the bath water had to be heated on the stove, so it took forever to get lots of it.

Suzy and I dutifully stripped and got into the tub. We splashed and laughed and played with the floating rubber toys and the Ivory Soap. We scrubbed each other's back. We soaped ourselves all over, making mounds of suds in our hair, giggling madly, while pulling shapes like horns and ears from our lathered heads. Then we used big sponges to rinse off.

When Suzy pulled the plug and as the water started to recede, I was utterly mortified. I wanted to go down the drain with the dirty water when I saw the look on Suzy's face as she watched a rather dark, rather thick ring of ugly, brownish gray scum remain on the walls of the tub as the water subsided. Suzy, never having been very dirty, had never actually seen a "ring" around the tub, at least not one of that magnitude.

Her eyes widened and she gulped in surprise. After a short pause, she quickly and kindly made some funny remark to soften my embarrassment. In fact, she drew some clean water and we both rinsed ourselves off again. After that, while making jokes about walking barefoot and getting dirty feet, we also washed down the tub and ended up laughing about the incident.

When we finally put on our nightgowns and climbed into bed, we spent half the night giggling and whispering. But even while laughing and joking, a small knot of pain would form in my stomach each time I remembered the ring around the tub and the look on my friend's face. I never forgot it. I wonder if she did.

The last and truly most indelible and unforgettable experience occurred the next day. It was a sunny, warm, and glorious Saturday. After a delightful breakfast of orange juice, pancakes, and bacon, Suzy and I were sent outside to play. (I found it odd to be served orange juice for breakfast, since the only time my mother served it was with castor oil, in order to make it less oily and to kill the taste.) Suzy suggested that we should go out in the rowboat again, just the two of us.

Leery from the near-drowning incident that was still fresh in my mind, I hesitated at first. But then, remembering the incredible beauty of the lake while on that boat ride the day before, and trusting her to take care, I carefully lowered myself into the rowboat and we pushed off. Suzy rowed.

When we reached the middle of the lake, she stopped rowing and the boat drifted slowly. The beauty of the lake was starting to work its magic all over again and I sat entranced and serene, gazing and listening.

"Sadie?" Suzy's voice had a strange lilt to it. Eyes squinting in the sunlight, I looked at her in puzzlement.

"What? What is it Sue?"

Suzy paused and savored what she was going to say next. Then seeming to relish each word she asked,"Do you know what sex is?"

Surprised at her question my eyes widened as I answered, "Sex? Sex? What do you mean? Like 'Sexy', like Lana Turner or Gypsy Rose Lee?" Suzy looked at me gravely, her deep green eyes seemed to grow an even deeper green. She looked around, furtively, as if someone might be listening.

"No! I mean, do you know where babies *really* come from?"

WELL! I must tell you that while I had no idea of where

or how, I DID have a healthy and terribly growing curiosity about the subject. To my disappointment, I had discovered that no matter how many times I asked any grown-up where babies came from, they would always give me that dumb stork story. I knew that there had to be more to it than some bird bringing babies, but never could I get anyone to tell me the truth.

Believing I was about to finally learn the truth, I laughed in exultation. "No, I don't know where they come from. Hey! You mean to tell me, YOU know where they come from? You actually *know?*"

With a look of triumph, Suzy grinned a wide and wickedly gleeful grin. Again looking around cautiously, in a low voice she said, "You have brothers. Did you ever see that funny thing that they pee with?"

I felt my face flush remembering the time when I had peered down from the hay drop to the cow stalls below and watched as one of my brothers relieved himself. It appeared to me at the time that with one hand he was holding what looked like a rather large, deep pink sausage that was protruding from his crotch. From the tip of that strange appendage, clear yellow fluid was squirting with great force. I realized as I watched, that he was urinating. I was so surprised!! How he did it was so different from how I did it. I was also fascinated. It seemed strange to me that he did not have to squat. Then it occurred to me that this might be what was meant when I heard grown-ups say that boys were different from girls.

I had never seen any of my brothers naked and thus was not aware of the physical "difference" between us. Totally intrigued, I continued to watch as he waved his "sausage" about, making wet patterns on the cement floor of the barn. Suddenly, like a jolt, something within me made me aware that I should not be watching him. That watching this was something my mother would call "dirty" and something that I should not be seeing. Besides, I was old enough to know that bathroom activities were a private matter. Quickly, I silently withdrew, tiptoeing out of the barn so that my brother would not hear me. Once out of the barn door, I ran back to the house as fast as I could.

"Hey, aint'cha listening to me?" Suzy's plaintive tone of voice brought me quickly back to the subject at hand. Now, finally, I would learn at last where babies really came from. I nodded impatiently, "Yes. Yes, I know about that funny thing between boys' legs. So what? Go on, go on."

"Well," Suzy said, pausing and enjoying my pent-up curiosity. Searching to find the right words to describe what she wanted to say, trying hard to choose exactly the right ones, impatient, she finally blurted it out! "Lissen, you're not gonna believe this, but when you get to a "certain" age, some man has to put *his* peepee "thing" inside of you, where *you* pee from and if he *doesn't*...then...*you will die!* You will *actually die!*"

It took a moment to sink in, but I, of course, responded exactly as Suzy thought I would. Horrified, I shrieked! "*What?*"

My "What?" could be heard clear across the lake. I was incredulous. I was in shock. Then disbelief set in. "It can't be! It can't be! What if I won't?"

"Well, then they send you to a doctor and he puts you up on a table and then HE does "it" to you. Yup! Every woman that is walking around alive today in the *whole world* has done 'it.'" Suzy's eyes danced with delight over my reaction. Then she added, "An then after that, you can have babies when you get married. Then your husband does 'it' to you all the time. Yep, every woman walking around alive has had 'it'!"

For the first time in my life, I was speechless. I sat almost paralyzed with disbelief, reflecting on what Suzy had just said. Then in a voice filled with pained incredulity I wailed, "You mean *Rita Hayworth* has had it? And, and *Judy Garland*?" (After a long pause, I continued on.) "And all our *teachers* have all done this with some man?"

Suzy nodded sagely,"Yes, all of them! EVERYBODY!" Suddenly a new and far more horrible thought hit me. "Oh my God! You mean MY MOTHER and YOUR MOTHER and our FATHERS do 'it' all the time?"

"Sure, dummy, how do you think WE got here?" It was all too awful to contemplate. I felt dizzy and almost fell out of the boat, such was my state of shock and amazement. I could not remember feeling like this at any time in my whole life. Her words were very, very upsetting and totally unexpected!

Suzy was thoroughly enjoying my discomfiture since she too had gone through the same state of amazement and agitation when she had first learned about "sex." Patiently, she had waited for the chance to share this giddy knowledge with someone. I, however, just couldn't give in to this monstrous idea.

"Well Suzy, I don't know about you, but I'll die first. I'll just die first before I EVER let somebody do 'that' to me! Besides, I think it's a sin to do anything like that! I'll betcha it'sa sin!"

"Well, I dunno if it's a sin or not, but I feel just like you do. Yeah, me too Sadie. I'll die before I ever let somebody put that funny looking thing inside of me!"

"Aw, who told you all this dumb stuff anyway? It sounds too dopey to be true."

"Some girls in seventh grade were in the bathroom and they were talking and didn't know I could hear them. So I know they were telling the truth, cause they were just talking about it like it was almost nothing."

We were both very quiet as Suzy rowed the boat slowly back to shore. I was getting more upset by the minute, because if what Suzy said was true, I sincerely believed that someday I might have to sin mortally and greatly in order not to die.

My mother had always warned me that men can do "bad" things to little girls and that I should never let anyone touch my body, especially "down below." Not anyone, ever! It would be a terrible sin and I would go straight to hell when I died. She said I wouldn't even be allowed to stop in purgatory for a while to get used to dying or to atone for my sins.

I got more and more disconcerted and confused as I weighed in my mind what I had just learned. After a while, it was all too overwhelming and confusing so I tried to think about other things. But hard as I tried, "sex" kept popping back into my head. Suzy rowed back and we were both unusually quiet, each filled with her own thoughts. When we reached the dock and disembarked, we walked mute and subdued back to the house. Suzy realized I did not think it was funny.

After this last and final of the three incidents, it seemed that I would never again see the world with the same eyes. Now that I knew about sex and where babies came from, somehow I felt "different." Grown-up, I suppose. Loss of innocence affects us all in different ways.

I was delivered home safely early that evening. The next day I went back to feeding the chickens and doing the laundry while Suzy and her mother probably went shopping or off to visit some friends.

On that particular Sunday, however, as I did my chores my mind was filled with all the new events I had experienced in the home of my non-Sicilian friend, my closest friend, who was Jewish. Our lives were so different. I was especially surprised over how Suzy's father and brothers treated her and her mother. It was so different from how my father and brothers treated us, the females in our family–my mother, my sister, and me.

Suzy's father and brothers didn't give her or her mother orders or command them in any way. They all seemed to live together so peacefully and Suzy's father treated her the same way he treated her brothers. In fact, he was nicer to her! Suzy's mom smoked, wore lipstick, and even spent money to go to the beauty parlor! All rather bad things a "good" Sicilian woman would not dream of doing, aside from not being allowed. But Mrs. Marks was such a nice lady anyway.

I wondered greatly about all that I had seen and heard. This wonderment was the beginning of questioning. It marked the beginning of a new awareness. As a young girl growing up in a Sicilian household, I learned, at an early age, the unquestioned superiority of the male. Although no one admired a stupid woman, no matter how intelligent, quick, or talented my gender, our potential was not that important. Basically, my Sicilian upbringing taught me the following; that a female strictly and without question obeys the men in her family, be they brothers, father, or husband. That she was expected to carefully follow orders, work hard, cook, clean, and take good care of the house and all of the people in it, especially the children. Above all, she was to be virtuous beyond question. Aside from all that, not too much more was expected of her.

Insofar as physical appearance, she was never considered an ornament in any way. Lipstick, pretty shoes, dresses, or fancy hairdos, all, were the sign of a *'putana'* or a *'tappinara,'* both of which meant whore. Besides, money was not to be wasted on self-adornment. That was a sign of vanity and thus a sin.

Should a female in the family bring disgrace upon her family by acting in any way like a "loose woman", she could justifiably be beaten bloody, crippled for life, or, in some instances, even killed by the men in her family. Merely being disobedient or showing lack of respect could often result in a beating or some other severe form of punishment.

Thus, during my growing up years, I was both obviously and subtly programmed to feel inferior to my male counter-parts. Paradoxically, I was made to feel that being a woman was a very special thing. To become a mother was the height of wonderfulness. There were "men" things and "woman" things and I had to learn to accept the role in which I was cast due to gender. I had to understand my "place" which was always subservient. Above all, I was never to question or challenge the men in my family, especially my father...God forbid!!!!!

An obedient and pliable child, I learned early on to accept my lot with little complaint since doing so, along with all the other dogma, is what was expected of a "good" Sicilian female, young or old. Needless to say, not all Sicilian men and certainly not all Sicilian women accepted or fit the "mold" described thus far. I can speak only of my experiences and recall and record them as accurately and honestly as possible.

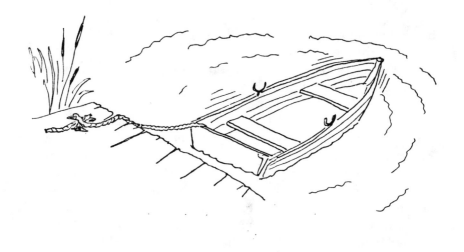

chapter 5

Mama's Tree

Spring and then summer came again. Each winter, as far back as I could remember, Mama would say, *"Si veni la primavera e'non muoro..."* ("If spring comes and I am not dead...") and then she would end the sentence with what she hoped to do come spring. Her list would include planting an asparagus patch or another fig or peach tree. Mama could make anything grow, whether flowers, vegetables, or trees; trees of all kinds–fruit, nut, or floral. All things green prospered under her care.

This mention of trees reminds me of the very first time that I ever saw my mother cry. In a Sicilian family, children may cry, babies may cry, but adults? Never! To cry was a sign of weakness and considered beneath one's dignity. Only the most serious or disastrous happening was cause for crying.

Certainly, when death occurred, many tears, much screaming and carrying on was not only acceptable, but expected. After all if you didn't cry, it meant you didn't care. Never mind that "stiff upper lip" stuff, a loss through death was no trivial thing and one let it all hang out.

True, some tears were also permitted if one was in really great pain (a severe injury or a "good lickin'" at the hands of Papa). You see, after he had more to drink than usual, it was his habit to lie down and take a nap for a while. However, after waking from his nap he would be grouchy and find some trivial reason to lash out and swat any person or animal near him. He was usually sober enough to connect! At those times, upon hearing his footsteps approaching, we all would scatter in fear and apprehension.

I did not consider it unusual to see my father strike my mother if she happened to annoy him in any way. I had seen it happen ever since I could remember and so I believed that it was "normal." I disliked seeing it, but believed it was her due for displeasing him in some way.

He would "punish" her, for instance, if she did not move quickly enough to do his bidding or if she had kept something from him in order to protect one of us from his wrath. For any of those reasons and, sometimes, for what seemed no reason at all, he would become quite angry. Although he did not beat Mama severely, he would, however, cuff her, sometimes just once, other times repeatedly.

When "punished" thus, my mother would put her arms over her head and hunch over, head down, to ward off the blows. She accepted the punishment passively as her "wages" for having been stupid or careless enough to have done or said something that displeased her husband. A victim of tradition, Mama never dared object to, nor would she even dream of, questioning his right to punish her in any way he saw fit and for whatever reason he found necessary. He was, after all, her husband and it was his "right." Her "rights"? She had none.

Back to the very first time I ever saw her cry. It began late in the afternoon on a lovely day in late spring. On that day, not easily forgotten, I came in from feeding the chickens and the half-grown baby chicks and was in high spirits. Spring never seemed "real" to me until the arrival of the baby chicks in early April. There seemed to be hundreds of them and they were delightful! The looks and smells of the tiny, golden, fuzzy babies filled me with wonder. Each day, they grew visibly bigger and bigger. I enjoyed caring for them and was astonished by how quickly they grew and developed into long-legged, feathered chickens. The early feathers were rather scruffy looking. It took about six to eight weeks for smooth white feathers to form.

That particular day, however, upon finishing my chores, I had run quickly to the kitchen in order to relate to my mother how very fast the chicks were growing. As I mounted the kitchen steps two at a time, I heard shouts and screams coming from within. Alarmed, I pushed hard against the creaky old door to the kitchen. It gave way and swung wide open. From the dark interior, the sounds of sobbing and shrieking pierced the air. My eyes, still filled with sunlight, could not see, but I was suddenly paralyzed with fear! "That sounds like Mama!! Could that be Mama crying? No, it couldn't be! Mama *never* cried, never! Yes! It *was* Mama."

Eyes straining to see, I quickly tried to assess what had occurred. Papa, probably, after too much wine in the afternoon, had awakened from his nap and beaten her harshly. Either that or someone in the family had died. I froze suddenly since either of the two thoughts were too terrible to even contemplate. I looked up toward heaven and prayed, "Oh please, PLEASE, God, don't let anyone be dead or don't let Mama hurt too much from a beating."

As my eyes adjusted from bright sunshine to the darker interior, I saw my mother sobbing and shrieking. Furtively, I looked about. My father was nowhere in sight. Caroline had one arm around our mother and was trying to calm her by stroking her hair.

Mama, seated in a chair near the old black coal stove, was wiping her eyes and crying out in Sicilian about the cruelty and injustice of it all. Although her crying surprised and upset me, what I found most disturbing was that my mother (a woman who was pious and never cursed) was now using the worst kind of language to describe Papa, whom she was supposed to honor and respect no matter what! I had no idea she even KNEW any of those words. The worst I had ever heard her say when she was absolutely furious was "Ah, SHEET'ta!"

"Figlio di butana, disgraziato, animale, animale! Ci'va venir'un boto di sango!" (Son of a bitch, disgraced one! Animal, animal! He should die of a blood clot!)

I watched in fascination since her shrieks and the waving about of her arms seemed to "feed" her sorrow and anger. It appeared that the more she cried out between sobs and tears, the more the tears flowed, and the greater the string of shouted insults. Frankie and Joey stood by looking helplessly, first at Mama, then at Caroline, and then at each other while shrugging their shoulders and rolling their eyes upward.

By now, I was thoroughly confused and frightened. Relieved that my mother was not a bloody mess from a beating and certain that no one had died, I wondered what awful event could have brought on all this hollering and cursing. As I watched the tears stream down Mama's cheeks, all at once I experienced a numbing sensation of pain in the pit of my stomach. Now I, too, started to cry from the grief of seeing my mother, who was always so kind and caring, now unhappy and crying as if her heart was broken.

Sobbing, I ran unhesitatingly to her, jumped up on her lap, hugged her, and in a voice filled with sympathy and pain pleaded "Mama, oh Mama, don't cry. *Non piangeri Mama.* (Please don't cry Mama), *Ti voglio bene* (I love you), I love you. It will be alright."

However, to my shock and dismay, Mama, who had never once raised her voice to me, her "baby" and who had always had the patience of a saint, pushed me aside as she would a kitten who had jumped unbidden on her lap. She continued hysterically, seemingly unaware of my attempt to placate her.

My poor little body bounced a little as it hit the floor and I am sure looks of surprise, wonder, and hurt registered on my face all at the same time. "Boy-o-boy, whatever happened must've been awful for Mama to act like this!" I mumbled to no one in particular. Then I jumped up quickly and nervously brushed off the seat of my pants. I went over and took a place beside my brothers, who, eyes filled with pain and compassion, looked even more helpless and perplexed than before. Mama kept repeating in Sicilian over and over, "It took so long and now it's gone! Such a long time! And in one minute, it's gone. It can never be brought back again. How could he do this, he knew, "*disgraziatu*" he knew!"

On and on she went! Waving her arms and shaking her fist toward the barn, she continued her tirade against her husband. "*Figlio di butana, L'i'ammazzari. Disonuratu!*" (Sonofabitch, I'll kill him. Dishonored One!) (Be aware that "*Disonuratu*" is about the worst thing you can call a Sicilian.)

I bit my lip in perplexity as Mama continued to call out all those bad names and continued using those awful words! I found it hard to believe she was actually cursing Papa? Of all people, Papa? She *couldn't* be carrying on all this while about Papa? *How did she dare?*

Thinking of Papa and his rages started a small splinter of fear stabbing at the base of my spine. The fear rose until it reached my skull and then I could feel my whole body flood with the searing heat of terror. I feared my father more than anything or anyone.

My very first memory of him occurred when I was old enough to first recognize his footstep at the door. Whenever I heard him approach, I would run, heart pounding with dread, and hide under the bed. Occasionally, I would find myself joined by the youngest of my brothers, Joey, and sometimes by my sister, Caroline. Most often, however, I would be there crouching under the bed all by myself.

I even remember a few times when all five of us would be there, huddled under the bed, hearts wildly beating and flooded with fear... listening. That was an unusual occurrence and happened only when he was in a really violent rage. That's when everyone scattered and ran to avoid his wrath.

When hiding thus, we would carefully note the tone of Papa's voice as he entered the kitchen. If it was calm and he wasn't shouting, we would quickly emerge from beneath the bed lest he come in and find us hiding from him for no good reason. However, if he sounded belligerent or angry, we would all remain under the bed until summoned or at least until he sounded like he had calmed down a bit. I always remained under the bed until Mama or Caroline would come and coax me out.

When Papa called for someone, he never expected anyone to say: "What is it? " or worse yet, "What?" When he called us, we were expected to run to him immediately and ask, *"Si, Papa, che voi fatto?* (Yes, Papa, what do you want me to do?)"* Lord help the one who did not run *immediately* to answer his call!

As the youngest child, it was my duty each night to remove my father's shoes and fetch his slippers and the box of "Di Nobili" Italian cigars he favored. (Frankie referred to them as "Guinea stinkers.") They were the *most* Godawful smelling cigars!! Each one resembled a small, twisted, old, brown piece of rope, which, had he actually smoked old ropes instead, probably would have smelled much better.

After working in the fields all day, each evening as Papa entered the house the first thing he would do is remove his work gloves. He never did any kind of labor without wearing gloves. As a result he had smooth, creamy white, rather lovely hands, except for a curious and rather ugly growth on the fore finger of his right hand. It looked to me as though the middle of his finger had grown into the shape of a head of garlic. The growth was slightly lumpy and from it, the tip of his finger just below the nail, emerged, smooth and normal, in sharp contrast to the grotesque, disfiguring lump. To my young eyes, it looked as though he had poked his finger into a head of garlic and was wearing it like some sort of monstrous ring. The skin covering the growth was smooth, shiny, taut, and translucent. Actually one could clearly see round, strange, blue-green shapes like giant peas embedded beneath the skin, along with some pearly white shapes, similar to cloves of garlic.

The ugly growth on Papa's hand both fascinated and repelled me and often I would stare at it intently. Occasionally, I would reach out a tentative finger and carefully touch the tumor (for that is what it really was). Papa would smile at my curiosity and then stroke my cheek gently with his other hand. There were a few rare times when he exhibited love and caring, but very few and very far between.

After removing his gloves, he would sit down in the chair at the head of the kitchen table, turn sideways, and put one foot out. He did not have to say a word. I would rush to him, kneel down, and untie his shoes. First one, and then as he put out his foot, the other.

Papa's shoes always intrigued me because they had little hooks instead of grommets in the upper part of where they were laced. I always loved the feel of pulling the laces tightly around the hooks when I had to tie his shoes. I especially enjoyed unhooking the laces. Somehow the hooks made it seem more like playing with an unusual toy rather than tying or untying shoelaces.

In removing his shoes, I would first undo the laces and loosen them far enough so that each would slip off easily. However, as I started to pull off a shoe and it started to give way, the thick, pungent aroma of sweaty socks, smelly feet, and moist leather would rise up and...whew! They stank!

To avoid the acrid, unpleasant smell, I would try to turn my head, imperceptibly, so that Papa would not notice and feel offended that I found his smelly feet offensive. Soon I invented little ways of trying to tactfully avoid the full force of his odorous foot. Turning my head one way, or else cocking my neck in another way, I did my best to keep my nose out of the mainstream of the air rushing upward from the now freed foot. I often wondered about the tiny smile that played about my father's lips and the mischievous gleam in his eyes as he watched my sly maneuvers.

As soon as the shoe was off, I would pop his slipper on, very quickly so it would sort of trap the smell and thus make it less of an ordeal to remove the other shoe.

The sound of Mama's hysteria brought me back to the moment at hand. Mama was still at it, continuing her raving tirade against Papa. I glanced toward the door, fearful that my father might enter at any moment. I was certain he would be so furious at Mama's behavior and show of anger toward him that he would in a fit of anger kill his entire family—with his bare hands!!

You see, whenever my father got really angry, he would look around at all of us and very quietly and ominously say, "I end up ina'lectric chair!" At that time in America, the death penalty for murder was in full force. His message was very clear. There would always be a long and ominous silence after that. Trembling, and as soon as we felt it safe to do so, we would quietly disperse. He certainly must have been bluffing, but we believed him and obeyed him unquestioningly.

But for now, consumed with curiosity about Mama's anger and tears I wondered,"What awful thing could Papa have done to make her so angry that she would dare to defy him in this way?"

By now, Mama had worked herself into a frenzy and had given over completely to uncontrolled rage. She was even preparing herself to attack Papa should he dare enter her kitchen. Intrigued, I watched as my mother, a woman of infinite patience and gentility, now stood up, reached over, and picked up a large cast iron skillet. Standing there, still venting her anger, she was now brandishing the skillet and threatening to use it on Papa's head should he come anywhere near her.

Meanwhile, after some whispered questioning, I finally learned what had precipitated this unusual outburst of frenzied anger. It so happened that a few years earlier, someone returning from a visit to Sicily had brought Mama a gift— a small twig from a black mulberry tree. She was delighted to be given the twig because, properly planted, it would grow into a mature, fruit-bearing mulberry tree.

Now you must understand that my mother was a good, kind woman, who had few pleasures in life. Her joy over this gift was boundless because the twig brought back fond memories of when she was a young girl. Back then, black mulberries were her favorite fruit and black mulberry trees grew in great profusion in Sicily. But here, in America, in upstate New York, where we lived, there were none.

A woman with an incredible knack at gardening, she planted the twig in the ground, watered it, and nursed it. She bundled it up and covered it in winter and fed it in spring. During the next few years, she lavished much attention on the little twig. It had finally grown into a small, but healthy and sturdy tree. Her excessive care of the tree was almost an obsession. So much so, that it had become a family joke. When everyone teased her about the concern and attention she bestowed on the tree, she would grin and respond with happiness and great satisfaction, "You wait 'tila you tasta them! Dee-lish'!" and she would put her thumb and forefinger together and rub them in a twisting motion on her plump right cheek to signify a tasty morsel.

After three years of growth and a great amount of attention, the tree was finally ready that summer to bear its first fruit. Thick clusters of almost ripe, pinkish-white berries hung in abundance from the branches. There had been plenty of rain early that particular spring. By mid-summer, the trees and grass on the farm were rich shades of green, lush and thick.

Just as Mama's tree was her pride and joy, Papa, too, had a favorite-a huge young bull named Joe. (Papa's name translated in English.) For obvious reasons, Joe had to be kept separate from the cows. Daily, he was tethered to a stake in various locations on the property, always in the midst of tall and tender grass. Joe would graze and munch contentedly as he circled the metal stake to which he was bound by a chain attached to a ring through his nose. When he had eaten everything within the parameter of the chain, he would have to be moved, otherwise he would pull on the chain, lift up the stake, and wander at will.

Although young, Joe was an enormous bull. However, he was easily led about by the ring through his nose. The chain attached to the ring was easy to handle which made Joe so gentle that even I took my turn at untethering him and leading him to new eating places. His appetite was voracious and he had to be moved to new locations a few times a day. We all took turns at moving him around. Keeping him tethered in this way gave him access to the best grass. Most of all, it kept him separate from the cows.

On this fateful day, however, when it came time for Papa to move the bull, he either inadvertently, or on purpose (perhaps as a sick joke) tied Joe next to the little mulberry tree, now finally ready to bear its first fruit.

As the ripening season approached that summer, Mama's mouth had watered for the sweet, luscious berries that turned one's mouth purple. She had not eaten black mulberries since she had been a young girl in Sicily. The great joy of her life that summer was that she would once again taste the fruit of her childhood and share it with her children. (Papa disliked mulberries, white or black.)

She went out to the tree on an almost daily basis to check the small fruit as it changed from white to pink. Soon the berries were a deep rich pink, only days away from picking time. There was not much in my mother's life that gave her joy and the contemplation of picking and eating the ripening fruit made each day a day of anticipated pleasure. A small pleasure to be sure, but big to her.

On this particular day, she took her customary walk to the tree to check the ripeness of the mulberries. As she approached the spot where her tree was planted, she was puzzled for a moment. What she saw seemed very odd! Standing where her tree should have been, was Joe the bull, knee deep in a heap of branches and twigs. Quickly she drew closer to see better. As she did, her heart sank and almost stopped.

The branches and twigs on the ground were all that was left of her mulberry tree. It was broken and splintered beyond recognition. Every one of the mulberries, from the deepest pinkish-purple to the unripe greenish-white, had been crushed and ground into the dirt and grass. Since Joe had been chomping and milling about that particular area for at least two or three hours, there was not one mulberry to be salvaged.

The young bull had first consumed most of the leaves and then much of the fruit. Moving around and around in the confining parameter of the staked chain, he totally splintered and crushed the tree. Stomping on it over and over, his chain tore it apart as he repeatedly circled. Sadly, just as the tree was totally shattered, so for Mama was the pleasure of eating the fruit and sharing it with her children.

After a few moments, the enormity of what happened sank in. The complete destruction of her precious mulberry tree became reality and she was filled with a sad and aching feeling in her heart. The feeling spread and filled her entire chest. She began to breath very heavily. Then she wondered,"But who would do such a thing? Who would tie the bull that close to 'my' tree? Certainly the tree was big enough to see, even in the tall grass." Like a thunder-bolt, a thought suddenly came to her. *"Po'essere ca Pippino lu facci?* (Could Joe have done it?) It had to be him! It had to, because all of the children were hoeing tomatoes in the south meadow that morning.

Oh, *Dio mio*, how, how could he do this? *Mio marito!* (My husband!) *Perche'? Perche'?* (Why? Why?)"

Her eyes rolled up toward heaven. She put her fist up to her mouth and bit her knuckle to stop from screaming out loud. A strangled, muffled cry emerged; half scream, half moan. Her deeply ingrained traditional upbringing took over automatically and made her control her anger at her husband.

Since earliest childhood, she had been thoroughly brainwashed. She had been taught that a husband is the "head" of the household and has absolute power to do whatever he pleases. He is never to be questioned or disputed, on pain of being punished. Thus, she stood and stared, first at the decimated tree and then at the hateful creature that had destroyed it.

Her first impulse was to vent her frustration and anger by picking up one of the broken branches and beating the young bull with it as hard as she could. However, being an inherently gentle and kind person prevented her from doing this. She fully realized that the bull was not at fault. How was he to know one tree from another? The real fault lay with her husband. HE was the person who had tied the bull that close to the tree. HE was at fault! HE, and he alone. The tears started as she thought to herself, *"Como lu potiva fare sta cos'amia?"* (How could he have done this to me?) "Will his cruelty never end? Am I destined forever to be treated like a dog (*como nu cane*), unhappy, robbed of even the smallest pleasures? Will he never show some kind of caring or concern? How many more years of misery with this man do I have to look forward to? *Accusi av' esseri per tutta la vita mia?"* (Will it be like this for the rest of my life?)

She moaned to herself as she remembered that he had never, in almost forty years of marriage, been a kind or loving husband. He let her know, almost immediately upon marrying her, that he had only married her for spite. The woman that he really had wanted to marry had rejected him for another. So he had turned to my mother, his junior by seven years. When they married, she was eighteen and he was twenty five.

Just as he had never shown her any kind of warmth or affection, neither did he express any concern about her emotional needs. There had never been even an iota of romance in their marriage. This was really tragic, since my mother was an incurable romantic.

In his defense, I must admit that he did work very hard to provide food and shelter for his family and whatever else was expected of him as the head of the household. He did it as his duty. It was what a man of "honor" did to provide for his own. A man who did not provide for his family was considered lazy and despicable. Papa provided well, if not lavishly.

As Mama thought about it, she realized she had always been nothing more to him than a vessel to bear his children, to carry on his name, and to give him hands to help him in his work. She realized also that she was a vassal to do his bidding-cooking, cleaning, taking caring of the family and the house. She was to work at whatever needed to be done.

The workload increased tenfold when we moved to the farm. Even then, never did he show sympathy, appreciation, concern, or affection for her, no matter how hard she worked. As she thought of his lack of appreciation, the tears flowed copiously down her cheeks. Wearily, she turned away from the site of the ruined mulberry tree and the young bull happily chomping on the grass. Her feet dragged through the tall grass as she headed slowly back toward the house.

As she walked, head bowed, her shoulders contracted in violent shudders as deep, wrenching sobs made her whole body shake. The tears continued. They ran down her cheeks and dripped off her chin and on to her dress. Her nose was so full, she almost choked from the profusion of tears and mucous. Reaching down, she took the hem of her apron, pulled it up and blew her nose. Then, using the rest of the apron, she dried her face and eyes. Unable to control them, the tears began again and she continued to cry and sob into her apron.

Her tears were tears of mourning. Not for just a shattered tree, but for a shattered life! The heartbreak she was feeling was devastating. Somehow for the first time, this giving, accepting, sweet woman, who for years had been physically and mentally abused, was suddenly aware of what a meaningless and cruel play her marriage had always been.

Giving it real thought, for the first time she realized the emptiness of it all. She tried hard, but could not remember her husband, even once, providing any pleasant or happy times.

Her life had meaning and direction only because of her children. "Life" itself consisted only of work and sleep. What little pleasure came her way was from the unconditional love and loyalty she felt for and received from her children. There was really nothing else. You may say that should be enough, but we do not live by bread alone. We all need different kinds of love to be fulfilled.

My mother, whose name was Antoinette, Nina for short, had been sent to America at the age of fourteen as "punishment" for being in love with and wanting to marry a young man who had a speech impediment. He stuttered. Her parents packed her off, by steamship, to America, in the company of a woman from their village named Giuannina who was sailing to America in order to join her older brother, a man named Giuseppi.

When they disembarked, Giuseppi met them at the boat with his horse-drawn wagon. After loading his sister's and Nina's (Mama's) trunks on his wagon and seating them beside him on the front seat, he proceeded to deliver them and their trunks to their destination. He charged Nina only a quarter, half what he usually charged others for the delivery, primarily because she was with his sister.

In his thick knit, cream-colored, turtle neck sweater and with his curly, jet black hair, carefully combed and parted on the side, he was indeed an extraordinarily handsome twenty-one year old Sicilian. His face, tanned from wind and exposure, was clean shaven and smooth. His eyes, the color of deep brown chocolate, seemed to bore into Nina's and see down into the bottom of her soul each time he turned to look at her. As his horse clip-clopped along, Giuseppi sang Neapolitan love songs all the way to their destination on the lower east side of Manhattan.

Obviously, he made some sort of impression on the young fourteen-year old who had just arrived from their mutual hometown in Sicily. Four years later, after a very brief courtship, they were wed in a short and simple ceremony. There were not even any photos taken.

When Nina and Giuseppe married in 1907, many marriages were arranged and were anything but a love match. People married primarily for convenience and to carry on tradition and the family name. Few ever promised, nor did many really expect, marriage to be a happy, joyous union. One knew it involved work and commitment and if love and joy were a part of it one could consider oneself lucky. Lucky, Mama obviously was not. Thus she had spent a lifetime of unhappiness which culminated in this day of pain and sorrow.

Earlier in the day, Mama had been inconsolable over the broken mulberry tree. By late afternoon, though, she appeared to have calmed down a bit. She got some degree of satisfaction from the fact that Papa had not come in for lunch, which was unheard of! This made her certain that he was aware of his dastardly deed. The "knowing" made her quiet rage simmer even more.

By the time my father entered the kitchen at supper time, his face was pale and his mouth was set in a tight straight line. His eyes glittered and looked even darker than usual. Glancing over at him, Mama, standing in front of the old black kitchen stove, pondered over whether or not she dared vent the anger that was still consuming her. Should she even mention the tree or Joe the bull or her pain and heartbreak? Her heart began to beat very fast and she was nervous. She had never confronted him before. Should she risk his anger and the violent aftermath of it?

As he closed the door behind him, she turned abruptly from the pot she was stirring. The wooden spoon continued twirling by itself for a moment. It was ominously quiet in the kitchen. Taking a few steps, she stood directly in front of him. Fists on hips she confronted him, looking deeply and directly into his eyes. It was a rebellious, piercing, hostile look.

Although surprised at being confronted in this way by his usually pliant and subservient wife, Papa hid his surprise well and easily stood his ground. He folded his arms, slowly and deliberately, across his chest. Standing there, firm as a rock, he stared down at her with eyes even colder and more hostile than hers. They stood a long moment, eyes locked together, neither "giving." All at once, Papa, glaring, raised his right arm, hand toward his left shoulder, to give her "the back of his hand." Raising her own arm in a similar gesture, Mama stood, head up, facing him defiantly, eyes ablaze! After what seemed an eternity to those of us who were in the kitchen watching and who were almost paralyzed with fear, Papa finally laughed out loud and lowered his arm. Still chuckling, he deliberately turned away, nonchalantly removed his hat and gloves and took his customary seat.

Relieved, I rushed over, happy that violence had been averted. Kneeling down, I quickly removed his shoes and ran to fetch his slippers. Mama, back straight as a ramrod, turned slowly toward her stove and with great dignity walked back to the pot and continued to stir. There was a strained and eerie silence at the dinner table that evening.

With so much work to do from dawn to dusk, Mama had never had time to think about or assess her situation. She really never had time to ask herself if she was happy or unhappy. Questioning was not part of *"la vita"* (life). Her happiness did not matter one iota. Only the family, as a unit, mattered. Whether or not the family itself was happy or unhappy was not important either. The concept of "family" was sacred and, as such, was not to be damaged or broken apart in any way, ever! No one person's need, emotional or otherwise, was more important than the cohesion of the family.

Of course, there was strife. Of course, there was unhappiness and frustration. Of course, there was often a need to sacrifice your own wishes to the greater good. So what? That was life. You did what you had to do! That was the way it was and you learned to cope and make the best of it. (There were no psychiatrists or Advil.)

Along with the bad was the good; the warm, deep feelings of family unity. You knew at all times, no matter how hostile the inter-familial feuding, that if you needed any or all of them, the members of your family would be there for you, no matter what! You could be certain that you were loved and that you would be helped, protected, and nurtured. Whatever your needs, when called upon, the family would never fail you. It was a solid, dependable entity that made you feel safe and secure.

Despite unhappiness on Mama's part, it simply had never occurred to her to ever even dream of questioning the fact that her life revolved wholly around her husband's wishes and the well-being of her children. There was nothing to question as far as she was concerned. The way it was, is the way it was and always would be. She never knew she had a choice. From the way she was brought up and as far as she was concerned there never was a question of choice. She lived according to a proscribed code. Her primary measure of behavior in any situation was *"Che a'na dire le gente?"* (What will people say?)

During the first fifteen, childless years of her marriage, before she gave birth to her first of five children, my mother had considered leaving her abusive husband and her unbearable, unhappy marriage many times. But honor, hers and that of her family back in Sicily, was not to be taken lightly and had to be given first consideration above all else. Honor had to be protected at all times. The good "name" of her family was much more important than any of her needs. Her actions, even in far away America, would still reflect on her family back in Bivona, the small village in Sicily from whence both my parents had immigrated. Back in that village, one of her brothers was a priest and, as such, held a place of high esteem in the community.

As unhappy as she was, whenever Mama pondered leaving she would ask herself how she could ever do such a thing. A thing that would disgrace her family and, the worst sin of all, disgrace her brother, a priest! Anything she did that was out of the norm would reflect badly on him and the villagers would look at him askance. To bring disgrace upon your family was unthinkable.

In Sicilian culture, at that time, you were your brother's, mother's, father's, and sister's keeper. Everyone was responsible for everyone else's behavior, always! Nothing you did was ever your behavior alone. You shared both the guilt and the triumphs, the faults and the virtues with your family. Like it or not, good or bad, that was how it was.

Back then, not just among Sicilians I am sure, there was no valid or legitimate reason for which a woman could leave her husband. No matter what the cause, if a woman left her husband, she would be judged as a "bad" woman and one whose family was dishonored. Even if she was terribly abused physically, whatever action she might take to protect herself or to better her life would only heap dishonor and disgrace on those she loved and respected. There was only "divorce, Italian style" (the death, sometimes murder, of the wife).

Therefore, due to her upbringing, Mama preferred to accept her lot rather than be known as a "dishonorata", as bad a word as "tappinara." Well, almost as bad. The first means "woman without honor" and the second means "whore." The two are equally repulsive to Sicilians.

Thus, in her married years, Mama had endured, for all that time up until now, beatings, insults, degradation, and frustration. She suffered silently...and alone, so very, very alone. Perhaps there were some super strong cells in her genes or maybe it was her incredible patience. *Something* within enabled her to bear the unbearable and tolerate the intolerable. How sad! What harm we do in order to shape those we love, teaching them to accept and endure great pain.

Sicilians of that generation were, if anything, zealous believers in tradition. Things had to be done as they had always been done in the past. There was to be no deviation in behavior or beliefs. One was obedient and bowed to authority and/ or to those "in charge" with no questions asked. To question or ask was to be disrespectful. Disrespect was looked upon as a major "sin."

My mother, doing what she felt was right, did her best to inculcate in her two daughters the same beliefs and upbringing that had shaped her. My sister Caroline, however, did not always listen. I guess maybe she inherited a different set of genes and was smarter than I. She was strong-minded and followed her own path. For sure, she marched to a different drum.

I, however, (mostly to avoid getting hit at all costs), was more easily molded and more compliant. From an early age, I unquestioningly did as I was told. There was no rebellion in my nature.

An obedient child, my philosophy of life was definitely shaped by two phrases my mother, almost up to the day she died, repeated over and over to me. They were almost a litany. The first of the two, and the one that probably shaped my outlook on life more than any thing else was *"Pazienzia figlia mia."* (Patience, my daughter.) It was my mother's standard reply to all complaints. The second phrase was *"Che a'na dire le gente?"* (What will people say?) These two phrases were burned into my head as sure as if a branding iron had been used. They certainly had the same impact.

All my life, it seemed to me that no matter what my complaints were, whether it was having to work all day Saturday and Sunday picking up hateful "brush," having to slaughter young pullets, having to wash mounds of dishes, do laundry all by myself, or if I complained of being "picked on" by others, no matter what the complaint, Mama's reply was always the same. "Pazienzia figlia mia."

And patient I was, almost to a fault. This "patience" enabled me to complete even those chores that I absolutely hated. Above all, despite my distaste, I had to complete those chores properly and in a way that was satisfactory to my father.

Of all of the chores, the one that repelled me most was when I had to slaughter pullets. Caroline refused to do it. I don't know how she got away with it, but she did, and so the task then fell to me. She did not plan it that way, that was just the way it happened. I was nine years old at the time.

Our summer boarders liked to purchase pullets (young chickens about eight weeks old). Freshly killed, they were extraordinarily tender and tasty; everyone's favorite. In early morning, the boarders put in their orders and then the chickens had to be delivered by mid-afternoon. Thus, when it fell to me to slaughter the pullets, I dared not disobey Papa's orders to "chop off their heads."

The fluffy little baby chicks of early springtime had grown prodigiously. Leggy and feathered, they were now the eight-week old pullets that I had to slaughter. Approaching maturity, the cute, yellow chicks of early spring had also grown rather ugly. Scraggly, undeveloped feathers sticking out all over, no longer "cute" they were still not so ugly that I could kill them with equanimity. Of all my farm chores, I found that this was the only one that made me want to disobey my father. I didn't dare to, however.

One day, he took me aside and matter-of-factly demonstrated how to kill the young chickens. He showed me how to pull firmly on the feet of the pullet after placing its head between two nails partly sunk in the flat surface of the cut-trunk of a large tree. Holding the pullet taut he instructed me on how to use a large ax to chop off their heads (hopefully with one stroke). Once their heads were off, I was to fling the headless chickens on the ground. Even with no heads, those pullets would run frantically through the grass for quite a few minutes, I suppose until their hearts stopped beating. Running about in this way would drain all the blood from their carcasses before they died and would result in clean, white meat when cooked.

However, I abhorred chopping off their heads and leaving bloody stumps where once were beaks, eyes, and bright red combs. It really pained me to see them run headless until they keeled over in the tall grass kicking until their life and blood drained away. After slaughtering the last one, I would then have to search for them in the grass, and as I found them, I would gingerly pick up their blood-spattered bodies. One by one, they would be deposited in a burlap bag and then delivered to the women in the summer kitchen, who had already paid my father for the pullets earlier in the day.

He charged extra for plucked chickens. Usually, Mama performed this task, but when she was busy, this task also was assigned to me. My mother had instructed me that before plucking their feathers, holding tight to their feet, I would first have to plunge the slaughtered young chickens into, and then quickly remove them from, a pot of boiling water. The quick emersion in hot water made the feathers come off quite easily. Just as quickly, I discovered that I could not stand the pungent smell of the feathers when they were soaked with hot water. It was an extremely unpleasant smell, like dirty wool burning and until I finally got used to it, it always made me gag.

As I performed the various chores assigned to me, some of which I enjoyed and others that I detested, I sometimes wondered if my whole life would have to be spent often doing what I did not want to do. I especially resented being ordered about, having to do as I was told and being slapped if I did not obey quickly enough.

Because I was the youngest and had to take orders from everyone else in the family, I also wondered if the time would ever come when my life would be my own. I saw myself only as the slave of the rest of the family. As the youngest, I accepted my lot. Now in retrospect, I wonder why, all those times that I was filled with rage and frustration, oddly enough, I never questioned or rebelled. At least not openly and certainly not at that point in time. Because of the great amount of work I was assigned, I felt put upon and I resented the fact, and rightfully so, that I had so little time to play. In fact, I had hardly enough time to do homework.

Since there were so many chores to do on the farm, I often got the feeling that they were an endless string of tasks that I could never complete. All of the outside work had to be finished by sundown. After that, it was time to help prepare supper and set the table. After supper, by the time the dishes were washed and all the pots were scrubbed, dried, and put away each night, it was well past ten o'clock. But always, when I turned to Mama for sympathy I heard, *"Pazienzia figlia mia."*

Sounds simplistic, right? And repetitious? Right? It was! However, it ingrained in me the realization, at a very early age, that there were situations in life that one had to overcome and things one had to do, no matter how difficult or repellent. You did as you were told, no matter what! You did not question. To be good and obedient was not only expected, but demanded! At the same time, my mother and father taught us to take pride in our accomplishments. When given a task, you were expected to do it to the best of your ability. Careless or incompetent work was not accepted. Sloppily done tasks were met with punishment—swift and forceful! Complaints and pouting were not tolerated. Being forced into the mold of growing up Sicilian and female was exacting, sometimes discouraging, and often times bitter. It did, however, teach me discipline, to wait out anger and pain. It apparently helped make me strong enough to cope with what life held in store for me later on.

chapter 6

Tanti Cosi (Many Things)

My very fondest memories of school were those times when the teacher read us stories. Some of the stories told of mothers who bathed their children each night and dressed them in night gowns or pajamas with "feet" in them. After being given a glass of warm milk or Ovaltine they were tucked into bed, read a bedtime story, kissed goodnight and left drifting off to dream. The same kind of thing happened in the movies and it all seemed like pure bliss. Bliss which I would never experience. Sitting in my underwear–which served as bedclothes–and before climbing into bed, I would daydream as I gazed out the fan-shaped window of my small room beneath the eaves. Outside was an ancient maple tree. Staring at the moon through the web of branches woven against the deep blue of the evening sky, I would fantasize that my mother bathed and then dressed me in a pretty nightgown and read me a bedtime story. It was my favorite fantasy even though I was well aware that my mother could not read.

One day I asked my sister,"Caroline, how come kids in stories and in the movies always have somebody giv'em a bath, put a pretty nightgown on'em 'n give em warm milk to drink 'n then read'm a story? How come nothin' like that ever happens to me? Boy, I sure would like to have somebody read me a bedtime story sometime?"

I guess she took the hint because the next thing I knew she came home one day with a book. While she could not provide a nightgown (and to tell the truth, I found warm milk unappetizing), she had decided to make me happy at bedtime by reading me a story.

The title of the book was *Ferdinand the Bull*. Almost every night, Caroline would read the story to me and I never tired of hearing about a bull who would rather smell flowers than fight with the matador, the picadors, or with anyone for that matter. I can still see, (in my mind's eye), the colorful illustrations of Ferdinand smelling the flowers while the matadors and picadors were going crazy because he refused to fight. No matter what they did, Ferdinand just smelled the flowers and just about anything else in sight that looked fragrant, including the slick matador!

Caroline stopped reading when the book finally fell apart. But by then, I had learned to read well enough and had discovered the school library. I do believe that eventually I read every single fairy tale and myth that it had to offer. (It was not a very large library to begin with.) We had no books in our house but I managed to get quite a few, through what might today be called "reverse cultural accumulation."

One year, my father hired a man to work on the farm full time. His last name was Jones and he and his family lived in the tenant house down in back of the main house as partial exchange for his labors. He had a wife and six children. The only one I remember was Maceo. Maceo Jones. He was a very pleasant, polite boy, my age. His skin was as smooth as milk and the same color but with cocoa added. With dark brown eyes and straight white teeth he was indeed a handsome boy. We went to school together, were both in the fourth grade, shared the same classroom that year, and became good friends. Maceo was a bright child, but extremely shy.

My father respected Mr. Jones, he was a hard worker, and Papa was happy to have him working on our farm. I don't know why, but the family did not stay very long-only a year.

They were only the second family I can remember that ever occupied the tenant house. Right after they moved, I went down to the house to see if they had left anything behind. The house was empty except for a large number of books. You can imagine my delight! (I noted that some were from libraries in towns I had never heard of.)

I carried all of them home, making many trips from the tenant house, back and forth to mine. It was a very warm time of year and even now I can remember sweating profusely as I climbed up the hill, arms loaded down with heavy books. I continued to sweat as I carried them up the various flights of stairs to my room. It was well worth the effort. Thereafter, between chores and on rainy days, I reveled in *The Jungle Book, The Works of Victor Hugo, Tarzan and the Apes, Little Women, Treasure Island*, and lots of other short stories and novels. Those were the first and only books in my house aside from *Ferdinand the Bull*.

In the years before I started school, I was the lone and constant companion of my mother. Completing her chores with me at her side, Mama filled my days by reciting to me Sicilian folk tales, anecdotes about modes of traditional behavior, superstitious beliefs, and religious teachings. Throughout all of the tales and teachings, evil was greatly punished and good greatly rewarded.

The consistent exposure, at such an early age, to the teachings of my mother probably influenced my thinking to a large degree. It certainly made me absorb much more of her traditional philosophy and strong religious beliefs than did my brothers and sister. This also might have accounted for my unquestioning obedience in my childhood, youth, and early adulthood.

My brothers and sister had been born only one and a half to two years apart and Mama did not have the time to lavish on them which she lavished on me, the baby by five years, a so-called "change of life baby."

By the age of thirty-three, after fifteen years of marriage my mother had proven barren. During that "empty", painful time, she had endured much verbal abuse from my father about her "rotten insides" and other rude and cruel remarks.

Papa was really getting desperate for children after all those years. He probably wanted to prove to all that he was a "real" man who could procreate. Finally, he sent his maligned and barren wife to doctors in Italy. (I suppose in the thirties, medicine in Europe was more sophisticated than in America.) Anyway, upon examination, the Italian doctors discovered she had a tipped womb. After inserting some sort of device to straighten it out, they sent her home. Thereafter, she dutifully produced four children in five years. First a son, Bernard, then a daughter, Caroline then much to her husbands delight, two more sons, Frank and Joseph, Jr.

Although my parents did not practice birth control, five years passed before Mama, at the age of forty-two, was again with child. All her *"amici"* and *"comare"* (both near and close friends) advised her to *"Tirar e'te su bambino, si troppo vecchia."* (Tear out that child, you are too old.) Smiling gently, Mama replied, *"Lu Signoruzu m'l'manato stu bambino e l'av'ere, maccari si moru."* (God has sent me this child and I shall have it, even if doing so, I die.) Of course, they thought her foolhardy. When her time came to deliver the child, it was decided that due to her age, she should go to the hospital rather than have the child at home, as she had done with the others. For the ten days that Mama was in the hospital, it was left for Papa, alone, to care for his brood. Totally inept at anything domestic, on his first day without his wife, Papa cooked an enormous pot of lentils and pasta. That is the only food his children ate for the entire ten days that their mother was away.

Because it was early in January, there was no problem with refrigeration. He just put the pot of lentils out on the fire escape. Dishes were never washed, he just threw them out! The window! At least, that is what I have been told. His frugal nature makes that story hard to believe.

Meanwhile, back at Governere Hospital, where much of the staff was primarily Jewish, each time I was brought in to nurse at my mothers breast, the nurses would say,"Here's little Sadie." I suppose the name became fixated in my mother's brain. Soon it was time for her to go home.

Mama entered carrying me and was greeted joyously at the door by my brothers and sister. They had been waiting impatiently for her return, not only because they were thoroughly tired of lentil soup, but they could not wait to see their baby sister. As she came through the door, my brothers and sister, jumping up and down, shrieked and shouted in unison, "What's her name, what's her name?"

"Sadie," replied Mama with a small helpless shrug of her shoulders. And Sadie it remained, even though a short while later I was baptized "Rosaria" (an even worse name than Sadie). Occasionally, during my childhood, Caroline would tell me that my name was not really Sadie, that it was "Jemale" since that is what she remembered having once seen on the birth certificate. Thinking "Jemale" was a rather silly name, I never gave much thought to it.

It was not until thirty-one years later, when, curious as to what my "real" name was, I sent for a copy of my birth certificate from the board of health in New York City. When it arrived, I carefully examined the faded writing on it. It was difficult to decipher, but for the first time in my life I learned that my name was not Sadie. For the first time in my life, I learned that I *had no* name, for on my birth certificate was written "female Penzato." But the hand-written capital "F" did look like a capital "J."

Unfortunately, no one had ever bothered to ask my illiterate, Sicilian mother what name she wished her child to bear. Probably due to the large number of children born to all the "foreigners" in that area, it was the custom in those days to often designate only the sex of the child on a birth certificate, not the name. Perhaps language was a barrier. I wonder if English-speaking parents were sent home with the same kind of birth certificate for their children. This, of course, is only conjecture on the my part, but since telling this story to others born of immigrants, they have recited the same experience concerning gender listed on their birth certificates rather than a name.

Being the youngest by five years, I was cuddled and played with and almost spoiled rotten. Paradoxically, discipline and proper behavior were drummed into me by everyone since I was at the bottom of the pecking order. However, although I was constantly disciplined and ordered about, I have to admit that I did love all that attention, both good and bad!

As mentioned previously, the most attention came from my mother. For when all the rest of her brood were in school, or out tending to farm work, Mama, whether baking bread, making pasta, dusting, washing or cleaning, found me constantly at her side. Everywhere she went, I followed. I was like her shadow.

Many years later, when Mama was old and frail, her children took turns "sharing" her. She often came and lived with me for months at a time. By then, our positions were reversed. Wherever I went or whatever I did around the house, there would be Mama following me about. She was my shadow. One day she said, "Ah you rememb' when you a lil'la girla, you follow me ev'ry place, en' now, I follow you all ova' the house. Aah, you mine ee' when I do that?"

In my studio, working on a painting at the time, surprised at her words, I turned to her, to where she was seated on a chair and gently said, "No, Mama, no, I don't mind at all. You can watch me and follow me around all you like. You know how very much I love you. *Io saccio quanto tu me voi bene.*" (And I know how much you love me). "No, Mama, no, *cara Mama mia*" (dear mother of mine), "I don't mind at all."

Still holding my paintbrush, the tip of which was coated with Burnt Sienna oil paint, I walked over to her and looked deeply into her soft brown eyes, eyes that were almost the color of the paint on the brush, eyes which were nearly hidden behind rimless glasses. Looking at my mother, whose life had been so filled with pain and sorrow, quietly I said,"All the times I was a little girl, you were always there for me. You rarely scolded and you never hit me. Always patient and loving, you made me feel so good about myself. Maybe sometimes, too much so. *Vosi'a stattu la ciu melglia matre di tutti.*" (You have been the best mother of all.)

Reaching over I put my paintbrush handle bristles-up in a jar. Then I stooped down and hugged my mother's frail, seventy-three-year-old body close to me. I kissed her gently on the cheek. With my lips against her thinning, white hair, I said, "No, Mama, I'll never mind you following me around. I only hope you are here to do it for a long, long time." Sadly, she died a year later.

During the 1930s, on the farm, Mama's life was an endless series of cooking, canning, gardening, cleaning, and laundry. The house was more often messy than neat. Because it was such an enormous house, by the time the last room was thoroughly tidy the first ones were again in need of cleaning. Caroline and I spent much time at this never-ending chore.

Dinner in my Sicilian household, according to nutritionists in the 1930s, would not have been considered a properly "balanced meal." Each meal was, however, quite "balanced" in its own way. In many Italian and Sicilian households, back then, some form of pasta was served every single night with dinner. Pasta was inexpensive (10 cents a pound). It was filling and went far when mixed with other things.

The sauce for the pasta varied each night: garlic, vegetable, or meat-tomato. This was called the *"primo piatto"* (the first plate). Each family member would consume two or three dishes of pasta. Besides a variation of sauce, the shape of the pasta would vary from night to night. On Monday, it might be *"tupatedi"* (also known as *ditalini*). On Tuesday, it might be *spagettini*, and on succeeding nights, it could be *buccatini*, small shells, *margharita*, or any other number of pasta shapes available. They were numerous and made each meal interesting.

Four or five pounds of pasta would be cooked in order to satiate the voracious appetites of my hardworking family and the regular farm hands. One or two nights a week, the pasta would be served as a soup dish: *minestrone*, thick with fresh vegetables and small macaroni or as a rich, thick, chicken soup, filled with *Orzo* or *Semen'd Melone*. Lentils, escarole, red or pink beans (*past'e fasole*) and chick peas were also served with pasta.

The second plate (*secondo piatto*) was either meat, chicken, or fish and was always accompanied by a salad. In summer, our salads often consisted of chickweed (a fleshy weed which grew in abundance throughout the farm). Thick, green olive oil with homemade vinegar liberally flavored with salt and pepper was the only dressing I ever saw my mother use. Mama used her hands to tear the greens apart and mix the salad, *never* utensils.

Pasta came in different shaped boxes–rectangular of varying lengths and sizes. The pasta that came in long, thin, boxes was always wrapped in a sheet of white paper. I learned, early on, to salvage each sheet of paper, smooth it out, and save it to draw on.

Mama's favorite brand of pasta was "La Rosa" which had photos of a rose on each side of the pasta boxes. The roses were a form of "coupon." They could be cut off the boxes and saved. When a certain number of them were collected, they could be exchanged for gifts that were pictured in the "La Rosa" gift catalog. These included toasters, waffle irons, dishes, and the like.

Needless to say, due to the enormous amount of pasta that was consumed daily, there was a great accumulation of rose coupons. In fact, a slot had been cut into the wall next to a closet door in the kitchen. Into this slot, the torn coupons were deposited. Once a week, the small chamber fed by the slot was emptied out and the family, seated about the kitchen table, would spend the evening counting roses and sorting them into small bundles of ten, held together by a rubber band.

These bundles of rose coupons would be redeemed the next time that Benny, my oldest brother, drove to the city and went to the redemption center. It seemed like magic to me. Here Benny would go off with sacks of torn rose coupons and then he would miraculously return with an electric iron or a toaster–and they were *free*! To a small child it seemed indeed a miracle.

Mama's cooking was fabulous, but her meatballs were especially incredible: light, juicy, fragrant, filled with grated cheese and bread crumbs, eggs, parsley, and much garlic. My brother Frankie, the family comedian, dubbed them "garlic balls." The name stuck, just as the smell of garlic "stuck" on one's breath if consumed in great quantity.

Because of this nasty, clinging habit which garlic possesses, often, at school and sometimes elsewhere, some unkind children or adults would make nasty remarks about the terrible breath of "those wops and spaghetti benders." As a result, we children would often come home bruised or with a bloody nose, hurting, yet defiant and proud of defending our eating habits and ethnic roots.

It is with a sense of keenly remembered embarrassment and unhappiness that I recall lunch time at school. In those early years, I always carried my lunch to school in a brown paper bag, in what-ever size was available from the bags Mama diligently saved. There were no packages of lunch-sized bags in the stores at that time. If there were, spending money to buy paper bags, when they could be saved from shopping, would have been considered a waste of money.

As for my lunch bags, one day it might be an enormous bag, with the top folded over so many times that I could barely grasp it with my small fingers. Another day, I might have a bag so small that the lunch would be popping out of the top of it and the bag would look like a large stuffed sausage. Whenever a proper-sized bag was found, Mama would admonish me to save it and bring it home each night. I did as I was told and certain sized bags were used until they wore out and fell apart.

The cafeteria was six flights up from my first floor classroom. With the rest of my classmates, I would get in line and be led by our teacher. We would quietly (no one was allowed to talk) make our way down the halls. At the center of the building, we would turn down a small corridor, walk past a wrought iron enclosure leading to a mysterious place called the basement, after which we would climb up a small set of stairs in the middle of a long wide hall. Halfway down that hall we entered a large metal "exit" door that opened to the stairwell leading to the cafeteria. The gym was on the top floor, six sets of stairs up and just one floor above the cafeteria. I believe I can trace my current aversion to climbing stairs to those daily trips to lunch and gym classes.

Being first in line was considered a great privilege. Often, the teacher would use where she placed students in line as a method of reward or punishment. In fifth grade, I was often put at the very end of this line and made to hold Sammy's hand. I absolutely hated being at the end of the line or at the end of anything, for that matter. I always prized being first. Years later, when I found myself constantly seeking the front seat at college lectures, on buses, in classrooms, at baby showers, anywhere and everywhere, I seriously wondered how much of this front row obsession had to do with my years of being placed at the end of the line in school.

But, it was the Kindergarten line I remember most. As a Kindergartner, when the line of children had marched up floor after floor of stairs and finally arrived at the cafeteria, we were led to a special section. It had smaller tables and chairs than those in the rest of the room. In this special section, we, the smallest of students, took our seats, six to a table. Dutifully we took out our lunches and prepared to eat.

I seem to remember that most of the children had lunch boxes. Their lunch boxes were colorful and had little, pretty, matching thermos bottles that were filled with cold milk or hot chocolate according to the season. The teacher would supply each child with a tan-colored paper towel. Each of us would then place our lunch on the towel which served, I suppose, as a placemat. Most of my classmates had dainty little sandwiches, which had been cut in quarters. Some had ham, some had peanut butter and jam, others were made with cheese or baloney with lettuce and tomatoes. Many had a cookie or banana for dessert. If really affluent, a child might even have a "Yankee Doodle."

Hesitantly, I would take out a large, wax paper-wrapped sandwich made of thickly, sometimes crookedly sliced, homemade Italian bread. At least Mama had the good sense to cut it in two, though sometimes she forgot. Although I occasionally got peanut butter or baloney, most times my sandwich filling would be Mama's famous "garlic balls," oozing thick tomato sauce. Or worse yet, sandwiches of eggs, scrambled in thick, virgin olive oil, the smell of which pervaded the entire Kindergarten area. The egg sandwiches were especially distasteful and unappetizing to eat, since once they were cold, they had a really strong, unpleasant, greasy, olive oil taste and smell. The olive oil Mama used was like none of that "sissy" supposedly "virgin" oil they pan off on us today. No! The oil Mama used was sent from her parents' farm in Sicily and Frankie wisecracked that it looked like crank case oil. It was a deep green! Powerful stuff, whew! So rich and thick was this oil that Mama added vegetable oil to it, in order to cut it and make it thinner.

My lunch milk was not in a thermos, it was always in a mustard or jelly jar. When warm weather came, the milk would sometimes smell of mustard or turn sour. It was milk straight from the cow, unpasteurized or treated in any way. When it had a sour smell, I would dump it out in the low drinking fountain near the tables and then get myself a glass of water. Sometimes the teacher would offer to buy me milk, but I would have none of that watery tasting stuff that came in small milk bottles that they sold to the other students.

As you can see, lunch time for me was typically not the pleasant respite in the humdrum day of school activities that most of my other classmates found it to be. Actually, besides a time of distress it was a longing for what others were eating. Rarely did I look forward to lunch time.

At home, dinner was a time of talk and specifically described experiences, both pleasant and unpleasant. It was also a time for me to help Mama put dinner on the table. Having accomplished this, I would rush to my seat and try to get food on my own plate before it was all gone.

My mother, Caroline, and I were always the last to be seated. There were never any leftovers after dinner. If anyone left a bit of food on their plate, Mama would eat it, not out of hunger, but because it was considered a serious sin to waste food. (We never ate "leftover" food. Those few times there was a lot left over, it went to feed the pigs. They ate *everything!* I truly did not know what "leftovers" were until I got married.)

As a result of her extra-curricular eating habits, my mother was quite plump. As she "cleaned" up the dishes, Frankie used to tease her and call her the "human garbage pail." I did not like to hear Mama referred to as such, but decided he was teasing playfully. Papa never reprimanded him, however, so I figured it was OK. Still, it bothered me a great deal when I heard him refer to her in this way, even if in jest.

I could also not understand why my brothers referred to our parents as "the old man" and "the old lady." Old they were, but not THAT old. It was, of course, a brand new and "cool" term at the time and eventually worked its way, to a much greater degree, into the everyday slang of later years.

My Sicilian family did not quickly adapt to the community, not only because of our foreign looks and habits. What compounded the problem was that we were "city people" and very, very different from our farmbred counterparts. My brothers suffered from a plague of New Yorkese, with their usage of "dese, dem, and dose" grammar. Along with their different way of dressing and combing their hair, they certainly were looked upon as different. Besides being Sicilian and proud of it, we "city folk" also had a veiled kind of contempt for "hicks" and those that could not dance well or did not "know" music. "Knowing" music meant being able to recognize bands and singers such as Glenn Miller, Tex Beneke, the Dorsey Brothers, Russ Columbo, and later on, Dick Haymes, and Frank Sinatra. If one was ignorant in these matters, one was considered "square!"

There were often battles in town and at school. Some with out-of-town youths and many with in-town youths. My brothers were "citybred" Sicilians, street-wise, strong, and able fighters. So much so, that on those days when Joey, the youngest and scrappiest of my brothers, came home with his shirt bloody and torn, my mother would wring her hands and say, *"e 'n'autra camissa, oh Dio Mio, n'autra camissa!"* (Its another shirt, oh my God, *another* shirt!) Joey would laugh gleefully at Mama's distress. We still laugh whenever he tells that story. However, since she sewed the shirts, it meant that much more time and work for her to replace them and her sometimes feigned distress, while amusing, was often real.

Much of the conversation around the dinner table often revolved around this fight or that fight. Fights resulting from what we "newcomers" perceived as slights to our ethnic background or remarks and gestures which my brothers regarded as insults to their manhood, either of which was considered reason enough to beat up someone.

Most of the fights were justified, since Papa was adamant in his council. We were *never, never* to start a fight. But should anyone insult us, pick on us, or start a fight with any of us, it was imperative that the challenger should be beaten as severely as possible. We were also expected to support and help any member of the family that needed it. Papa reasoned that if his children did not start fights, but were victorious when challenged, there would be fewer challenges in the future and thus fewer fights. Papa was right.

Those early years on the farm and at school were exciting, enlightening, and never dull. The events we shared, the tears and blood that we shed, the unity of the family in the face of bias and bigotry shaped us. The bitterness gradually faded for me, but not so quickly for other members of my family. They were older and treated more harshly than I. They paved the way for me. Prejudice, however, is a bitter, bitter morsel and can poison one forever. The poison takes a long time to dissipate.

chapter 7

Educashe' and Food

I am not certain when, but at some early point in my life, I got the distinct impression that education was not an area that my father considered important. Both of my parents were illiterate, even in their own tongue. (Though, after my father died, my mother taught herself to read when she was 60 years old.) Papa used to boast "Educashe, educashe', who needee? Looka me! I gotta no educashe' ana looka what I do." (Indeed, having purchased such a fine piece of property at the height of the Depression was a great accomplishment and he prided himself on this.) The following incident occurred one day and served greatly to reinforce his negative attitude toward education.

It was mid-morning in early spring. A young man stopped by the farm. He was conducting a Farm Bureau survey and announced, proudly, that he was a college graduate and needed information from my father. "OK," answered Papa. "What you wanna know?" The young man, pencil poised, asked, "What is your name?"

"Giuseppi Penzato" answered my father, head held high and eyes riveted on the young man.

The young man blinked, gulped, and said, "Would you kindly repeat that, sir?"

Loudly, this time and with an impish twinkle in his eyes, my father replied, "Giuseppi Penzato!"

"Uh, could you, uh, please spell that?"

Papa looked at him in disbelief! First he laughed. Then he said, "You shoulda know how. You wen'a to college!".

Caught off guard, the young man's face turned red. Obviously uncomfortable, he then had to try to figure out the spelling of our last name. Just as the immigration officers years before at Ellis Island had misspelled it, he too now probably put a "z" where an "s" should have been.

After that, Papa, delighted over the highly educated young man's discomfiture, never tired of telling the story. It probably reinforced in us the idea that an education did not really add to one's intelligence. My father declared that the young man, despite his degree, appeared stupid. Another encounter that my father experienced added to his belief that my brothers were "wasting time" going to school.

Hard work and brains were his formula for success and the following encounter made Papa's beliefs even more ingrained. During his first year on the farm, knowing nothing about apple farming, he went next door and asked a neighboring apple grower, Mr. DuBois, for some information. Mr. DuBois smiling widely said "Why, Mr. Penzotta, there's nothing to it. Jes' read yer *Agricultural Farm Bulletin* each month. It'll tell you all you need to know." Disappointed, my father shrugged his shoulders, thanked him, and left.

Years later, after my father had built the first cold storage plant in the area, Mr. DuBois came by to store some of his apples. Comparing his apples to those of my father's, and seeing how much larger and more rich in appearance they were than his, he turned to Papa and said, "Well, well, Mr. Penzotta, you sure do have some fine looking apples, I must say. Could you tell me what I could do to get such a fine looking crop?

Smiling broadly, my father answered, "Fa sure! You justa reada the *Agricultchi' Bulletin*, lika you tole me. It'sa gooda ting. You justa reada tha *Agricultchi' Bulletin*, Mr. DuBois, that'sa whatta I do. I reada da *Bulletin!*"

It took quite a while before we were no longer looked upon as total "outsiders." My father's integrity, hard work, and ability to take a run down farm and make it successful soon earned the respect of the community. He paid his bills on time, was law abiding, and was willing to give others a "hand" when needed. People saw that we were an addition to the community, not a detriment and while not accepting us into their bosoms as one of them, nonetheless, they did respect my father's "good name" and of that he was very proud.

Papa had his hands full, trying to manage the farm and Chico and my brothers at the same time. As I stated elsewhere, they did have ideas about what they wanted to do, but Papa instilled a fear in them...and respect. So they listened when he spoke and obeyed his orders without too much question. Joey was the bane of Papa's life. Although Papa adored his namesake, Joey was such a devil, always getting into trouble and misbehaving, that Papa was forever having to reprimand or beat him to make him behave. Whenever Papa hit any of us, Mama would wail, *"No 'nda la testa, no'nda la testa!"* (Not on the head, not on the head!) It seemed to be her constant refrain, since we were always wrestling, play fighting, and being hit, if not by Papa, by one another. One day Joey did something that really set Papa off and there he was, chasing Joey with a broom. When he caught up to him, cursing and shouting, he whacked him over the head, and in doing so, broke the broom handle. Mama came roaring from out of somewhere, screaming at Papa.

"Che ci sta faciennu? L'mmazzare! Ti tiro lu couri si tu che stru'pia la testa!" (What are you doing? You will kill him! I will tear out your heart if you hurt his head!)

Papa took off and left Mama in the dust. Joey was delighted at seeing Mama chasing Papa–and Papa, actually running from her! (It had to be a mock chase for Joey's benefit.) Thereafter, Joey did all he could to enrage my father, to the point where Papa would want to break another broom over his head. Joey wanted to see Mama chase Papa again. It was not to be.

There was a nice balance of work among us. We all had our chores and knew what was expected of us. We never argued over who did what or if someone did less or more. Somehow, when Papa assigned us our tasks, we unquestioningly completed them. There was a routine in our lives and a stability that connected us to one another. Growing up is often easier when you know what is expected of you, there are certain boundaries you do not cross.

Each day, when I got off the school bus, I would quickly change my clothes. As usual, I donned my brother Joey's old, outgrown pants and shirts. The change was mandatory since I had to "save" my good clothes. "Work clothes" were for the times I fed and watered the chickens, gathered eggs, or lugged the heavy milk pail up to the house. It was unheard of to work in one's "good" clothes. The habit of changing into old and even scroungy clothes in order to do any kind of physical labor has stayed with me for my entire life.

Carrying the milk pail home each evening, despite its weight, was one of my favorite chores, primarily because of the time of day. No matter what season of the year, milking time took place right after sundown when the cows were brought in from the field. Thus, winter, summer, fall, or spring, it was a little past sunset when I carried home the milk (still warm from the cow).

My house was often framed against a beautiful sunset whenever I walked up the driveway from the barns across the street. On those evenings that Mother Nature decided to grant our valley a splendid display, the sky, where it touched the earth's rim, would be drenched in myriad shades of silver, gold, soft pinks, and deep corals. Other times, mauves, purples, deep blues, and hot pinks dominated. The beauty and wonder of those vast evening skies sometimes made me remember and recite to myself a phrase learned from one of our apple pickers from the Bowery. "Red sky in the morning, sailor take warning. Red sky at night, sailor's delight." (It was, and still is, a surprisingly accurate weather forecast.) On those evenings, as I trudged up the driveway, I never ceased to marvel at the beauty before me. Silhouetted against the glorious pink and gold panorama of the sun as it set over the Shawangunk Mountains, the house and trees looked much like black, exquisitely cut-out paper patterns. Magnificent!

On rounding the south corner of the house, the lights of the kitchen windows would come into view. To this day, nothing on earth has surpassed the delicious and pleasant feelings that enveloped me whenever I saw those warm, soft, golden-yellow tones glowing at twilight. I knew that when I pushed opened the kitchen door, divine and familiar smells would greet my nostrils. My mother would turn her head and greet me from in front of the kitchen stove with a warm smile. Plump and usually perspiring, she would then return to her stirring and continue to orchestrate the various pots and pans that she moved about on that wonderful, old, black stove. Upon entering, I would place the milk pail on the table and then run to get dishes and silverware. Setting the table was "my job." Caroline (unless assigned to give my brothers a hand that day) helped Mama cook.

Each night, supper was served to at least eight people. There were seven in my family and always one or two hired hands who shared the dinner table with us. We had one regular hand named Carl, who stayed on winter and summer. He was a tall, husky black man with a warm, kind face and the whitest teeth in the world (or so they appeared to me). We all loved Carl. He had been with us for as long as I could remember (I think he came with the farm) and was practically a member of the family.

One year, for Halloween, when I was a very little girl, he brought me a cellophane bag full of small, odd shapes. They were all identical and each one was wrapped in silver foil. Protruding from the top of the wrapped foil was a tiny strand of white paper with blue letters on it. Carl unwrapped one of the "odd looking things" and handed it to me. "Here, Sadie. Taste this an' sees if you likes it."

I stared at the small, brown shape in his big, brown palm. They were almost the same color! Tentatively I reached out, picked up the odd-shaped morsel and popped it into my mouth. I waited for something to happen. The morsel began to melt. Instinctively, I pushed my tongue against it, squeezing it against the roof of my mouth. A sweet and delicious film of chocolate began to spread. Slowly it oozed over my tongue and down my throat. "Mmmmmmmmmm! MMMMMMMMMM!!!

Never had I tasted anything so utterly luscious. "What is this Carl?"

"It be a candy kiss."

"A kiss?? A *candy* kiss? It made no sense to me. I knew each night I had to "kiss" Papa and Mama on the cheek before going to bed, but this? A kiss? I had seen people "kiss" on screen at the movies, but this? A kiss? However puzzling it was, it was much too delicious to question. I accepted and enjoyed the candy. I have never forgotten Carl. Hershey's chocolate kisses have remained a lifetime favorite.

In our family, there was a ritual. From as early as I could remember, before going to bed or leaving Papa's presence, we would each have to kiss him on the cheek and say, *"T'sa benedica."* To which our father would reply, *"Sant'e ricca."* or *"riccu"* to my brothers. This held true for *all* the children of the family, no matter how old we were, male or female, this was required of us. Mindlessly repeating the phrase, beginning from when I was almost too young to understand the language, I never gave a thought as to what it meant. I had, however, learned that it was a "rote" kind of thing that was required on threat of punishment if ever omitted. The incident that taught me how important it was occurred as follows. Eager to get to the movies one Saturday night, on my way out of the door, I forgot to kiss my father and say the phrase. Papa came roaring after me and struck me soundly across the face. In forceful Sicilian, he berated me for my lack of respect and my shallowness. I covered my head with my arms and cowered as Papa struck me again and again. Thereafter, I never forgot to kiss him and ask him for what I eventually discovered was a benediction. *"Tsa'benidici"* means "Give me a blessing" and *"Sant'e ricca"* means "Grow saintly and rich."

In our Sicilian household, as in most others at that time, the father was the undisputed head. He was king, president, and dictator. His was the final word in all situations. There was no appeal. Usually, the mother of the house (*this* house, at least) was powerless. Mama was not literally, but **actually** Papa's slave. To a great degree, my sister and I felt we were "slaves," too! In everyday situations, we had no recourse if punished and absolutely no choices. (But then again, who was given much choice in childhood?) During all of my growing up years, I totally believed that as females, we were there to serve the men, help them when needed, and do their bidding.

At our dinner table, Papa was always served first and got the best and choicest of every dish. Benny was served next and then the others were served according to age. Caroline often was served after our youngest brother. Mama and I were served last and often shared the wings and neck of the chicken. *"Lu giussariu"* (the gizzard) was a delicacy. Papa knew how much I liked it and occasionally would share it with me. When my mother cooked a chicken, she cooked everything but the feathers and the beak. After disemboweling it and setting aside the heart and gizzard, its intestines were carefully split open, scrubbed, rinsed repeatedly, and added to the soup. The feet and comb were scrubbed, parboiled, scraped, and also added to the soup. Occasionally, an old laying hen would be "tapped" for supper. The cluster of soft eggs inside her cavity, with shells not yet developed, would be added to the soup and they were *truly* a gourmets delight.

I hate to say it, but Mama simply "murdered" the Thanksgiving turkey. After carefully cleaning all the pin feathers, she would cut small slits in the skin, all over, and stuff pieces of parmesan cheese and slivers of garlic into them. Then she would rub olive oil over the entire bird. Next she would stuff it with homemade Italian sausage meat mixed with parsley, eggs, breadcrumbs, and cheese. Naturally, we had spaghetti to go along with the turkey, and, along with much other food, sweet potatoes, cream soda, wine, espresso and cannoli. Yes, it was delicious, but I never tasted turkey gravy until I first had it at the home of my mother-in-law.

I had forgotten, but Joey reminded me that Mama's first efforts at making homemade bread were disastrous. It took her a while to learn and once she did, her loaves were crispy and deliciously light. Before that, they could be used to sink battleships–hard, yellow-brown crusted and doughy inside. We survived, however, and suffered in silence. No one wanted to hurt her feelings.

When Mama made minestrone, it was a labor of love. Early in the morning, she gathered vegetables from the garden. From a bushel full of broccoli, string beans, lima beans, and tomatoes, Mama would end up with only enough greens to fill a large, white enamel stock pot. (She would never use aluminum pots, certain they were unsafe for human consumption.) It took many hours to peel and clean the vegetables, especially the broccoli. Mama would bang the cut stem of the broccoli on the table top a few times and lots of little green worms would drop off. Seeing them, I would shudder in disgust at the thought of eating those worms if Mama had not had the good sense to get rid of them in such a clever way. Her minestrone was a symphony of vegetables, garlic, and olive oil. Thick and rich, it was an entire meal when accompanied by a loaf of homemade Italian bread. How times change! Back then, olive oil, garlic, and pasta were considered strange, exotic foods, smelly and probably not as nourishing as a nice roast or mashed potatoes with lots of butter and fresh milk. Today, garlic is thought to inhibit cancer growth, olive oil is low in cholesterol, and pasta is a newly discovered "wonder" food. As I look back, nutritional changes wrought in the last fifty years make me feel I grew up on a different planet.

Each autumn Papa would make wine from his own, farm-grown, Concord grapes, mixed with grapes from California. He also pressed apple cider. When it got "hard," (fermented) Papa sold it. One could get pretty drunk on it. By early November, there would be five or six barrels of new wine, and at least six or seven barrels of cider in the huge, cool cellar of the house. During late autumn, a wine barrel from the previous year would be tapped. It became a ceremony of sort, for there would be much sniffing, tasting, and lip smacking when friends visited. Much discussion and many comparisons would be made over this year's vintage as opposed to last year's.

Because I was the youngest, it fell to me to fetch the wine. My brothers and sister had all taken turns being wine bearers and had, at one time or another, experienced the fear of gloomy, spooky cellars. Whether in New York City or on the farm, in those days, cellars were never pleasant places to be. They were NOT basements. I dreaded those times I had to descend the steep, dark, cellar stairs and enter the mysterious, frightening, rooms of the cellar. They called to mind the dungeons I remembered from the haunted houses in the movies.

The cellar walls of our house were built of enormous cut blocks of grayish white stones fitted together without benefit of mortar. The few windows that were visible, were completely covered with dust and cobwebs. The little daylight that filtered through, had an eerie, misty quality as it shone through the opaque glass of those windows. For illumination, in each room, there was only a small, naked, pull-chain, electric bulb, hanging from a wire. Each lit the way to the next room, and led finally to the furthest room, where the wine and cider barrels were stored. In that room, was yet one more bare bulb dangling from the ceiling. Sheets of cobwebs draped the cord from which it hung.

Despite many, many trips to fetch wine and cider, I never lost my fear of the cellar. Each time I had to descend those steps I would start to whistle as loudly as possible. Why that helped to dispel my fears, I really did not know. I had learned, however, from the movies that people always whistled in the dark, when they were afraid, or when they thought they were being followed.

At the bottom of the stairs, to the left, was a small room with bars on the small, square window of the door. I always imagined that some giant, monster of a prisoner was in there, lying in wait for me! As soon as I got past that first, terrifying obstacle safely, I prepared myself to face the huge, main room–a place that held even more frightful creatures. I imagined them lurking behind boxes and hiding in the dark shadows formed by the light of the meager bulb. Running through as quickly as possible, I would finally reach the last room. Besides being filled with barrels of wine and cider, it held an enormous cistern–large and mysterious. Gazing at its thick cement walls made me feel that at any moment, emerging from its open top, horrid, ugly creatures would leap out, ready to rip my body to pieces should I stop whistling, even for a moment. I reasoned, if my whistling stopped, my family might realize I was being attacked and come to my rescue.

After filling the wine bottle from the wooden spigot tapped into the bottom of the front of the barrel, I had to brave the same frightening return trip. The heavy jug slowed me down, but I passed as quickly as possible through the dimly lit cellar, and ran swiftly up the stairs. Breathless upon reaching the top, I was relieved, and welcomed the safety and warm comfort of the kitchen. After delivering the wine to the table, and taking a seat in the corner, I had to wait there patiently until the bottle was emptied. The whole fearful routine would then be repeated for as long as Papa and his friends needed refills.

One of the more frequent visitors was a Gypsy. He had purchased a few acres of land from my father. It was up the road, a short distance from our house, and was situated between the dirt road that began at the foot of our driveway, and the main highway. Too rocky and hilly to make good pasture or orchard, it had been sold. This Gypsy would usually come over on a Sunday afternoon. During those long social conversations, he and Papa never tired of talking about the strange, and, to their way of thinking, "stupid" ways of the "Americans."

The Gypsy was a short, squat, heavily built man. His face was round and florid, with a small stubby nose, a deep cleft chin, and deep creases like long dimples in his cheeks. What was left of his hair, which was light brown and curly, surrounded an exceedingly shiny pate. He would always pat me on the head in a warm and friendly way whenever I passed him on my way back from refilling the wine bottle. That would make me a little bit nervous because in stories I had heard that Gypsies steal children. However, I was secure in the knowledge that my father would never let any one steal me!

To this day, my brother Joey insists that the Gypsy had a slave. A black man lived, winter and summer, in a barn on the Gypsy's property and was seen working constantly. Joey said that a few times he had seen the black man being badly beaten by his master. Being quite young when he witnessed the beatings, Joey assumed the Gypsy had a right to punish his help. On second thought, he surmised that if the black man had a choice, he would have left the Gypsy rather than suffer the beatings and poor living conditions under which he labored. Besides, eventually, the Gypsy's son told my brother that the black man was a slave. If true, how little we know of the various strata that make up society right next door to us.

During one of the visits by the gypsy, my father said to him, "Ah you know, theesa crazy 'Mericani, would you b'lieve it, they lika they dog'sa more betta' than they lika they friendsa."

"You think so? Yeah? How come you say a thing like that? You doan mean they really like a dog more than a good friend?"

"Yeah, for sure. You watch'em whena some friend dies. They say 'Ah yes, he was a gooda man, but ita was his'sa time ana we alla gotta to die somatime.' But thena you watch 'm when they dog or cat she die, Madonna mia! They cry ana carry on likea it was they ona kid. 'Oh he was such a dearie pet, how I canna go on wi'thouta him. I lova that dog so." Papa would mimic some person and the two of them would explode with laughter, most of it from the influence of the wine.

Then papa would say, "Whatsa thisa word "lova?" Lova means eggs, in Italian. Whatsa thisa lova? They dumb they 'Mericans, yeah, they sure dumb." And the two of them would discuss the intricacies of eggs and of love which led to their next topic. The "sissy" attitudes some men had towards women and their children. Half-way through the conversation the Gypsy said, "You know Joe, you got really good kids."

"Nah, they all no good, they terrible. They lazy, they stupid. They ugly!"

Incredulous, his drinking partner replied, "Joe, Joe, what're you saying? You crazy? You got good, hard-working kids. They wonderful, good-lookin' kids. I wish I haddem!"

Papa smashed his fist on the table. Hard! The wine bottle almost tipped over and everything rattled and shook. "No! I say no!! They *no good* and they lazy!!!" Seeing my father's genuine anger, the Gypsy, baffled, fell silent. My father changed the subject and soon they both ended up laughing again, resuming the enjoyment and the camaraderie for the rest of the wine-filled afternoon.

My father's anger was real! Being extremely superstitious, many Sicilians believe that if you brag about something or become too proud or enamored of your possessions or your loved ones, you "tempt the Gods" and misfortune would befall you. *"Non sput'n celu, ca ti cathi n'da la fachi."* (Don't spit at heaven, it will fall in your face.) Whatever thing you were most proud of or loved best would be taken away or maimed. On the other hand, if you were humble and reviled those things you loved and were most fond of, misfortune would not befall you. In fact, it was believed that that with which you found most fault, would improve and become even better. Perhaps this might explain Papa's constant stream of uncomplimentary remarks directed at all of us most of the time. He found fault with everything we did, no matter how well we did it. I think that he sincerely believed that if he said anything wonderful or complimentary about us something terrible would happen. For example, if he bragged about how smart we were, that is when we would end up doing something stupid. Conversely, if he complained that his hard-working children were lazy and no good, we would become even better workers and become even more compliant and obedient.

I am not certain how common this particular superstition might be in other cultures and among other nationalities, but I know for certain that it was deeply ingrained in the Sicilian mentality of those days. Thus, denigrating the ones you loved most was really a positive rather than a negative act. An act, however, that might be misconstrued by those at the "receiving" end of disapproval.

On long, cold, Saturday nights during the winter, I made many, many trips to the cellar, but not to fetch wine. Oh, no! It was to fetch gallons and gallons of hard cider. Papa needed every penny he could earn in order to keep up the payments on the farm. Thus, each Saturday night, starting at around nine o'clock, there would be a knock on the kitchen door. Sometimes one, sometimes three or four negroes would be standing there. They would be welcomed, would enter and be seated.

Thus began the numerous trips down to the cellar, to bring up, sometimes a quart, sometimes a gallon of hard cider. The cider barrel did not have a spigot. Instead, it had a rubber hose, about an inch in diameter, which was poked into the cider barrel from a bung-hole in the top. I would have to suck, really hard, on the hose to siphon the cider out of the barrel. It took two or three really hard sucks and suddenly the cider would gush into my mouth-horrible, bitter stuff! I would quickly put the hose into the neck of the bottle and fill it, meanwhile spitting out that mouthful of awful tasting liquid. "Yuk," I thought to my self, "How can they drink this stuff!" But they did, and even enjoyed it! When the bottle was full, I would put my finger over the end of the hose, stopping the flow, holding it up in the air so the cider returned to the barrel. The hose would be left dangling, ready for the next refill.

By eleven o'clock in the evening, the kitchen would be literally "rocking" with ten to fifteen black men and women of assorted ages, drinking, singing, and dancing. I distinctly recall one man, named Jack Johnson. He would make an "O" with his mouth, and, using his knuckles and rapping on his head, would play a tune. Really! By changing the shape of his lips and mouth, he got different tones emanating from his scull. He could play "Row, Row, Row Your Boat" "Hail, Hail, the Gang's All Here," and other simple songs. He fascinated me to no end. Seated in a corner, waiting to refill the bottles, I would watch utterly intrigued by those wonderfully interesting people, so different from us, as they danced and sang the night away. Seated around the room in a circle, the dancing took place in the middle. The cooking stove, stoked with coal, warmed the room and the air was filled with a smoky haze and the smells of cider, perspiration and tobacco. The twang of a Jew's harp or a harmonica often accompanied the singing.

I enjoyed the warmth and friendliness of what seemed one, big, long party. Our visitors, dressed in their best, while noisy and animated, were also polite and well mannered. It was obvious that they thoroughly enjoyed their evening out. As the evening wore on, our clients, filled at different levels with happiness and/or drunkenness, would leave, two and three at a time. By the early morning hours they would all be gone. I cannot remember ever seeing a fight or anything disagreeable happening. Since Papa always stayed in the kitchen, with our guests, he probably fielded disagreements, if there were any, before they turned into anything more.

I especially enjoyed watching the women. They seemed to glow in their finery–with bright red lipstick, shiny red cheeks, slick, sleek, black hair, smooth creamy or chocolate colored skin, big dark eyes and thin eyebrows. They wore high heels and colorful dresses, dangling earrings and noisy bracelets. I found them beautiful and unusual. Daring! Some of them reminded me of exotic, brightly colored birds. Many seemed genuinely fond of me and very friendly. Each time I walked across the room to the cellar door to fetch the cider, I received many pats on the head, along with being told that I was very pretty or that I was a nice little girl. I, in turn, became very fond of all of them. They came regularly and after a while I thought of them as my friends.

Although those Saturday nights seemed like much fun to me, I believe we sold cider that way for no more than a year or two. I wonder, as I write this account, if my father ever gave a thought (insofar as to what we were doing) about whether or not it was legal or illegal. I do not know if selling hard cider to anyone was against the law at that time. Perhaps a permit was needed. Perhaps he had one. I shall never know. Whether it was, or was not, whether he did or he didn't, the memory of those evenings remains vivid.

chapter 8

The City

My father still owned the tenement building on Gaorick Street on the lower east side of Manhattan where we had lived before the move to the farm. Because of this, Mama often had to travel to the city to take care of business for him; collect rents, I suppose. Sometimes, she would take me with her. The remarkable sights and sounds of the city made me fall in love with it forever! All the wondrous and exciting things about New York City made me almost dizzy with delight. Raw clams were a penny apiece, opened, and I would pester Mama until she bought me as many as I could eat, maybe a dozen or two. She would always make such a big fuss over the fact I could eat so many even though I was so young and so small. I would always force down a few more than I wanted, just to hear her.

She spoiled me rotten by buying just about anything I wanted to eat. I would ask for Charlotte Russ' (a dixie cup-size, wonderful concoction of sponge cake, jam, and whipped cream in a round paper container), pizza, and egg creams. All of which were not available "upstate," in the country. Mama would shake her head and declare I had a stomach of iron. She did it in such a way, however, that I felt she thought I was extraordinary to be able to eat food in such quantity and variety and yet not get sick.

Although the exotic foods were what I loved most about the city, next best were the many, many open pushcarts which lined Rivington Street for as far a person could see. At that age, my head was probably even with a pushcart wheel. Looking up from that vantage point, the contents of those pushcarts seemed piled high as the heavens. I remember one in particular that was stocked with dolls of every size and description. When I came upon it I stood, rooted to the spot, enchanted. I coveted ALL of the dolls. I probably asked for one, but I don't remember my mother buying me one, which is surprising. Perhaps she had spent all her extra money on the "junk" food I had been consuming up until then. Then again, it was the time of the great Depression. Perhaps she didn't feel that she could spend money on frivolous things. Food, however, was another matter. Living on the farm insulated me, in many ways, from the privation and misery of the Depression. I don't recall hearing it mentioned and we always had ample food, clothing and shelter.

Some pushcarts were filled with only clothes or shoes. Others were loaded with all kinds of things I had never seen before. The color and variety of pushcarts, the noise, the people bargaining, the crowded sidewalks, and the wonderful, yet terrible smells convinced me. Rivington Street was an absolute wonderland!

Chinatown was near little Italy. As the two of us walked on Mulberry Street in Little Italy, I could get a glimpse of Chinese people or sometimes a store sign with Chinese characters on those far off streets. Chinatown appeared utterly fascinating, especially from a distance since it was so foreign and strange, so different from anything I had ever seen before. Curious, I begged and pleaded for us to walk over and see it up close, but my usually obliging mother would not take me there. She had lived many years in the Italian section of the Lower Eastside, very nearby Chinatown and felt that the Chinese were unconventional, dangerous people and not to be trusted.

In later years, when we suggested dining out for Chinese food, she would slowly shake her head from side to side and with a mysterious look on her face declare that the Chinese never buried their dead. The family was never quite sure of what she meant by that because what it implied was too awful to even contemplate. To her dying day, she would never consent to eat in a Chinese restaurant. When we thought about it, we laughed nervously, and agreed it was just another one of Mama's crazy ideas.

Descending the steep steps and going down into the deep and cavernous tunnels that my mother called "the subway" was something that always filled me with apprehension and fear. The roar of the huge trains as they emerged mysteriously from the dark tunnel left me breathless. Fascinated as they swept past, I cringed as they suddenly came to a whistling, grinding stop. Because I had never before heard such loud, piercing noises, my ears hurt. I also somehow feared that because I was small, the powerful, swirling gust of air from the motion of the train could sweep me off the platform. I remember clearly the first time that I was in a subway station. When the train pulled in, I winced and quickly wrapped my arms tightly around my mother's legs. Smiling and amused, Mama gently unwrapped my arms from where they were firmly anchored. Her hand, strong and steady, held mine as we waited to board the train. The moment it screeched to a stop and the doors slid open—hordes of people came pouring out. Just as quickly, we found ourselves propelled on board by the throngs rushing to enter before the doors slammed shut.

Imagine my surprise to find that due to the fact that there were so many people jammed on the train, the crush of the crowd actually held me upright, in position, next to Mama. Neither one of us could move. As the crowd shifted into place and the train started up, I was suddenly aware that we could be separated. Terrified, I clung fiercely to Mama's hand. Squeezing it, I held on tighter and tighter as the train started moving and gaining momentum. After a while, I realized that she wouldn't let go of me, so I relaxed a bit. As the train whizzed along the tracks, I looked up curiously at the people surrounding me and suddenly felt dwarfed. It seemed that I was in a world of giants as I stood there, gazing up, head only hip high to fellow passengers. My body was wedged in tightly between those of strangers. It was a very uncomfortable feeling. The legs and torsos of people were pressed tightly against me and the rough texture of their clothing felt scratchy against my face. Worst of all, some people smelled bad, really bad! Piu! I wrinkled my nose in disgust as their body odors invaded my nostrils. It wasn't the smell of clean sweat like from papa and my brothers after a hard day of work. No, it was a rancid, "dirty" smell.

Leaving the subway, we would climb the steep stairs to the streets above. Each street seemed to have its own distinctive smell. People of all kinds, shapes, and colors were rushing past, some carrying packages, others pushing things. Children played on stoops and on the sidewalk. Some were on skates and whizzed by, dangerously close. Small shops were stocked with myriad articles. It was such an alive and vibrant place to be. It was so alien from the quiet green, chirping, twittering expanses of the farm in summer and its cold, white silence in winter.

Never had I experienced so many mixed feelings before. It was unpleasant and pleasant at the same time. It was exciting, frightening, and unfamiliar. It all left a deep and lasting impression. It was a glorious place to be! Standing there that day on the subway platform I decided New York City was a wonderful and magical place and that somehow, someday I would have to live there. Perhaps someday I shall.

chapter 9

Spring Flowers and Memorial Day

The fact that our house in summer became a resort, of sorts, added greatly to the fabric and texture of our lives. A whole new world opened up for the entire family. After being confined to the house and barns during the long, cold, winter, we all looked forward to that kindest season. Spring arrived and soon Memorial Day was drawing closer and closer. On that weekend, the boarders started arriving for their first mini-vacation. For us, that was the beginning of summer. After that, the Fourth of July was the "real" slammer. But before then, there was much work to do to get ready for the boarders.

With the warmth of spring invading the rooms of the house, those which had been shut off for the winter were opened, windows were flung wide, beds were taken apart, springs were dusted, and wiped down, and mattresses were aired. Floors were mopped and walls washed down. Curtains and bedding were laundered and replaced. Everything was made spic and span for our summer visitors.

The dreaded annual "washing down" of kitchen ceilings and walls was the most unpleasant of all chores. Standing on a wobbly stepladder and scrubbing, first ceilings and then walls, with Lestoil is an unpleasant memory recalled with vexation. The ceilings were so thickly coated with fly specks that as I washed, clean expanses of cream-colored ceiling appeared, where before there was only a dark tan color. To this day, I find it incredible that mere fly specks, albeit thousands of them, could change the color of an entire ceiling.

Washing a ceiling was an exercise in patience and bodily contortions. The smelly dirty water from the accumulation of washed off specks would trickle down your arm or drip into your eyes and face. The strain of standing on a stepladder and reaching up to scrub a flat space above your head was difficult and made one's body and head ache by the end of the day. "Always begin at the bottom, so that streaks will not form from dripping water." The "washing" instructions on the Lestoil box were explicit. The unbelievably thick accumulation on the ceiling came from the incredible number of flies which congregated in the kitchen. The barnyard animals across the street bred enormous numbers of them. The flies were then drawn in even greater numbers, or so it seemed, to the cooking area of the kitchens in both the great house and in the summer kitchen used by the boarders.

All summer long, the screendoors would creak open and slam shut hundreds of times a day. With each opening, the hoards of flies which had congregated on the outside screen waiting to get into the cool kitchen area, zoomed in and lighted swiftly on any exposed food. Keeping the flies out of *any* of the rooms was a losing battle, but the kitchens were a hopeless case and were always abuzz with them. This, despite the fact that many, many, long thin coils of gluey paper were hung from the ceilings to entrap them. The gluey strands had to be changed daily since each would begin to be coated with flies almost before the thumbtack to keep them in place was wedged into the ceiling. Thus, by the end of the summer, despite the entrapment of thousands of flies in the glue, it was no wonder that the ceilings were literally "black" with fly specks.

Having seen flies in such great numbers, I did not give them, nor their layers of droppings, much thought. Their prodigious numbers were as commonplace to me as the frequent litters of kittens born each year to our many cats. Years later upon hearing jokes about Italians and flies, I would nod my head in recognition, smile wryly, and remember in embarrassment.

The time between Memorial Day and the Fourth of July was planting time on the farm. On one day, each year, in early June, we were greeted with the arrival of 500 to 800 hundred tomato plants. The entire family and workforce had to be mobilized. Everyone got out and planted the small scraggly stems that would, in six to seven weeks, grow into mature plants bearing hundreds of plump, ripe tomatoes.

It so happened that on one particular planting day, the tomato plants arrived on the exact same day that I was to make my First Communion. Numerous hours had been spent designing and sewing my lacy, fancy, white, communion dress. My veil with tiny mock orange blossoms, however, was standard. The priest had ordered them by the dozen from one store for all the female communicants. My dress, however, was like no other. It was an original, one of a kind, a fact I did not appreciate at all. As always, I longed for the luxury of a store-bought dress just like all the others in my group. It was not to be.

Early on that particular day, I got dressed in my finery. Caroline fussed and fussed over my hair and Mama kept arranging and rearranging my veil. Soon, we piled into the car and arrived at the church. There, I shared First Communion with the rest of the kids with whom I had attended "religious instruction." The rituals which we had all studied and practiced together for weeks and the studies for the same amount of time finally came to fruition on that day. I was happy and excited and had looked forward with great anticipation to that special day in the life of a Catholic. It was a lovely ceremony. Afterwards, there was chaos as pictures were being snapped and families were milling about. Not so with me. As soon as it was over, I was whisked home.

Sadly, for my Communion there were no photos, no party, no celebration such as my brothers and sister had enjoyed. They, however, had made first Communion in New York City and things were different there. Life on the farm could not be compared to life in the city. There was much more work to do and life was much harder. Therefore, because of the inauspicious arrival of the tomato plants, we had to head straight home immediately after the ceremony.

Arriving there, all of us: Mama, Caroline, me, and Benny, (the one brother spared from planting in order to drive us to the church) changed immediately into workclothes and rushed out to the fields to join all the others in the backbreaking task of planting the hundreds and hundreds of tomato plants.

Long furrows had been ploughed earlier by Papa, using a single-hand plow which was pulled by Katie, the largest, strongest workhorse on the farm. The workforce was divided into two groups. Each person from one group would take a large handful of the small tomato plants (stems, actually, with four or five leaves on top) and walking down the row would drop them one by one about a foot apart in the freshly ploughed furrow.

Then each person from the second group of workers would "follow" a partner, the ones dropping the plants into the furrow. The "followers" would then, on all fours, or squatting, or crawling on the ground, would stop at each "waiting" plant. Holding it upright with one hand, they would firm the soft ploughed earth around the fragile roots of the seedling until it stood straight and tall on its own. Looking ahead and up the row, one could see dozens of young plants lying at an angle on the fresh dirt of the furrow. Looking behind, one could see a long straight continuous row of what looked like tiny little green trees standing upright and reaching for the sun.

Down on my knees that were scraped and sore from the small stones and twigs that I could feel through Joey's old outgrown work pants, I thought ahead ruefully to midsummer when the truly backbreaking work of picking hundreds and hundreds of tomatoes would begin, never mind the laborious weeding that was also necessary in between. The planting went on until dark or until all of the plants were in the ground, whichever came first. Mama and I were allowed back to the house earlier than the others in order to prepare dinner. The remembrance of what was supposed to be one of the most important days of my life is a bittersweet one. I did enjoy wearing the lovely white dress and veil: that part of the memory is the most pleasant. Somehow, wearing pure white had some mysterious connotation, the purity of it, the sheer beauty of it. It made me feel special and significant.

Besides planting and extra work, spring was a time of days growing longer and peepers singing at twilight. They did so in glorious unison, a melodious chorus rising from the swamp in the cow fields behind the barns. Sitting on the front porch on a warm spring evening listening to them was a time, for me, that made me always wonder where I would be in springs to come. Would I always be listening to that chorus? What would I be doing and who would be with me?

It is with a warm sense of nostalgia that I recall the air, still warm from sun-filled hours, brushing against my skin and soothing me. The smell of growing things stirred dormant sensations and filled me with the joy of being alive and able to savor the beauty of sounds and smells. Perhaps it was because of all these things that each April I suffered a severe case of Spring Fever. I felt the need to break out of the routine and explore new areas of experience and feeling.

Starting from the time when I was about six years old, each spring in early May, after my chores were completed (and before all the work of Memorial Day began), I would take off for the woods–we had acres and acres. Leaving the house, I would walk down the barberry-lined stone-paved walk, cross the road, and enter the barnyard. From there, I would go past the clucking hens who would pause and watch me with their heads cocked and one eye carefully following my movements. Trained at having me feed them, they expected me to fling some chicken feed in their direction as I approached them. When I did not, they clucked loudly in protest, but continued scratching in the dirt. I smiled at the sight of the silly chickens which had regarded me so solemnly.

Soon they were left behind as I made my way toward the pig sty where the contented grunts of its inhabitants could be heard as they mucked about in the mud. The smell of their sour and ripe compound was overpowering and always caused me to gag. I held both my nose and my breath for as long as it took for me to race past them. Behind their pen was the barbed-wire fence which confined the cows to the enormous meadow stretching out for what seemed miles from the rear of the barnyard. Small and thin, I easily wriggled under the fence and then struck out across the field, careful to avoid the many, large, soft cowflops that dominated the meadow.

Soon I reached the small swamp in the middle of the field. I had to cross it in order to reach the woods. This is the point where I played "pretend." Leaping from clump of dry grass to clump of dry grass, each surrounded by oozing mud, I made believe that I was escaping from someone who was pursuing me in the Florida Everglades. At that age, to me, a swamp was a swamp. I had learned about the treacherous, dangerous Everglades in school and imagined that it was like "my" swamp, only wetter and bigger, and with funny looking trees and killer alligators.

As I leaped from clump to clump, occasionally misjudging my step, one foot would sometimes land ankle deep in the oozing mud surrounding the high clumps of grass. The sensation of slimy mud seeping around my foot was a yucky, unpleasant feeling. Pausing to shake that foot to get the excess mud and water out of my hole-filled sneaker, I would continue on. In a short while, my favorite spot on the entire farm would come into view: the small pond nestled at the edge of the swamp.

The pond was a place of endless fascination and the source of all kinds of imagined adventures. Squatting at its rim, I would wait patiently. Staring at the opaque pond water, my imagination would picture an alligator swimming about beneath the surface. After a while, convinced there was some "creature" hiding there on the verge of attacking me, I would jump up quickly to "escape" his sharp teeth and huge jaws. Running off at top speed I would not stop until I was out of breath and sure "IT" had been left far behind. Flinging myself on the ground and breathing heavily, I would lie quietly and rest on the soft moss at the edge of the forest. When my heartbeat slowed and I caught my breath, I would rise and continue on to the shadowy quiet of the woods.

At other times, the pond provided hours of quiet fascination. The tadpoles and frogs, especially, were creatures I never tired of listening to or watching. I especially liked the large bullfrogs, who, sitting on large, exposed rocks serenaded me with a symphony of croaks. I, in turn, made believe that they were singing or sometimes talking to me and invented all kinds of conversations with them. The shiny slivers of bait fish that glittered in the sun as they sped through the water were another source of wonder. What made them so silvery looking? What did they eat? Where were their parents? Do they grow any larger, or is this as big as they get? Were they mere babies?

When I first noticed that tadpoles developed legs, I was astounded; even more so when they lost their tails. It was all such a mystery. Before long, I started asking so many questions both at home and at school that I am certain a few people, including some teachers, were ready to strangle me. Most of those I questioned did, however, try to satisfy my curiosity.

After getting my fill of playing near the pond, I would continue on and go deep into the woods in order to find the first flowers of spring. Wandering about and coming upon the beauty of a bed of dog-toothed violets or the gorgeous sight of a solitary bloodroot rising from the leaf-covered ground filled me with inexplicable pleasure. To find them, I had to descend the dirt walls of the creek to reach the moist, grassy banks below. Very carefully, I would let myself down the steep inclines leading down to the creek. Pretending I was an Indian scout, I would hang on to small saplings as I slipped and slid down the rock and soil covered creek walls arriving safely at the bottom. Down near the water, where the soil had been filled in and was rich in humus, one could find all kinds of wild flowers.

Jack-in-the-pulpit was another favorite among other flowers that bloomed in springtime, though they came a bit later than the very first flowers. Wild red columbine also arrived at a later time, but they bloomed only on rocky hills along the main highway. My primary quest for wild flowers was to pick a bouquet and bring it home to Mama. Come springtime, I would always bring my mother flowers, either nosegays of white and purple violets, large handfuls of columbine or, because they were rare, one single beautiful bloodroot. Early on, I had discovered that dog-toothed violets would wilt before I could get them home, no matter how fast I ran. Eventually, once I had picked my fill of flowers to bring to my mother and when the flowers stopped blooming, I no longer went out to the fields and down to the creek. That is, not until the long, hot days of summer drove everyone to the cooling balm of the crystal clear water of the creek.

Wide and beautiful, it swirled around large boulders and bubbled gently over small rocks. Small pools formed in some places and low waterfalls in others. It was on such hot summer days that I found myself carefully picking my way down the sides of the creek again. But this time, I had to endure the constant admonitions of my brothers and sister who watched over me carefully and cautioned me not to fall down the bank. They were certain that since I was so young and so little, I did not have the stamina and strength to make it safely down. Besides, they were certain that if I fell, I would be badly hurt or swept away by the water and bruised by the large rocks in the creek.

Thus, being protectively guided, I smiled to myself in satisfaction, wondering what they would say if they knew that I had ventured this way alone and unaided many times. Besides, I thought to myself, in springtime the creek was an angry swirling body of water, not the benign and gentle flow it became by summertime. I chuckled in delight and self-satisfaction at what I perceived as my "bravery."

The farm was a wonderful, glorious place to grow up. It was a large spread and there were many nooks and crannies to examine. When my chores were finished, or when I was not drawing, one could always find me exploring buildings, tramping through meadows, climbing trees and hills, or sitting quietly watching the animals, both domestic and those in the woods. My brothers Joey and Frankie told me that if I sat quietly and hit two stones together, the sound would mesmerize small animals and after a while many would come and sit by me.

I couldn't wait to try it. The next day my wrists were sore from banging the stones together. Tapping and tapping, I waited for the squirrels and rabbits to come. After a long while, I realized I had been "had." Annoyed, that evening during supper, I questioned them. Joey grinned from ear to ear and Frankie gently ruffled my hair and said, "We were only kidding, we didn't think you'd believe us! Sorry, Miss Prim."

"Yeah, who thought you would actually do it? Maybe it would work if you used bigger rocks!" said Joey. I made a face at him. He laughed. We all did.

In childhood we are all naturally curious and filled with wonder, with a compulsion to question, look at, and examine everything. Those strong learning traits remain with many of us, often, even into old age. It is the continuation of that wonder which leads us down new paths and which fulfills and enriches our lives and (if we are lucky) the lives of others. Like many others, I have spent much time searching, seeking and trying to achieve certain goals. I like to believe that growing up Sicilian and female gave me positive traits and specific strengths that enabled me to cope with and overcome adversity. More so, perhaps, than had I grown up as something else. I suppose each person who takes pride in his or her ethnicity feels the same way. It is a conundrum to which I shall never find the answer. Suffice to say, I would not change a moment of anything, even the painful and unhappy times, since we truly are the sum total of all we experience.

chapter 10

Jello and the Summer Kitchen

I used to love to climb down the steep five steps that led from our huge kitchen down to the woodshed attached to the main house. The eerie semi-darkness and wonderfully pungent smell of old wood filled me with curiosity and fascination. Upon reaching the foot of the stairs, I would find myself in what seemed to me an enormously cavernous and dimly lit room. The windows were frosted with layers of white dust that had accumulated over many, many years. Cobwebs hung in profusion from the huge, exposed, whitewashed beams overhead.

Rarely did I venture into the further ends of the building, primarily because the high mounds of piled firewood seemed insurmountable. Besides, in this first room, ankle deep with the chips cast off from splitting wood, there was the accumulation of many years of debris some of which consisted of discarded household articles. Curious, I found that when I dug or even scratched past the surface and probed down into the piles of wood chips I often found what seemed wondrous treasures.

Once, I found a tiny porcelain doll about six inches tall, with eyes that opened and shut when it was tipped backward and forward. It had only one arm, one leg, and no hair. Captivated by the doll's beautiful face, I took it to my room. There, I made a cape for it in order to hide its lack of limbs. I also sewed tiny bonnets and made small babushkas to cover her bald head.

On another occasion, I remember my excitement over finding a small bent gold-colored ring. Its ovoid shape prevented me from slipping it onto any of my fingers, small as they were. I tried prying it back into its original round shape, but had not the proper tool to accomplish this and soon gave up. Frankie finally straightened it out for me, but it was still too small to fit on anyone's finger. Other times, I found saucers and, sometimes, cups with missing handles. I would bring my treasures to Mama and together we would try to imagine who the past owners of the "treasures" were and how the articles had come into their possession. Invariably, my mother would praise me for my ability to find such marvelous treasures in such an unlikely place as an old, dirt-filled woodshed.

One year, Papa decided to take in summer boarders. He needed the money and people in the city needed a place in the country. To prepare for them, he converted the wonderful old woodshed (huge wooden barn would be a more descriptive term) into two spaces. One he turned into a large dining area. The other he converted into a smaller area which served as a community kitchen.

In the kitchen section, on one entire wall, he ordered the builder to install utilitarian plywood kitchen cabinets. Along another wall, he directed that a three foot high heavy-duty shelf be built. Upon this, he then had installed ten, small, four-burner gas plates. Across the room from the gas plates were two large cast-iron enameled sinks on legs. Each sink had double bowls, one of which was deeper than the other and had an enamel drain board over it. The deeper one of each could be used with a wooden scrub board to do laundry (like the ones in the tenement). Above the sinks were two windows which faced south. Immediately to the side of the windows was a door to the outside where a number of containers were stored next to the outdoor kitchen wall. They were used for garbage and had no covers (being old oil barrels with the tops removed). Here was another breeding ground of the flies I mentioned earlier. "Billions and billions of them!"

A wall with an archway at each end separated the kitchen from the dining area. In the center of the wall on the dining side area was a huge, white refrigerator–brand new. It was shared by all of the boarders using the kitchen. Next to it was an immense glass-fronted storage cabinet for dishes with drawers for silverware. The floor in both rooms was cement, painted battleship gray. All walls and ceilings were whitewashed.

The dining area had long, simple pine tables and benches that were placed at right angles to the room. The space between formed a large aisle in the middle of the room which was wide enough to allow a good flow of traffic–sufficient room for people to carry food to and from their assigned tables. It was a first come, first serve basis insofar as space allotment of cabinets, appliances, or anything that had to be shared. All of the boarders, being either Italian or Sicilian and thus rather emotional, would from time to time have an impassioned dispute concerning the sharing or waiting for a gas range or use of the sink or refrigerator. At those times, my father would be called in to mediate. Generally, however, the boarders worked things out for themselves. They usually posted their own guidelines and peace commonly prevailed.

It was in that summer kitchen that I discovered the never-to-be-forgotten first taste of chocolate pudding and of strawberry Jello. At the age of seven, I had not yet heard of desserts. One evening, when I happened to be in the summer kitchen, I noticed that the DeSantis family, who had the first table near the door, was busily eating something red and wriggly from small pretty glasses.

I stopped abruptly, fascinated, and stared wide-eyed with curiosity. I completely forgot Papa's admonition to never intrude upon or stare at people while they were eating. Seeing the look on my face, Mrs. DeSantis called out cheerily, "Hi Sadie, want some?"

"What is it?"

"What do you mean 'what is it?' It's Jello, silly, don't you even know what Jello is?"

"Is it like ice cream?"

"Of course not, it's Jello!"

Perplexed by it all, I wondered whatever could this red stuff called "Jello" be. It looked like soft red ice, which wasn't quite frozen. It shimmered and the color was very pretty. Never before had I ever seen food that was this color-well, maybe jam.

Strict orders from my father usually kept me from visiting the summer kitchen when the boarders were eating since most Italians and Sicilians, at that time, (and probably still) had an emphatic custom. If a family is eating and a person (friend or stranger) comes along, that person or persons must be offered whatever food is on the table. If those so invited refuse to eat the food, such refusal could be construed as an insult. Thus, one had to at least taste whatever was offered. Conversely, no matter how little food there was on the table for the family dinner, it must be offered. Since people had to take turns at the gas stoves and other appliances and parts of the kitchen, the dinner hour went on for hours. It was almost impossible to visit the place when there wasn't one family or another starting or finishing a meal. So there I stood, caught!

Before I realized what was happening I found myself holding a cup filled with pieces of red gelatinous matter in one hand and a spoon in the other. Thanking Mrs. DeSantis for her kindness, I self consciously put the spoon into the red blobs and tried to scoop one small piece out and place it in my mouth. The ornery stuff would not hold still! I finally got some of it to stay on the spoon. Bringing it up slowly to my mouth, as I was ready to pop it in, the red gelatinous matter trembled on the spoon and suddenly rolled off. SPLAT! It lay on the gray cement floor like a tiny red sun with rays emanating from its center. Fearful, I looked up quickly at Mrs. DeSantis, worried that she would scold me for making a mess.

Even worse, at the same moment I realized with trepidation that the Jello lying on the floor was food. "Food was God." He too would be angry at me for dropping Him on the floor. Was there no end to my problems? Instead of anger or annoyance, Mrs. DeSantis' eyes, when thy met mine, were filled with merriment, good humor, and compassion.

"Go on Sadie, try again, you'll get used to it. Put it up to your mouth a little faster. Go ahead. That's it. Don't be afraid."

Relieved, I tried again to get the Jello to behave. My efforts brought forth good-natured laughter from the whole family and the surrounding tables as I grappled with it. After putting the spoon in this way and that, I learned to balance the bouncy stuff and finally got it safely into my mouth. The taste was so rewarding that I patiently continued. Everyone cheered and laughed when they saw the look of divine enjoyment which crossed my face as I savored the sweet, delicious flavor of strawberry when that first spoonful of Jello, partially melted, slid down my throat.

Almost the same thing happened with chocolate pudding, except for the fact that it was relatively easy to eat. After I discovered Jello and chocolate pudding, I quickly convinced Mama that she should order cases of both from Mr. Cimino, the man from whom we bought truckloads of food and supplies.

About four times a year Mr. Cimino would drive up to our house in his shiny new car. Dressed in a dark suit, white shirt and dark tie, he would sit at the kitchen table writing orders for food, dictated by my mother. Her list included the following (approximately, it was a long time ago): four or five cases of pasta-vermicelli, spaghetti, ditalini, ziti, and various other kinds: one hundred pounds of flour; a case of *Tunno* in olive oil (Italian tuna fish); a five pound box of salted anchovies; cases of cut corn, peas, string beans, *capponatina* (an Italian delicacy); cartons of Rice Crispies and Corn Flakes (Kellogg's); twenty-five pounds of sugar; pounds and pounds of black coffee (brown for the hired help); cases of Jello and chocolate pudding; canned tomatoes (in case she ran out of those she had canned herself); and a case each of soap powder, face soap, and bleach. Those were staples. We grew and harvested or slaughtered whatever else we needed to augment our meals.

As Mama recited her list, I would sit at the table, elbows propped on it and chin in hands, watching, as Mr. Cimino took her order. I remember staring at him all the while he did so. Having a stranger to study for any length of time was an interesting break in routine–something different to look at for a while. A big diamond ring on his right pinky glittered as he wrote. Fat, white fingers, nails carefully groomed, held down the corner of his pad. A yellow pencil scribbled away as fast as Mama could talk. His looks fascinated me, since he dressed so differently from the men in my family and resembled no one else I could think of. His closely shaved, owl-like, round face, glasses, and a double chin made him seem neither young nor old. His hair, thin, brilliantined, and combed sleek, looked almost like a tight, jet black beanie, so closely shaved was the lower part of his head, especially his sideburns. Near his chin, just below and to the left of his mouth was a small, brown wart. He had a habit of wetting the tip of his pencil with his tongue every few minutes. I never did understand why. He also pursed his small, but full lips a lot, which made him appear "fish-like" to me. Despite all that, he was pleasant and spoke impeccable Italian (which I had trouble sometimes understanding). After taking the order, he would place it in his battered, leather brief case, put on his fedora, and, after profuse thank yous and regards to my father, would leave. A week later, a large truck with "Cimino Importers" in gold letters on a green background would drive up to the kitchen door and unload our order. I don't remember my mother ever going to the store for groceries until the 1940s.

chapter 11

The Movies

*I*t was Saturday night. Late in the afternoon, I had begun ironing my brothers' white dress shirts so they would have them to wear to go out that night. After working hard on the farm, seven days a week, all of us, Benny, Caroline, Frankie, Joey, and I always looked forward with great pleasure to Saturday night. That was the night Papa gave us money to go to the movies.

Admission was a quarter, 15 cents if you were twelve years old or younger. At a nearby candy store, one could "fill up" for the movies. Nothing in the way of refreshments was sold at the old New Paltz Cinema. At the store, they charged a nickel for a Baby Ruth, Milky Way, or a chocolate bar. For a penny apiece, there was an enormous assortment of loose candy: banana cremes, rootbeer barrels, Tootsie rolls, bubble gum, tiny sugar "dots" stuck to paper, and many, many others. Neither soda nor popcorn was available at either place.

There was usually a double feature. The second feature was always a "B" picture, often a cowboy film. They usually starred Hopalong Cassidy or Gene Autry. I was crazy about Hopalong but thought Gene Autry was a real "drip" (dumb and really "square"). The "movies" included a cartoon and a newsreel. Sometimes, there was also a "film short" and the main feature played twice (this was called a "double feature").

Everybody went to the movies. They were my favorite thing to do and I felt about them sort of how I felt about fairy tales. It was mostly make-believe and was only sometimes like the real world. Movies were "there" and they were enjoyable. Sometimes, they made you feel bad and sometimes they made you feel good. You laughed or cried. But, as you watched movies (or read fairy tales), you were aware at all times that they were eons away from the world that you were experiencing.

I did believe that perhaps somewhere, someplace women did dress in exquisite, expensive clothes and that some people did live in gorgeous homes with maids. Perhaps somewhere children were so squeaky clean they fairly sparkled. The lucky "movie" kids had tons of toys and were often taken to circuses and parties. Above all, they were spoiled, loved and pampered!

Yet, in other movies, just the opposite would occur. Some, or all, of the characters depicted lived in such misery and squalor and faced so many insurmountable problems that it broke your heart to watch. They too were unbelievable. Nobody could have that many problems or live in such horrible places! Sure, maybe some of those things happened somewhere on earth, but not to me and not where I lived or to the people I knew. And even when I grew up, which seemed so far off in the future at the time that I thought it would never happen, I saw the farm as the only place that I would ever live. I imagined myself there forever, a drudge, always under the hawk-like watchfulness of Papa. Because he was so "old fashioned", I was certain that never in my life would he ever allow me to do many of the things the other kids in school were allowed to do. Stoically, I accepted it as my lot. The fact that Papa permitted me to go to the movies every week made me feel grateful to him for being so benevolent. He really could just order all of us to stay home if he wanted to. It sure would have saved him some of his precious money if he ever did.

As I ironed, my mind was full of what I would wear to the movies that night. Now almost nine-years old, I had recently developed an even stronger awareness than before that clothes could do a bit more than cover a body and keep it warm. I had also become a little more aware of personal grooming and of trying to look pretty. At the same time, I had noticed that subtle changes were beginning to taking place in my body.

Lately there had been a feeling of tenderness and soreness on my chest all around the area of my nipples. Curiously, the area beneath my nipples had begun to swell, ever so slightly. Slightly or not, it seems that others had noticed enough so that I no longer felt comfortable running about in hot weather with my top off. Gradually I came to the realization that, someday, I would have a bosom just like "big girls." I looked forward to it with mixed emotions of both embarrassment and glee.

What made me cover my chest and be especially aware of the changes taking place in my body happened one day as I walked up the driveway wearing only shorts. One of the young, male boarders, named Sal, was walking toward me. He was very handsome and he came from Brooklyn. I had a big crush on him, but he never noticed me. I realized that to him, I was just a little girl. On that day, however, as I passed by, he was grinning devilishly, staring rudely and intently at my bare chest.

"Hey, Sadie! Are those little tits I see?" he remarked laughingly as he sauntered by.

I felt my face get all hot and knew it was probably a bright red. So embarrassed and insulted by his use of words, I wanted to run after him and punch him as hard as I could! Angrily, I thought to myself, "If I told my brother, Benny, what Sal just said, Benny would probably kill him. Yeah! Even Frankie or Joey would beat him to a pulp. Yes, and if Caroline heard him, she would break his neck! And Papa! Papa would shoot him!" Then, too late to hit him or to make some quick retort, I threw his departing figure my most angry "look." It did no good however, since his back was turned and he didn't see it. Too bad!

You see, being the youngest and smallest in the family I was powerless. However, at an early age I had learned that there was a sort of "power" in my dark brown eyes. They were almost black, like Papa's eyes. I guess my eyes must have been pretty expressive because whenever I was anywhere near the boarder ladies, they would take note of me, swish their hands back and forth at right angles to their wrists and remark out loud,

"*Tallia! Tallia l'occhi, ti parlanu.*" (Look! Look at those eyes, they speak to you.)

Thus, I made the strange discovery, at a rather early age, that by looking at someone, while strongly and deeply feeling an emotion, I could somehow convey to the other person my feelings toward them; anger, sorrow or pain...joy, affection or pleasure. Soon, I found that I was using my "look" to convey disapproval, anger, or dislike.

To my great satisfaction and surprise, my "look" became a useful tool. Most of all, I was amazed to find that a "look" could actually intimidate others. Why, sometimes even grownups, if they said something stupid, would respond to the "look" with an embarrassed grimace. The "look" could make other kids look away or try to look back. But their "looks" seldom worked, for a really "dirty look" took a certain sensitivity and a firm belief in one's strength of purpose.

The first time I realized the power of a "look" took place at the dinner table when I was about eight years old. Benny, my oldest brother, used to take strange delight in a small ritual. While passing by my chair, he would stop, spread his fingers and reach under to where my hair grew at the nape of my neck. Beginning there at the hairline at the back of my head, he would slowly push his hand up through my long black hair. As his fingers, gliding upward, caught on the tangles of the hair and pulled on the them, I, in an effort to lessen the pain, would rise up in my chair at about the same speed that his hand traveled upward. My brothers and sister would then roar with laughter at the comical sight of me, slowly rising from my chair, like a puppet on a string. I suppose the look of surprise, pained fury, and frustrated anger registering on my face, all at the same time, looked amusing.

As Benny's hand and hair-entangled fingers continued slowly upward, I would continue rising until I was on tiptoe and screeching in pain, at which point he would smile fondly at me and drop his hand, gently disentangling it from my hair. I am certain that in his own quiet, clumsy way he adored me and meant no harm. He just liked to tease me and get me angry. He would then whistle innocently and continue on his way to his own chair. All of this would take place in the space of only a few seconds. Although he had performed this little "ritual" many other times, this time, for whatever reason, I reacted! Up until that time, when I was the butt of family laughter, I would slump in my chair, look down, chin on chest and hide my anger. Seething, afterward, I would talk out loud to myself in my room, helplessly fuming with frustration, furious that I was not big enough nor strong enough to fight back. I would even fantasize that I was Superman or Wonderwoman and able to beat up everybody and get away with it! But this time, I did not lower my head. Not this time! I was so angry! As Benny seated himself, I stood up and pushed my chair back. Then I glared defiantly, for a long moment, at each one of my siblings one at a time. There was an anger from within and I willed my eyes to glow and grow glassy with rage. I stared at Benny for a longer time than the others and said not a word. A hush fell over the table and my brother Joey said, in quiet awe and with a weak smile, "If looks could kill!"

For a moment longer, I continued to glare at everyone seated at the table who had laughed at me. Suddenly, strangely, I felt stronger, bigger, and wiser than all of them. Suddenly, I sensed in myself a new feeling, like some sort of electrical charge. Probably for the first time in my entire life, for a few moments, I was in control.

It quickly occurred to me that I could stare coldly and meanly at those in my family (but not Papa, never Papa, I would never *dare* do it to him.) and "get away with it." I could pour all the pain, hurt, anger, venom, and dislike in a look and no one could really "do" anything about it. Recalling cuffs and slaps, some gentle, some hard, delivered when I misbehaved or did not move fast enough, a thought crossed my mind, "I mean, they can't really hit me just because I *look* at them, could they?" Imagine my sense of triumph when I discovered that they did not. I had challenged them with my eyes and nobody did anything to me. Wow! My head held high, I turned away from the table and marched quietly and with dignity out of the room. As I did so, Papa chuckled quietly to himself.

That incident and my ever-swelling bosom, made me feel less like a child than before. Life seemed to be changing. It was obvious to me, in my ninth year, that new and different things were taking place. That each day, each incident which occurred, instituted metamorphoses which brought me closer and closer to what I imagined being grownup was all about. After a while, as more changes took place, I wasn't so sure I wanted to grow up at all! For even though my brothers and sister were sometimes unfair or pains in the neck, other times it felt good just to be the "kid sister" and to be taken care of and loved.

All of these thoughts, memories, and experiences crowded my mind as I ironed my brother's shirts. Ironing was such a bore, but it was a good time to think about things. As I slid the heavy black irons over the surface of the cotton shirts, I derived great satisfaction from seeing the wrinkled material turn into smooth, flat areas. It seemed almost magical that with starching and ironing, the damp, limp shirts became crisp, new looking. I worked with only two of the four large black irons which were continuously heated at the rear of the coal stove in the kitchen. Quickly, I had learned which were the two heaviest and avoided them as I discovered that they tired my arm more quickly than the others. As I used it, the iron would cool. There were no gages on the solid flat irons and the only signal of a temperature change was when the wrinkles still remained after more than one pass of the iron. When that happened, I knew it was time to exchange a cool iron for a hot one.

I don't know why I experienced such satisfaction from the feel of the old, worn, black iron gliding over the silky white cotton of the shirt. This, despite the fact that the two grubby, old potholders I used to hold the hot handle of the iron made the chore a bit difficult, even awkward. I quickly adapted to the clumsy feel of the potholders and after ironing many shirts, became very proficient at it.

Ironing became my "job" when I was eight. Delighted at being assigned such a grown-up chore, I worked diligently. By the time I was nine, I could iron a shirt in six minutes flat. Often, I timed myself racing to beat my best time. In the beginning, Mama gave me careful instructions on how to iron a man's shirt. The collar and cuffs were to be ironed last because sometimes there was a bit of rust or black on the iron and if it came off on the yoke or back, it wouldn't be seen (collar and cuffs being most visible). For now, however, as I continued to iron and to think, I suddenly remembered that no one had mentioned what was playing at the movies that night. It really didn't matter to me what movie was playing, I loved them all and often would sit through double features every chance I got. Although I was a movie nut, my very favorite ones were those starring Hopalong Cassidy or Sonja Henie. Sonja Henie especially! She was utterly enchanting. I adored the way this "queen of the ice" would glide about in her exquisitely designed, fur-trimmed, or glittery sequined outfits. For some reason, I was especially taken by the way the short skirt of her skating outfit would flutter up over her waist whenever she would put one leg straight out behind her and glide backwards for what seemed forever. From beneath the fluttering short skirt, her firm, round rear-end could be glimpsed, covered by tights. At first this shocked me because when she exposed her behind in that way I believed it to be disgraceful and immoral because of Mama's admonitions about peeks at one's panties. Therefore, I could not imagine what kind of major sin was entailed in exposing your *entire* behind to the world. Life sure was a mystery!

I pondered her behavior. "Was Sonja Henie sinning by exposing her behind that way covered only by underpants? Well, they weren't really her panties, even if they were supposed to look like they were." I knew they were really tights and the fact that they were in full view did not seem to bother anyone else in the audience who was watching. So if it wasn't a sin, then I wished I, too, could someday have such a lovely curvy body and wear such beautiful costumes, gliding about on the ice with my skirt also fluttering in such a flattering and delightful way. I decided it probably drove men to distraction and wondered if that was the point of it all.

Maybe, just maybe, movies stars were special human beings. It appeared to me that many of them were able to perform feats that seemed far beyond the capabilities of ordinary mortals. Take Tarzan, for instance. He would dive off a very high, sheer cliff into a very deep, treacherous looking river. Right away you knew it was filled with all sorts of dangerous creatures. Sure enough! Soon, underwater, an enormous alligator would attack him and they would engage in a struggle. Tarzan would remain underwater, wrestling with the alligator for a very long time, time in which most "normal" humans would certainly drown. In fact, he appeared to be so deeply submerged that often I feared he would not have enough breath to make it back to the surface. At various movies and at various times, each time Tarzan dove into a river, I would hold my breath to see if I could ever stay underwater for as long as he could. No matter how deep a breath I took or how long I held it, Tarzan stayed underwater long after I had to take another breath. In fact, he stayed on, wrestling that alligator for so long that I would almost have an anxiety attack, either believing he would drown before he could re-emerge, or, worse yet, be eaten alive by the alligator. After viewing many Tarzan movies, most of which had an underwater struggle, I finally decided it was either a trick or he was a superman. Maybe he even had gills like a fish, hidden somewhere in his body.

All this musing had made time fly and soon I found myself ironing the collar and cuffs of the last shirt. "There, I'm finally done," I thought as I hung the last shirt on its hanger and looked with pride at the four white shirts (the fourth was for my cousin, Chico, who came from Italy to live with us in 1938), each hanging neatly and crisply on its own hanger. "Hmmm, I don't do too bad for a little kid, hey?" I mused, taking pride in a job meticulously done.

Beginning at an early age, I had been taught that one should strive for perfection in whatever one does. I learned that perfection brings praise. Whenever I completed a task and was praised for it, I simply reveled in it. In turn, I then tried to excel more to gain even more praise. In the Sicilian vocabulary, there is a word *"massara"* to describe one who completes assigned tasks with great care and does exceptional work. To be called *"massara"* was a great compliment. How I glowed with pride and satisfaction whenever I heard Mama refer to me as a *"massara."* Unfortunately for me, the family quickly learned that they could get me to do just about anything if they would just compliment me and rave about what a wonderful, perfect, and beautiful job I had done.

On the other hand, if they told me something was impossible and a task that no one could complete, dummy that I was, I would almost kill myself to prove that I could do it. In my adult life, I tried to understand why I had this insatiable need to be the best and to be "stroked", complimented, and praised. In writing this book, I finally achieved some insight as to its origin. The discovery was of some help in recognizing my past neediness. The "need" has finally diminished quite late in life.

"You got those shirts done?" I was still admiring my handiwork with the shirts when my brother Joey's voice drew me out of my reverie. I looked at him archly.

"Of course, what do you think? I'm lazy?"

"Boy, you sure finished fast."

"Well, yeah, so what do you expect, it's gonna take me all day?" While not complimenting me directly on a job well done, his comment on the swiftness of completion was gratifying. As Joey scooped up the shirts, I asked casually, "Hey Joey, what's playing at the movies tonight?"

"Don't worry about it, you can't go. It's 'Gone with the Wind' and you gotta be sixteen to get in."

Shocked by his answer, I was struck dumb! Quickly recovering, I asked in a high-pitched, angry voice. "What do you mean, I can't go? I ALWAYS go! Even when you say I'm too little to go 'n Papa makes you guys take me."

"Well, even Papa can't get you into this movie. Clark Gable says a bad word in the movie, so they won't let little kids in. You got to be sixteen I tell you!"

"But you're not sixteen so you can't go either!"

"Yeah, but I'm fourteen, so I could probably pass for sixteen. But you're right! I can't go either."

Greatly surprised I said, "You can't?" How come?"

"Because the movie is three hours long, so instead of 40 cents to get in, it's a dollar. Papa won't give me a buck 'cause I'm not sixteen. So you see, Miss Prim, you're not the only one who ain't goin' to the movies tonight." Joey turned away and walked out of the room, the shirts draped over his shoulder, the hangers held in the crook of his left fore finger. He headed toward the bedroom where he and the others dressed to go out. I was devastated! Why were they doing this to me? That story about having to be sixteen; that was stupid. They probably just didn't want me tagging along with them after the show. Besides, even if it was true that Joey couldn't go to the movies either, he, at least, could go into town and see his friends and buy ice cream sodas and candy.

Furthermore, I couldn't imagine Clark Gable cursing. He would never curse, at least not in the movies where everyone could hear it. No, no, not Clark Gable! He was a real gentleman. In my family, no male of any age would curse during ordinary conversation in the presence of any female. Certainly, men cursed when they were alone or with other men. I knew because I used to hear my brothers and others in the barn when they didn't know I was near. But a "real" man, a respectable man of decency and honor, would never be so crude as to show disrespect for a female by cursing in her presence (arguments and fights excepted). Yet, as taboo as it was for men to curse, it was much more so for women.

Religion taught that cursing was a sin that could easily be avoided. There just was no good reason to use obscenities. God forbade it and that was that! Children especially were expected to refrain from using "bad words." As a Catholic girl, I had been indoctrinated and made to believe that there were two spirits that were always with me. My catechism taught me that on my right shoulder sat an angel, all in white. On my left shoulder, clinging fiercely, was a small, red, devil-angel with bat-like wings. I sincerely believed this as actual fact and felt I even knew what they looked like since there were pictures of them in my catechism book. I had been taught that the red devil-angel was there to tempt me and to get me to sin.

The white angel was present to prevent my temptation and keep me from sinning. I sincerely believed she kept me pure of heart and "good." Right now though, after what Joey said, that red angel was seriously at work, doing his best to get me in trouble. Because I couldn't go to the movies, I could feel him trying to make me scream and cry and stamp my feet and say a lot of the words I had heard in the barn. I even wanted to throw things and, yes, even kick my brother as hard as I could.

I was even tempted to run after him, catch up to him, and grab the beautifully pressed shirts and stomp on them. An anger was building in me. Suddenly, the desire to run up to Joey and kick his departing behind was overwhelming. More than anything, I wanted to...kick his ass...yes! His ass! The urge was powerful and I glanced defiantly toward my right shoulder. "Yes, angel! You heard me, I'd like to kick his...!" Suddenly, my hand shot up to my mouth to keep the bad word from tumbling out. That white angel was having a time of it trying to make me behave. Shortly, however, the influence of the white angel on my conscience and the phrase that had been recited over and over to me *"pazienzia, figlia mia"* (patience, my daughter) overcame my anger and disappointment. My shoulders sagged. I felt an ache, deep in my heart, and a pain in my gut. I knew with certainty there was no way I would be going anywhere on this particular warm and balmy, summer Saturday night. I was "stuck home!" Worst of all, there was nothing I could do about it. As I realized it would be another whole week before I could go out again, I felt even more frustrated. To a child, a week is a long, long time. The thought now gave me an even more hollow, funny feeling in the pit of my stomach.

The movies were the only pleasure I could look forward to which alleviated the drudgery of my life. I felt that to have it taken away in what seemed such an arbitrary manner was unfair. Summertime was no vacation for me, so going out on Saturday night was a real treat. While most kids looked forward to summer, to me, it was just a much longer workday and time; seven full days instead of two, and in heat, dust and dirt. On really hot, muggy days, the chicken coops were like ovens and reeked of manure and damp feathers. Often, I had to hold my breath, to keep from retching while gathering eggs or while feeding and watering the chickens. And the pig sty? Whew! No, summer was certainly no vacation. The movies meant the world to me! It was a catastrophe that I had to stay home on this Saturday night.

Thoroughly dejected, I thought about searching out my friend Frances (Frannie) Calderone. Yeah! Frannie would listen to my sad tale and commiserate with me. I remembered, though, that I would have to finish my chores before I could go find her. Frannie was a year older than me and lived in Brooklyn. It seemed that most of the boarders came from Brooklyn. "Brooklyn." It was a funny sounding name and at first I found it strange to pronounce. It felt so foreign on my tongue compared to other English words I had learned. Mama, as did all the other Italians and Sicilians, referred to it as "Brookolina." People always chuckled or laughed when someone said "Brooklyn."

Frannie was taller than I. But while I was thin and wiry, she was as plump as a plum with no discernable waistline. Her body was very round with arms so chubby they were dimpled at the elbows. Although she was broad and thick, her legs were not fat. She had a pretty face, except for the fact that she had inherited a slightly smaller version of her father's nose. His was quite large and had a definite hook at the end of it. Her lips were generously curved and pretty, but she had an ample double chin! Despite all this, I thought she was quite attractive since, except for her nose, she had a lovely face, beautiful green eyes, and the most gorgeous, long, wavy, strawberry-blond hair. It hung down to her waist. I would have given anything to have that beautiful hair; the waves alone, if not the glorious color.

Each morning Frannie's mother would brush and comb her daughter's hair and dress it in twists at the top held with barrettes; a different pair each day. I had never seen barrettes before since my mother used ribbons, bobby pins, or rubber bands to hold my hair. Curious and fascinated I asked Frannie, "Where do you get those things you've got holding your hair in place?"

"You mean my barrettes?"

"Is that what you call 'em?"

"Yeah, an you get'em at the Five 'n Dime."

I was perplexed, but not wanting to appear stupid because I didn't know what a "Five 'n Dime" was, despite the fact I had heard the term often, I just nodded sagely and said, "Oh yeah, right. At the Five 'n Dime. Sure! OK." Finally, my chores were completed. Just thinking about my friend made me feel a little bit better. I went in search of her. Soon I found Frannie in the dining part of the summer kitchen playing Monopoly with four other kids.

"Frannie, I have to talk to you."

"Sure, Sadie, what'sa matter?"

"No, no. Not here, I have to talk to you alone." Frannie looked up and, for a long moment, gazed directly into my face. She might have noticed signs of agitation, but possibly dismissed them as her own imagination. "OK, but I got to finish this game and you know how long it takes to play monopoly. Can you wait a while?" she asked as she moved two hotels and one house into her space. I turned away, my head downcast. Over my shoulder I called out, "It's OK, I'll see ya later" as I walked toward the screendoor of the kitchen. I could hear the clatter of dishes and pots being washed, dried, and put away by some of the mothers. Some called out a greeting to me from the left, inside doorway. I smiled at them wanly, waved, opened the screendoor of the dining area, and went out into the warm summer night.

Since Frannie was too busy playing Monopoly to talk to me, I left the summer kitchen and walked around the side of the house to the front. I sought out my favorite spot–the hammock. It was situated in friendly solitude on the south front lawn, shaded by many trees. While the north front lawn was always occupied, the boarders never sat or put their chairs on the south side. Because it was an unused and quiet spot, my brothers decided it was a perfect place to hang a hammock. They chose a place in the center of it where two young trees grew about twelve feet apart. Taking three large, heavy, burlap feed bags and cutting holes in the corners they threaded two ropes through the sides of the bags and tied the rope ends firmly to each tree. Thus, they fashioned a make-shift hammock; rather crude and unattractive, but practical and above all, strong enough to take the wear and tear that it would have to endure.

Soon grass beneath the hammock disappeared. Very fine dirt appeared in its place from the endless scuffing of feet, rocking the hammock back and forth. There was almost always a "waiting list" for that hammock. At times, there would be fights over who got there first, who would use it, and for how long. Often three or four of us would share the hammock and swing in unison and sing songs. But, tonight there was no waiting list. It was deserted and I was glad.

On my way to the hammock from the summer kitchen, I pulled on a ripe piece of tall grass. There was a gentle squeak as the long silky shaft where the seed-head was attached separated from its base. I loved the sweet crunchy taste of the soft, tender end of the shaft. All summer I chewed on grass right up to the time it became hay. Tonight the sweet, crunchy taste comforted me. Feeling totally rejected and unhappy, I wanted to be alone to think. The deserted hammock suited my purpose. The many trees surrounding it made it comfortingly still and dark despite the large outdoor light affixed to the huge oak tree nearby. The shadow of its leaves formed a lacy pattern on the burlap of the hammock and on the ground surrounding it. Still chewing on the grass, I plunked myself down on the hammock, with one leg hanging over. Facing the big house, I started to rock gently back and forth.

The windows glowed golden from those rooms where the lights were on. Pretty soon my brothers and sister, who were going out on this Saturday night, would be gone. They would pile into cars, happy and dressed in their best. After a week of hard work, they certainly anticipated a fun-filled evening. And I? I would be left behind feeling sorry for myself, in fact, consumed with self pity. Whenever they left me behind, for whatever reason, it always made me feel rejected and unloved.

As I rocked slowly back and forth I thought to myself, and sincerely believed it, "They don't love me. Nobody loves me! Here I am, all alone and by myself. I work so hard and try to do whatever I'm told to by *everybody*, I mean *everybody!* Here

I am, home and on a Saturday night! And they won't even take me to the movies! After all I do for everybody, they won't even take me to the darn movies. They just leave me here like some dog!"

Tears began to flow. Running down my cheeks, they quivered on my chin, then splashed onto my lap. I broke into sobs. It felt simply wonderful to cry and feel sorry for myself. In fact, the harder I cried and the more I imagined myself as unloved and alone, the better I felt. It was such a relief! I wailed! I really did! Wallowing in my misery and filled with self-pity I thought, "Sure, they don't care about me. NOBODY cares about me. Why I'll bet if I died tomorrow they would all be glad. Sure, sure! Then they wouldn't have to bother with me or take me to the movies 'r anyplace anymore an' I wouldn't be such a pest anymore. They're always sayin' what a pest I am. Boy, I should really die, like get killed by a truck or drown, like fall down a well or something. They wouldn't even be able to find me for a while. Boy! Then they'd be sorry!"

The thought of dying and how sad my family would be when I was gone made me feel even sorrier for myself. The image of being separated from those I loved made the tears increase. I was sobbing long, hiccupping sobs. My whole face was wet. My nose was running. To keep the mucous from running into my mouth, I snuffed a long, deep, snuff and wiped my eyes with the sleeve of my shirt. Then I reached out with my tongue as far as it would reach and licked at the tears that were coursing down each side of my mouth. At the same time I thought, "Sure, what do *they* care that I'm not going out? Boy, if *they* couldn't go out you'd hear about it. But heck, who cares if some little kid can't go out. They never want to take me with them anyway, not anyplace, ever! They say I'm too little to go. Boy! Just wait till I grow up, I'll show 'em! I'll go *everyplace* an' I'll never take them anyplace, ever! I'll leave them home, just like they leave me. I'll bet they just hate me, that's why they leave me home all the time."

The sobbing and tears of self-pity were now subsiding and tears of anger were taking their place. I found myself pushing harder and harder with the one foot that touched the ground. By lifting it and putting it down farther and farther back, the hammock was soon swinging so high that it started to squeak and twist where the ropes were tied firmly to the tree trunks.

It was at this point that Frannie approached. Darkness had fallen, but the light in the tree about thirty feet from the hammock illuminated the area enough so that she could see a figure swinging wildly on the hammock. Because she could hear me talking to myself and crying she recognized who was swinging so recklessly. As she approached, running the last few feet, she stopped directly in front of the hammock forcing me to come to an abrupt halt.

"Gee, Sadie, what are you doing here? Aint'cha goin' to the movies tonight?" This brought on a whole new flood of tears and Frannie was appalled. She knew how much I prided myself on being tough and strong–a tomboy! She also knew that I did not cry easily for one day she had witness my father slap me really hard across the face in front of a group of people. I, humiliated as well as hurt, shed not a tear but just bit the inside of my lip and looked down. Frannie mistakenly thought me very brave not to cry or look askance at my father. She did not realize that had I stared back at Papa without crying, it would have been taken as an act of defiance and I would have been severely beaten then and there in front of everyone for being disrespectful.

You see, I had learned at a very early age how to avoid pain and punishment. One learned never to answer back and to try to do precisely and exactly as one was told. All tasks were to be completed as quickly and perfectly as possible. Total obedience was expected, no questions asked!

I realized that Frannie was bewildered and was wondering what could have happened to me, who was usually so strong and who now sat crying so uncontrollably. Even in the semi-darkness, I could sense her feelings of helplessness as she looked down sadly at me. While not able to clearly see the pain on my face, she could sense it as she heard me wail through muffled sobs. I could repeat my anguish out loud and now there was somebody to hear me.

"Nobody loves me, nobody, nobody! Nobody cares that I'm out here crying! Nobody. I work so hard 'n nobody cares. I'm all alone! So alone! And (sniff, gulp) nobody cares."

Dismayed, Frannie tried to sit down next to me on the hammock; no mean feat, since it was still rocking. I scrunched over to make room for her. The poor hammock, sorely overloaded, creaked and sank much closer to the ground. Frannie put her arms around me and hugged me close, trying to make me see that someone did care about and love me. She lay her cheek on the side of my head, against my hair and I could feel her soft breathing next to my ear.

Suddenly, I was jolted by her closeness! Immediately, I realized no one besides Mama, Caroline, or maybe an aunt or two had embraced me in this way. I was so close to Frannie that I could smell her hair and skin and even the odor of garlic and onions on her breath. I felt uneasy being that close to someone else, our bodies touching. The intimacy made me very uncomfortable. It was a strange feeling that I could not really understand. I felt, in a subtle way, that we were doing something wrong. My enemy, the red devil-angel seemed to be telling me to sit there and enjoy the sort of warm feelings I was experiencing. At the same time, the white angel was telling me to "get up quick; there was danger."

So, ever obedient, I bounced up, and out of the hammock. It rebounded and poor Frannie almost fell off backward. Her substantial frame, however, stayed put in the swaying hammock. Surprised by my action she said, "What'sa matter? You don't like me anymore? I can't even hug you if you're cryin'?"

"Gee, Frannie, I donno'. It's not that, it's just well, uh, well uh, I gotta go to the bathroom! I'll be right back." Confused, I turned abruptly, running off through the semi-darkness and into the brightness of the huge halo of light illuminating the driveway. Taking the porch steps two at a time, I quickly crossed the porch floor, opened the screen door and disappeared into the wide hallway of the main house. A few moths sneaked in before the screen door banged shut behind me.

Meanwhile, Frannie sat quietly swinging, thinking, while carefully contemplating the hordes of moths that fluttered wildly about the lamp in the tree. There were so many of them that they looked like a cream-colored cloud swirling and surrounding the light bulb. The rays of light that filtered through seemed to merge the fluttering moths into a magical, glowing and golden mist. Frannie was so fascinated by it that, for a just a little bit longer than a moment, she almost forgot me and the fact that I seemed so burdened with sorrow and unhappiness.

While waiting patiently for me to return, she thought, "That was bologna, having to go to the bathroom. She's really acting funny." Frannie scratched her head in puzzlement. "But she's my friend and no matter what she does or how she acts, I won't get mad at her, no matter what!" Her brow was furrowed in remembering and she giggled a little, "Besides, she's the only one that never makes fun of me for having such a big nose." Laughing out loud, she said, "Well, her nose is kind of big too, so I guess maybe she understands." Pondering my hysterics and baffled by them, sympathy emerged, "I sure wish I could do something to make her feel better. Poor Sadie!"

As Frannie sat rocking gently in the hammock she recalled the fun things we did together like our hikes down to the creek to swim and then how we would lie on towels in the hot sun of the meadow to dry off. She thought of how I let her help collect the eggs and throw corn to the chickens. Once, I even shooed a chicken, flapping and squawking, off its nest so she could feel the wonder of lifting a warm, still moist egg, out of it. Other times I would take her to my "secret" place up in the hay loft where a small nest of tiny kittens would be mewing for their mother. Most times, they would be rolled up into a large furry ball with tiny noses, ears, or feet protruding from it here and there. The kittens were the most adorable things Frannie had ever seen. We would cuddle, pet and talk to them for hours and pretend they were our own little "babies."

There were rainy days, when I couldn't do chores out of doors. In the afternoon I would visit the summer kitchen. As the rain played a serenade on the tin roof, seated at one of the tables and using cardboard from old gift boxes, I would draw and cut-out paper dolls with foldback tabs on the sides of their feet so they could stand up. Then, tracing the figures of the dolls on white paper I would design, draw, and color-in wardrobes for each doll. I especially enjoyed designing ice skating outfits like those of my idol, Sonja Henie. I even drew little white ice skates with tabs to hold them firmly on the doll's legs. Because store-bought paper doll's clothes often fell off, I learned to put extra tabs on the dresses, hats, and coats in order to keep them on. I drew, she cut. She was my best friend. I always made sure Frannie would be included in everything.

By now, the poor girl was getting nervous. At least, she believed she was nervous. She had heard her mother talk about "getting nervous" so she assumed what she was feeling was a case of nerves. Anxiously, she kept looking toward the front door waiting for me to re-emerge. Finally, after wondering about my absence and thinking, "She couldn't still be in the bathroom, not after all this time. Maybe she's in her room. But why isn't she coming out again when she said she'd be right back!" she shook her head trying to figure out what was going on. Impatient, she decided it was time to go in search of me and find out what was wrong. It took no small effort and much grunting to finally get her ample, solid body up and out of the low slung hammock. The hammock groaned and squeaked in protest. Pulling on the back of her skirt in order to yank it away from where it was stuck between her cheeks, she walked toward the house. By now, only one small light was on in the hall and the house seemed deserted. Many people were out on the lawn, out for the night, or in the smoke-filled, summer-kitchen dining room playing cards, checkers, or Monopoly. Some were getting ready for a campfire on the hill in the meadow. As Frannie climbed the long, wide staircase, she wondered where she would find me. As she reached the top landing, she could see the door of the bathroom was ajar and the light was off. "Well, she must be in her room." At the top of the stairs she turned to the right toward my bedroom door and, as she approached, she could hear muffled sobs coming from the other side of the closed door. Without knocking, she opened the door and peering into the darkened room said, "Sadie? Sadie, where are you? Then, in an exasperated tone, "What'sa matter? You mean you're STILL crying? C'mon, what's wrong? You can tell me."

At that the sobs got louder and increased. Frannie reached over and flicked on the lights. She saw me curled up in a ball on the bed facing the wall, my arms wrapped tightly around a pillow, my head buried in it. My muffled voice wailed from the pillow, "Leave me alone, I don't need you, I don't need *anybody!*" The words were loaded with self pity and sorrow. I was pleased that she had come in search of me. Wailing loudly, I desperately needed her sympathy. Remembering *all* those other times I had felt shunned and rejected, I was even more upset now than before. There had been times in the past, many times, that my brothers and sister took part in activities that could not include me because I was too young. But I could not, or would not comprehend the "too young" thing. Whenever denied what I believed was my due, my immediate response was that I was unloved and unwanted.

My sorrow and pain that evening made me dwell on past hurts–those times my father embarrassed me in public–the fact that as the youngest in the family, I was at everyone's beck and call. The frustration that filled me with venomous resentment all those times when I was commanded to stop whatever I was doing in order to do the bidding of others. My longing to be free to do as I pleased. The cold realization that it could never be, burned in my chest. But by far, what distressed me most was when I would be happily drawing and Papa would come upon me. After a tirade of invectives, he would slap me, tear up my drawings, and reprimand me for wasting time on *"cosi stupidi"* (stupid things), "stuppi t'ings" rather than working. When that happened, if Mama was around to see it, she would look at me with sorrow-filled eyes. In an effort to sooth me, to ease my pain and frustration, she would gently say, *"Pazienzia figlia mia."*

Her words usually calmed me and made me control myself. But this night, I was having none of that. It just didn't work. "Sure," I thought. "Patience my foot! What good is it? Where does it get you? Crap on that!"

For whatever reason, not going to the movies that particular night compounded all those past hurts and magnified them to a very great degree. It made the recollection of all of those acidly remembered times coalesce and merge into a bitter rage. It was grossly unfair! Children feel utterly helpless when treated unjustly and that feeling of helplessness is devastating!

Cruelly, on that unusually hot summer's night, it seemed to me that I was being punished, not rewarded for my labors. The injustice of it all kept returning to my thoughts. What compounded my confusion was the fact that it had been drilled into my brain that virtue and obedience were always rewarded. But now, I could only see that it was all for naught. It was a difficult thing to understand or to accept.

Now armed with hindsight, I can see that one of the reasons for my overreaction was, perhaps, that I was growing up and beginning to question. Another reason could be my great disappointment after great anticipation. Whatever the reasons, I was traumatized. That night of crying and self pity marked a moving moment in my life–a night that affected me far more profoundly than I realized at the time. It seemed an inconsequential happening, one that I appeared to have soon forgotten. However, in late adulthood I traced some of my supersensitivity and difficulty in handling rejection, in any form, back to that one unhappy evening. That discovery was a total surprise!

Looking down at me and seeing my sorrow, Frannie wanted nothing more than to talk to and comfort me. She sat down on the edge of the bed. Her sudden weight made the mattress sag so much that I instantly rolled toward her. Our bodies thudded together. We both exploded into giggles. Quickly, I sat up. As my red, swollen eyes looked into Frannie's gray-green ones, I could see hers filled with merriment. Our giggles exploded into laughter. Poking each other, we roared. Something seemed awfully silly and soon we were wiping away tears of mirth. We, of course, had no idea about why we were having a fit of laughter, we only knew that we could hardly stop.

"Y'er really crazy, Sadie! I swear, there's nobody as crazy as you! First you're cryin' like it's the end of the world an' then you're laughing like a hyena. I jus' can't figure you out."

"No, Frannie, I'm not crazy. It's just that some things happen that make me laugh. Sometimes, they make me cry. An sometimes I just do nothin'." Breaking into a loud giggle, "I mean, gee whiz, if we ever had to sleep together, I'd be rolling over to your side of the bed all night. I would have to hang on to the edge of the mattress all night long." After a pause, I laughed out loud and said, "Geez, Frannie, you better not marry a skinny guy!"

With that, we broke into more laughter and continued to talk and giggle. After about fifteen minutes, we heard heavy footsteps coming quickly up the steps and toward the door of the bedroom. The door burst open and there stood Papa! Barefoot and wearing only his trousers he paused to catch his breath. His chest was heaving from running up the stairs so quickly. Eyes on fire with anger and face distorted with rage, he hissed at us in Sicilian. *"Non poso dormiri con tuttu la battaria che facchiti. Ts'ti'ti, subito!!"* (I cannot sleep with all the noise you are making. Shut up, *quickly!!*) *Massino, te fazu vethidi!* (Otherwise, I'll show you!)

With that, he bounded toward us. We watched, terrified and paralyzed with fear! He reached the bed and grabbed my arm. With one hand he held my wrist and with the other clutched my elbow. As he brought my forearm up toward his face, our eyes locked. His were filled with rage and I could see his open mouth. His bared teeth were close to my arm. I could smell the odor of wine and DiNobili cigars and then...and then....he bit me!

My throat closed with fear, I did not even scream. Raising his head, eyes ablaze with anger, they looked deep into mine! Staring back, mesmerized, I shivered!! Then he gave me a shove which sent me flying. I hit the wall with a thump. Meanwhile, poor Frannie had quickly jumped off the bed and was cowering in a corner. She had seen my father's wrath before and was now trembling. She lay there quivering, like a mass of Jello, eyes shut tight, praying; afraid she would be next.

As quickly as he had entered, he was gone. Only the slight odor of wine and his "Di Nobili" Italian cigar remained. The smells lingered in the hot night air of the room like the ghostly remnants of a barely remembered nightmare. The door creaked, closing slowly as if moved by some invisible hand. His footsteps going down the stairs grew fainter and fainter.

Slumped against the wall, I looked down at my forearm and was horrified! The skin was just barely broken, not bleeding, but the imprint of my father's teeth showed up as a large and perfect bite mark. I squeezed my eyes shut, but the tears trickled out anyway and spilled down from my tightly closed eyes. They were tears of pain, of fear, and, mostly, of shame. I could not bear to look at Frannie.

To think that my own father had behaved in this dreadful, savage way made me want to die. I was mortified that my friend had just been witness to the awful conduct of this man. This man, who was my father and who had acted like some wild animal. Or worse yet, like some small, stupid, spoiled child, not at all like a sane, grown man. How could Frannie ever understand the behavior she had just seen. How could anyone? How could one ever explain it?

Warily, I sat with head bowed and shoulders slumped. After a few moments, I looked over cautiously at my friend. Frannie looked back with great compassion. We stared at one another for awhile in disbelief. Then she got up, walked over, bent down, and hugged me really hard. She brushed the top of my head with her lips, rose, turned, and left the room.

Alone now, my mind was still reeling from the unnerving experience. Frannie's father came to mind and I thought about how very different he was from mine. Mr. Caldemarra was a quiet, heavyset man who wore glasses. The glasses, alone, made him "different." To me, he always seemed to be the model of what a father should be. He showed great affection for his wife and children and I never once heard him raise his voice to anyone, let alone his family. A prosperous, kind, and generous man who owned a dress factory in Brooklyn, he was forever bringing boxes of unused materials, buttons, and partially used skeins of thread to the farm (all of which Mama was delighted to receive). He was what I considered an ideal father, a Papa one could love.

Then, I told myself, Papa, my Papa was not like anyone else's as far as I could see. But then I remembered. No, that is not true, for there were other fathers who came with their families to board at the farm who were very much like my father in their dictatorial ways. Many Italian, not only Sicilian men were of that bent. Years later, I heard a description of an "outside angel" and realized that it fit my father and those others also. I got little comfort from learning that there were many, male and female, who fit that species; warm, friendly, and charming to strangers, yet cruel and mean to their own blood.

Meanwhile, still in shock, I was not aware that my father's bite was not actually that harmful or ferocious. As vicious as it seemed, it was only a tad stronger than gentle. It was a bite done in lieu of beating me. He probably was aware that in his rage, he could have harmed me seriously, so he vented his fury by biting. I was told by my sister that this was something he occasionally did to punish his children without risking bodily harm to them. Needless to say, the biting was quite effective. While it actually did us no harm, it sure scared the hell out of us!

Of course, not all Sicilian men abused their wives and children. Yet, how else to establish ones unquestioned place as head of the household? Obviously, not all men took this course to maintain control. I am sure that some found other ways (of which I am unaware).

In Sicilian culture, back then at least, any man who could not "control" his family, especially his women, was looked down upon with contempt by others; male and female alike. Because of this, I knew that while Papa liked Mr. Caldemarra, in some ways, he did not respect him. Papa considered him a man who was "too" kind to his family and who appeared to let his children rule him. Papa disapproved of the fact that Mr. Caldemarra publicly showed great affection toward his children; he loved them "too much." What was even worse was that he treated his wife with much affection–even in public! Surely he would spoil them all. A sure sign of a weak man! I guess I will never remember Papa as a "weak man!"

Curiously, many Sicilian women greatly disapproved of those few women who dared to assert themselves–and there were a few! Those strong-willed women who would not allow themselves to be mistreated and thus had some sort of control in their homes. Especially frowned upon were those who ordered their husbands about. They were considered anathema. In a perfectly understandable way, that kind of behavior on the part of women was felt to threaten the fabric of the family and jeopardize the many unquestioned years of tradition.

I cannot repeat often enough the importance of *virtue* and *obedience*. You think I overstate their importance? No. They were zealously and constantly touted as the most desirable of qualities to which females should aspire. Especially in the face of cruelty or adversity, those traits were considered almost saintly. And speaking of saintliness, the church played a great part in the lives of Sicilian woman. Religious teachings were the primary source of the overall preoccupation with virtue and morality. We must not forget, however, that Sicily was occupied by various people living on the rim of the Mediterranean Sea. Different factions were in residence over great periods of time. I have been told by many (in Sicily) that the Arab occupation, especially, had tremendous influence concerning male attitudes toward making females subservient.

These attitudes of domination and male superiority inculcated in me during my growing up years, distorted my opinion of the opposite sex. I believed that men who were kind, caring, and considerate were "sissies." I had no respect for such men. Additionally, my concepts of male and female behavior were shaped, I am certain, from overhearing the conversations of my father and his friends. Conversations overheard during those times when I had to stay nearby in order to refill the wine bottle when visitors were present. The very fact that I had to be constantly available in order to wait upon their every whim was, in itself, a message of strong relevance. "As the twig is bent...."

chapter 12

Campfires and Camaraderie

*T*he toothmarks took almost a year to disappear and I never mentioned the incident to anyone else. Frannie never brought it up, so I decided she had forgotten about it. I'll never know.

After she left my room, I sat alone in the darkness and continued to think about my father, her father, and lots of other things. I didn't feel good, sitting there brooding. Then I got restless. The evening had really just begun and I didn't want to sit in my room for the rest of that Saturday night. Once again I went in search of Frannie. I didn't have to go very far. She was right across the hall in her room, reading a magazine.

"Hey, Frannie, want to go down and see if anyone has started a campfire? It's better than jus' sittin around, doin' nothin'."

Frannie looked up at me in surprise. Then she smiled, nodded yes, closed her magazine, and walked toward me.

"I'm sure glad to see yer not cryin' anymore. C'mon, let's go."

We tiptoed out of the room and slipped quietly down the two flights of stairs. Stealthily, we crept past my father's room and went quietly out the front door. We followed the flagstone path that led down the center of the lawn. As we did, we could see the flames of a campfire across the highway, far off, on the top of a hillock jutting up out of the southeast cow field. We could barely make out the figures seated around it. There was not much traffic on 208 at that hour of night, so we quickly crossed the highway, crossed the strip of grass that separated it from the field and then slipped under the barbed-wire fence. I slipped through the wires easily, but had to hold the them apart so that Frannie could fit between them. The sharp barbs could inflict a really nasty gash on soft human skin, let alone on the hides of cows. Some of the boarders carried scars for a while because they were unaware of how vicious a barbed-wire fence could be.

We picked our way carefully across the darkened field toward the fire and soon could hear the voices of people singing. When we reached the base of the hill, we chose the rear, less steep, part to climb up. Reaching the summit, we approached those seated around the campfire. It was a disparate group, people of all ages. Some were sitting on apple boxes, others on blankets, some even holding infants. The entire group was in the midst of singing "Marie Alena" at the tops of their lungs. It was the number one song on *The Hit Parade* at the time. Someone motioned to us to sit and we did so on their blanket.

The smell of corn, steaming in husks charred by the hot coals, potatoes baking, and marshmallows roasting, filled the air as palpably as the music. Someone handed me some marshmallows. I noted what others were doing with them. So,in turn, I handed them to Frannie. "Here, hold these while I make something to roast them with." While Frannie held the marshmallows carefully in her chubby hands, I reached back and broke two long sticks off a bush. Painstakingly, I peeled off the bark, took the marshmallows from her, and threaded them carefully onto the bare twigs, two marshmallows on each. Handing Frannie a "loaded" twig we proceeded to hold them over the flames and toast them.

We almost burned our mouths as we started to eat the blackened, puffy marshmallows. My first marshmallow oozed out, dripped down the stick and burned my fingers when I tried to eat it. I learned quickly that eating a hot marshmallow can sear your lips as badly as the burn on the roof of your mouth from eating a hot slice of pizza. I ate only one toasted marshmallow, I decided I preferred them "raw."

While roasting food, drinking, and eating, we took turns telling jokes, stories, and riddles. In unison we would sing well into the evening. Songs such as: "Way Marie," "Hail, Hail, the Gang's All Here," "Oh, You Can't Get to Heaven," "Moonlight Cocktails," "I'm Gonna Sit Right Down and Write Myself a Letter," and "Tangerine." However, the favorite song was *"Ci'e la Luna Mezzo Mare"* ("There is a Moon Half-way Over the Ocean"). Adults always sang it accompanied by much rolling of the eyes and knowing grins. This seemed to imply secret meanings and actions which we younger children did not really understand. Not until many years later, as an adult, did I learn that the song was more than highly suggestive. It was rowdy and filled with a great deal of sexual innuendo. Probably that is why it was always such a favorite and sung with such gusto by adults. I always wondered why they laughed so hard over verses I thought were silly and meaningless. *"Si che ven'un pesciatori edu va, edu veni, sempre pisce e'mmano te'ne."* (If a fisherman comes seeking you, he goes, he comes, always holding his fish in his hand.) So what was so bad about a fisherman holding his "fish" in his hand all the time. Adults! Who could figure them out anyway?

After the singing, it was time to tell ghost stories. Each person told the scariest one they knew. The evening would end with a long dirge recited by all in unison. It began very quietly, "Who stole the golden arm? Who stole the golden arm? "Who stole the golden arm?" The phrase was repeated over and over building from almost a whisper to a loud climax at which everyone would turn to the youngest in the group, point, pause a moment, and then scream in unison "YOU, stole the golden arm!" Thereupon, the person pointed to, would practically jump out of his or her skin! It was all so deliciously scary and such great, good fun.

Around midnight, all of the firewood was gone and only dying embers remained. That was the signal for everyone to stomp out the campfire, clean up the area, fold their blankets, pick up their apple boxes, and walk carefully through the rough meadow back to the barbed-wire fence. There, they held the fence apart for one another to climb through, emerging onto the grass strip along route 208. A short walk and the crowd would arrive back to the flagstone steps and the walk leading to the house. A few people returned to the summer kitchen and made coffee while most others went to bed.

The summer kitchen dining area was the heart of social activities, especially on rainy days. Adults would play cards, children would play checkers, pick-up sticks, or jacks. Others would just sit, drink coffee or espresso and chat. It was a great place for parties. Especially birthday parties. To my never-ending sorrow, my birthday was in January when there was nobody around to give or come to a big party. In July, however, Frankie and my cousin, Chico, both had birthdays, which fell only days apart. A huge double birthday party was always celebrated.

Usually one or two girls who had crushes on Chico or Frankie would start the ball rolling. They would plan a surprise party. The kitchen would be decorated with streamers and balloons. We would buy gallons of ice cream and soda and the boarders would bake lots of cakes, as well as one great big birthday cake. Everyone would bring some kind of gift.

After the cake and the singing, it was time to open the presents. Everyone was amazed over the variety of packaging and the wily jokes perpetrated on the birthday boys. I remember with glee one enormous, beautifully wrapped box that was very, very heavy. It was for Chico, from an anonymous admirer. He smiled with great pleasure and was absolutely delighted with the size and looks of the box. It was with obvious relish that he began to open it. He had great expectations. Within that box however, were six other succeedingly smaller boxes-surrounded with rocks! When the final, smallest box was opened, inside was a can of pork and beans. The hidden message was explicit. Everyone got totally hysterical with laughter over that one. Giving gallons of money was another favorite. But the gallon would be filled with sand and there would be only a few nickels, some dimes, and lots of pennies hidden inside. Much laughter and shrieking went on as the gifts were opened, one by one. I was tempted many a time to lie and say my birthday too was in July. I longed to share in the fun and delight of a summer kitchen birthday party, but it was never to be.

Summer evenings on the farm were filled with children playing *hide and seek* surrounded by the myriad twinkling of fireflies glowing amongst the trees and hovering above the lawn. The many trees, the great number of parked cars and the nearby bushes made it easy to hide, but difficult to find anyone. It took hours to play a really good game of *hide and seek*.

On other evenings, much time was spent trying to catch fireflies and put them in jars. I learned quickly that if you squatted down in the grass and looked up, the fireflies were silhouetted against the sky during that interval that their "lights" were off. Thus they could easily be seen and caught in between "flashes." Once I learned that, I captured lots and lots of them. Tag was another fun game as was ring-o-leavio, a "city game" I never did get to figure out.

Despite the large numbers of people thrown together, people of diverse ages and social standing, altercations or quarrels were rare. There was much fun and camaraderie, much affection and respect. It was an innocent time. A time when people had very little money. Little or no expenditure often brought great returns in enjoyment and satisfaction. I believe it all derived from that sense of respect and affection that we felt for one another. We were all of the same "kind" and felt comfortable in our sameness. In everyday interactions, there were also truly sincere moments of concern and love. It was a time of naivete. It was that time when World War I was a fading memory and World War II was imminent. None of us could begin to imagine how profoundly different the world would soon be. None of us gave any thought to the fact that the time we were in, despite some hardships, was a delicious and wonderful time. It was a time that would live, thereafter, only in songs, in nostalgic memories, and in faded photographs. Memories *are* voyages the heart takes.

chapter 13

The Bennetts and Dolls

M r. and Mrs Bennett lived down the road from the farm and since they had no children, had become extremely fond of me. They first noted me as I scampered across the meadows and orchards near their house. Other times, they would catch sight of me as I slowly walked along the dirt road which rambled from my house to theirs, seeking wild strawberries or wild flowers. Whenever I came upon their house, I would stand and stare. It was a curiosity, because it looked so small and the grass was always so smooth looking, like a carpet. There were also flower boxes adorning the front windows. It was painted a deep, dark brown. Because of its color it earned the nickname "the chocolate house."

One day, as I stood and stared, Mrs. Bennett came out and asked me my name. I told her, we chatted and thereafter became friends. I liked her right away because she was short and plump, just like my mother. Like Mama, her hair too was worn in a bun on top of her head. She was also dark haired and snub nosed, yes, she reminded me definitely of my mother.

I did not realize at the time how much joy I brought this childless couple, especially on those days when Mrs. Bennett could convince me to come in and help her bake cookies. It took little persuasion after the first time. "Sadie, shall we make chocolate or vanilla sugar cookies this time?"

"I don't know, I kinda like 'em both." would be my reply as I grinned, my mouth watering for her delicious cookies. My mother baked bread and only occasionally a cake. It would be a simple vanilla cake, baked in a rectangular pan. No frosting, ever! Therefore the first home-baked cookies that I ever tasted were the ones Mrs. Bennett baked.

Her eyes would sparkle when she looked at me. She made me feel that I was the prettiest child in the whole world, even though had a kind of pallid, olive-toned skin and wasn't even pretty. Cute? Maybe. When I smiled, I had one deep dimple in my left cheek which Mrs. Bennett always commented on. She told me often how much she loved my smile. Years later, Mama told me they once asked if they could adopt me. They even offered some money but Mama said no. No, she wouldn't give me away, let alone sell me, for all the money in the world. After I married, one day my mother turned to me, sad eyed, and said, "Whena you have a chile, you no take alla the money in the worlda for it. En thena, ona day, you end upa giva them away to somebody anyway-for nothin! *Accusi e la vita.*" (That's life.) Of course, the Bennets understood her refusal. It did not diminish their fondness for me. In fact, it was they who gave me the only other possession that I loved as much as my pencil box.

It was the evening of my fifth birthday. Mr. and Mrs. Bennett came over early, around 5 o'clock carrying a long, beautifully wrapped box with a large pink ribbon tied around it. Imagine my surprise when they handed it to me. I recall staring at it, then at them, and then back at the box, puzzled, not sure it was for me. When I finally realized that it was, I still continued to just stare at it for what probably seemed like a long time to the Bennetts. It was my first gift-wrapped present and I was struck by the beauty of the flowered wrapping paper and the large fancy bow. I also wondered why they were giving me a gift, since I had never before received anything for my birthday. I had not even had a cake with candles.

Slowly and carefully, I removed the ribbon and, without tearing it, the wrapping paper. Just as slowly and methodically,

I opened the box. All I could see was pink tissue. Carefully, I pulled away layers and layers of it and then shrieked with joy as the exquisite features emerged of a dimpled face, surrounded by long pale blonde curls. She was sleeping on a bed of pink tissue. I paused, breathless with happiness and stared intently down at the Shirley Temple doll. Her eyes were closed, and fringed with thick, stiff, golden lashes. A jolt of pleasure filled my chest so totally I thought my heart would burst as it began to beat wildly, joyously. I was breathing very fast, my breath came in short, quick puffs and I could feel my eyes fill with tears of gratitude. I put the box down very gently, then rose, arms open wide and ran to Mrs. Bennett. She bent down, arms wide too, to embrace me. Reaching up, I hugged her so hard around her neck, the poor woman almost choked. I hugged and kissed Mr. Bennett too. He grinned through the whole thing. After receiving that doll, I decided that there was nothing I would refuse to do for the Bennetts. I absolutely and unequivocally adored them. They, in turn, reveled in my love and appreciation.

I never tired of playing with that Shirley Temple doll, holding it by its hips and making it walk. It was the first new doll I had ever had. Before that, somewhere in the huge attic of the house, Joey, the youngest of my brothers had found a slightly battered baby doll. It was fourteen inches long and its head, arms, and legs were of pressed sawdust painted a flesh color. Its stuffed body was covered with gray cotton from knees to neck to elbows and it had no clothes. Approaching my mother, I asked if she would make some clothes for the it. Soon she found some time and made a dress, a bonnet, and little panties. How I loved that doll! I named her Mary after the Holy Mother. Every free moment I had, I rocked Mary, changed her clothes, cooed, and talked to her incessantly.

Then one morning in late spring, I went to play with Mary and couldn't find her. Then I remembered that I had left her somewhere outside. I ran to find her, racing down the hall and out the front door to the porch. It was a crisp, sunny, beautiful morning. I paused for a moment as the pungent and familiar fragrance of wet earth pervaded my nostrils. The scene from the porch overlooking the valley was lovely. The rain from the night before had left the grass still moist and it sparkled as if diamonds were sprinkled in it. On the massive trees, the leaves, wet and shiny, glistened. The whole world seemed freshly cleansed. Plants, barns, trees, everything fairly shimmered in the clear, fresh air of the summer morning.

I had been taught to believe that whenever it rained, God had washed the earth. I took a deep breath of the sweet, clean air as I descended the front steps of the house, eyes scanning the lawn. Then, far off, I saw my doll lying atop the stone wall which held up the sloping lawn. Smiling to myself with satisfaction, glad I had found her, I quickly jumped the last two porch steps and ran across the lawn to retrieve her. When I reached the stone wall and bent over to pick her up-I screamed and drew back in horror. Quivering, spellbound, I stood and stared at what had been my doll. Slowly, almost fearfully, I crouched down to more easily examine the skin on her face, arms and legs. Staring and frowning with concentration-intrigued-but still horrified, I strove to fathom what I was seeing.

The face of the doll looked especially repulsive! Bloated and disfigured, the skin had black cracks while ugly bubbles had formed on its skin. Even her eyes were ghastly and looked encrusted. The legs, the arms, all of the composition parts looked equally loathsome and the colors on the dress were running into one another. The stuffed body, visible beneath the dress, was soggy and lumpy. It did not take too long before the horror of my poor disfigured doll sank in. When it did, I quickly turned and ran screaming for Mama. Sprinting across the lawn, I mounted the porch steps two at a time. Still crying, I ran down the hall to the kitchen. There my mother, baffled at my tears and hysteria, knelt down, reached out, and held me tenderly while I cried. Hugging me closely against her warm, soft, ample body, stroking my hair gently, she listened intently and then comforted me until I had calmed down.

After a short while, she stood up and with loving concern, took me gently by the hand and walked me back to where the doll lay. When we reached the poor, disfigured thing, Mama gazed down sorrowfully at it. Squatting down and at almost eye level with me, she looked at me intensely. Her eyes seemed larger and a more velvety brown than usual. Eyes locked together, we stared at one another for what seemed a long time. Then, smiling softly, she hugged me, kissed me on the forehead and slowly stood up. In a firm, clear voice, calmly and matter-of-factly, she explained that the paint on the doll had merely softened in the rain and often that is what happened to that kind of paint when it got soaking wet. Putting her hands on my shoulders, she faced me. In a more serious but still gentle tone, she said that if I had really loved my doll, I would not have forgotten and left her out on the lawn all night. She told me that if you really love something, you had to take care of it. You had to make sure it was safe and keep it from danger at all times. You had to watch over what you loved, even when it was not giving you pleasure so that it would be there at those times that you needed it or wanted it most. That stated, she patted me gently on the head, and turned, and walked back to the house.

I stood there transfixed, devastated, and feeling as guilty as if I had purposely murdered my doll. Suddenly, I wondered if the poor thing was feeling any pain from the ugly wrinkling of her skin. Both the sense of guilt and sense of great loss caused me to cry for a long time that day. Even though it was too ugly to play with anymore, I couldn't bear to throw Mary away. Pondering what to do, I decided she had died and I would bury her they way we buried dead kittens. And so, I buried my doll, Mary, under the snowball bush on the southside of the house, near the sunroom. Deeply religious, I even made a small, crude wooden cross of twigs and stuck it in the freshly dug earth at the head of the grave reciting a "Hail Mary" and an "Our Father" as I did so. It made me feel somewhat better. However, I mourned many days. I missed my doll. Of course, receiving the Shirley Temple doll, a short time later, helped me forget completely, the loss of the poor disfigured Mary.

However, perhaps, in some strange way, because of this, my first painful experience with the loss of something cherished, I was learning to cope in reality with a subliminal form of death. Perhaps my grieving and then matter-of-fact acceptance of loss at such an early age might have been the beginning of preparation to help me face the far more painful deaths of loved ones later on.

chapter 14

Roots, Winter and Hygiene

Of all the times I shared with my mother, my favorite was watching her comb her long, dark brown hair. It was fascinating. She would first take out all the hairpins that held her hair in a bun (she called it her *"tupu"*). When her hair fell loose to her shoulders, she would take a regular comb and remove all of the tangles. After that, a *"pettinu streetu"* or fine-toothed comb, would be used to comb and comb and comb her hair for a full five or six minutes.

Using the fine-toothed comb in such a way was in lieu of shampooing. In the Sicily of my mother's girlhood, it was believed to be unhealthy to wash one's hair too often. Many believed that doing so would result in dry, itchy scalp, and weak, unhealthy hair. (Perhaps they were right. I have heard that in the past, the best hair for making wigs came from Sicily and China.) Thus, Mama washed her hair only a few times a year. However, the use of that comb did indeed keep her hair clean and shiny, if not fresh and fragrant.

As she combed, she would pause occasionally to remove the tangles of hair from its tiny, tight teeth. After removing the excess hair, she would wind that hair around her index finger, then carefully and gently pull the hair off and place it on the dresser. The hair, so wound, looked like a small cocoon.

She then completed her toilette by twisting her hair into a long coil which she then would again twist into a bun on the top of her head, carefully securing it with hair pins: some large, heavy ones and a few thin, fine ones. She never, never used bobby pins. When she finished, there was a neat pile of sometimes two, sometimes three "hair cocoons" on the dresser. The cocoons intrigued me. On Saturdays, when I had to clean and dust my mother's room, I always regretted having to throw away the accumulated pile of cocoons. For some strange reason, an eerie feeling would envelope me and make me feel that I was throwing away a small part of my mother. I shrugged my shoulders at such foolishness. My feelings, however, perplexed me and for a long time remained a mystery.

Many years later, at the age thirty-two, seated in a college classroom in a course about the Near East, I learned that one of the beliefs of the people of that area was that it was imperative that those parts of your body, such as nail clippings and discarded hair, were to be carefully collected and then personally destroyed. The professor went on to explain that the people of Iran, Iraq, and Egypt would wind their discarded hair into small cocoons. He demonstrated by wrapping imaginary hair around his index finger and then pretended to remove it, precisely the way that my mother had removed the hair from her finger so many years before. Further, he explained that those people would then burn all of their hair and nail clippings so that they would not fall into the hands of enemies; enemies who, possessing even a fraction of a part of a person, could then place a curse upon them or send them bad luck.

Curious, I questioned the professor and was informed that this practice probably dated back to very early times. It then occurred to me that my mother had, perhaps unknowingly, been practicing part of a ritual that she had certainly, through example or whatever, learned as a girl in her native Sicily. Although a ritual that had begun eons ago in the far, far distant past, its use was probably passed on by invaders and adapted by the native Sicilians. In the course of performance, perhaps a part of the ritual had either been lost or not been taught. If my mother was aware of the ritual in it's entirety, perhaps she saw no need to follow it completely through here in America.

Seated there in a college classroom in the second half of the twentieth century, I felt that I was a part of a specific and long parade of humanity. Of course, I am aware that all of mankind came from others before us, but suddenly I was much more cognizant of the fact that I was the end result of a people that sought to cope with a strange and fearful world by inventing rites and mores that would help them survive. Their beliefs and rituals helped them conquer their fears of the unknown, albeit in strange, primitive ways. Ways that had evolved over years and years of experience, repetition, adaptation, and learning.

I shook my head at the thought of the incredible numbers and variety of the ethnic groups who were either visitors to or invaders of the Island of Sicily. In ancient times, because of its incredible fertility, it was called the "breadbasket of the Mediterranean." Probably every ethnic group living on the rim of the Mediterranean, and even beyond, had dropped their seed at one time or another in Sicily. I sat there, trying to imagine whose blood was flowing in my veins. Which of the many invaders and conquerors might have begun my line? Just the thought of it gave me a rush; almost a feeling of power. The adrenalin in my body was at work as I listened in utter fascination and delight to the rest of the lecture. A new consciousness of a vague kinship to those Near Eastern people, described so well by my Lebanese professor, came over me. I recalled that whenever I had a deep tan, people would often ask me if I was Syrian or Egyptian.

Since I had to finish cleaning Mama's room, puzzling over her hair cocoons was a waste of time. I had much other work to do. Shrugging my shoulders in a what-can-I-do-about-it attitude, I decided that I had better get on with dusting the furniture and dust mopping the floor. First, I had to throw away Mama's hair cocoons. I gently dumped them in the wastebasket. Saturday was the day that bed linens were changed and all the bedrooms were cleaned. Caroline and I shared the work. We enjoyed pillow fights in each room, finding them the best and most efficient way to plump the feather pillows.

Winter was coming and I looked forward to it with both dread and delight. Delight because I found nothing more beautiful than to awake one morning and find trees, fences, bushes, and buildings clothed in a glittering mantle of white. In the bright early morning sunlight, the world became a dazzling fairy wonderland. I absolutely believed in fairies but doubted that they were ever present in the wintertime. It was probably too cold for them. After all, in stories, "fairy rings" were only found in the grass, never in snow. And I had never seen pictures of fairies dressed in warm coats and boots. Whatever would they do with their delicate wings? Still, winter was so beautiful that I loved to invent creatures to populate the sparkling landscape. When I woke on those brilliant, snow-filled mornings, my imagination conjured up a tiny ice queen gliding over the snow on the roof outside my window. She rode in a crystal sled drawn by ten pale blue-white horses with huge pale blue plumes on their foreheads. The queen would be wrapped in mounds of exquisite white fur and she would be beautiful beyond belief. Even more beautiful than Hedy Lamarr or Lana Turner. My imagination knew no bounds as she would whirl and twirl round and round the flat roof top, avoiding the large brick chimney over to one side. Hearing my mother call, I would turn to answer and the queen would fly off to the west and disappear.

Winter meant sleigh rides, Christmas, ice skating, and sledding down the steep hills in the nearby meadows. It meant sweet potatoes baking in the top part of the pot-bellied stove. It meant the smell of good things baking in the oven all the time. It meant hot Ovaltine. It meant jumping into high snow banks from fences and stone walls.

Winter also meant other, much less pleasant things. For practical reasons, the house shrunk in winter. From the entire house in use in summer, we reduced our occupancy to living in half as many rooms, mainly those that could be heated by the stove in the parlor on the south side of the house.

However, not all that were in use received heat, such as the upstairs bedrooms. My sister and I were assigned to those.

COLD! Those rooms were cold! Deep, penetrating, and painful. It was a cold that was absolutely dreadful. In fact, almost all winter long, the only time I felt truly warm was when I was in school. Because my room had no heat, I never looked forward to bedtime, especially that moment just before crawling between the frigid sheets. Sheets that seemed to delight in enveloping my small body within the frosty grip of excruciating cold. Lying there, curled up in a ball, it seemed an eternity before the ice-like sheets surrendered to the warmth my body finally generated and trapped beneath the layers and layers of heavy blankets, long johns, and heavy socks. I learned that by keeping my head beneath the sheets and using my breath for warmth, I was able to create a small hollow of heat and finally fall fast asleep.

The next morning, the war on cold began all over again. To leave the warmth of the bed for the cold of the unheated room was stingingly painful, but especially so on those mornings when the temperature had dropped to below zero. The speed I developed running from my cold room upstairs to the warmth of the pot-bellied stove downstairs probably explains why I was one of the fastest sprinters in my class.

Because the house had no central heat, bathing was even more limited in wintertime. A few times a week, I would take a small pan of water, which had been heated on the kitchen coal stove, into the south parlor and place it within reach on a chair. Wearing only my panties and positioning myself in the only really warm place in the house, behind the pot-bellied stove, with brown soap and a torn piece of old towel, I would soap my face, neck, arms, and legs.

I didn't often wash my feet since it was difficult to do so while standing up. Besides, bending over in the confined area behind the stove was neigh impossible. As I washed various parts of my body, I would ring out the cloth and rinse myself off. It took a lot of rinsing in order to remove all the soap. I found that I had to keep dipping the cloth in the warm water and wring it out, over and over. The soft, soapy, gray, bubbly film of dirt which began to form on the top of the water and which increased each time I wrung out the cloth, never ceased to amaze me. Since I could not actually see the dirt on my body before I washed, I wondered where all that gray stuff came from? I remembered Suzy's house.

The real reason I began washing rather often in the back of the pot-bellied stove was due to a humiliating incident in school. The fact that obtaining good hygiene was difficult in my cold house often caused me to fail "morning inspection" at school. My humiliation grew each time the teacher would berate me in front of the entire class because of my dirty neck, black fingernails, or dirty ears. Standing all in a row, holding out our hands, I along with my classmates would wait patiently to be inspected by our teacher, Miss Giddings. She minced no words with those (and there were others) who did not come up to her expectations of cleanliness. I recall a few really embarrassing remarks such as, "Young lady, don't you know what soap is?" Another time, "My dear young girl, do you realize that you can contract a terrible disease if you do not bathe regularly?" After that, "Dirty ears are the sign of a dirty mind." In exasperation, " What *does* your mother teach you?" And finally, "Cleanliness is next to Godliness!" Especially after that last remark, I made certain that my neck, the under part of my forearms, and my ears were always clean, never minding how clean (or dirty) the rest of me was.

However, I was still being scolded for dirty fingernails, until one day I found that a small nail or even the end of a bobby pin would suffice to clean them. Overall, I tried to conform to the concept of "cleanliness is next to Godliness" though I never really understood exactly what that meant. However, since God was mentioned, I was sure it was important and that I had to comply. Such are some of the painful and somewhat arduous experiences which many of us have to live through in order to become "civilized."

Perhaps some of my classmates felt sorry for me, if so, they did not show it. Perhaps, without a really close look, my dirty neck was not visible to them. I really did not notice that any of them seemed to be as bothered by my lack of cleanliness as was the teacher. When the teacher scolded me, it was almost as if they expected it, accepted it, and possibly assumed it was part of my being Sicilian. I was different in other ways, so why not in this way too?

As fate would have it, just as I resolved the morning inspection, another "beast" reared its head. One day, the gym teacher, Miss Bennett (no relation to my neighbors), made an announcement in class. Even now her image is still vivid! She looked very old to me, even older than my parents. Her hair was always worn in a mass of large, fat, golden curls on the top of her head in what was called an "upsweep" (the kind Betty Grable wore in that famous pin-up of WW II). In all the years I attended elementary school, Miss Bennett's hairdo never varied (we giggled when it was rumored that she wore a wig). Sneakers, socks over stockings, a skirt, and a sweater with a shirt underneath was her "uniform" and it never varied either. She first clapped her hands to get everyone's attention and then said, "All right children. You are all to sit on the floor in one long row and remove your shoes and socks. We are having foot inspection today."

Upon hearing this, I seriously considered throwing myself from one of the windows of the gym which was six stories above the ground. The windows, however, were huge, locked tight, and an impossible escape route. Frantic, I decided that perhaps I could plead a stomachache. But no, since I was rarely sick, the teacher surely would not believe me. There was no escaping this inspection. Seated on the floor, first I groaned. Then I moaned. Then I sighed a big sigh of resignation. Slowly-very slowly-I untied my shoelaces. I cringed at the thought of what those students next to me and what the inspecting teacher would think, after I removed my socks. How would they respond to the sight of the thin layer of gray that I knew covered my ankles. Enough so that it looked almost like another pair of sheer socks hidden beneath my real socks. Socks! They too were yet another source of grinding, implacable shame because of big holes in the toes and heels.

Shame! I felt drenched in it. There was so much, that I was ashamed of: that I was dirty when others were clean; that my kind, loving mother was plump and old compared to the slim, young stylish mothers of my classmates; that my parents spoke broken English and could not read nor even write (my brothers or sister had to sign my report card); and that I had straight, black hair when almost everyone else in class had brown, light brown or blond hair. I hated the handmade clothes I wore. Especially, I loathed the ankle length, itchy underwear Mama insisted I wear in wintertime. It was one long garment and had a drop seat with two buttons, one in each upper corner, which often came undone. Over the ugly long underwear, I wore unbecoming, thick, long, tan cotton stockings that reached to the middle of my thighs and that were held up with rubber bands. I was also ashamed of my disagreeable, smelly lunches and the fact that even what I ate was so different from everyone else. Looking back now, I wonder how I coped with the impossible. Somehow I did. What seemed at the time unbearable, now seems almost amusing.

As soon as I reached puberty and we had central heating, my bathing habits matched those of my peers. I even shampooed my hair three times a week. *"Cu l'anni veni lu giuthitsiu"* as Mama used to say (with years comes wisdom). Many years later I came upon a quote while reading. The words exploded in my brain, an instant revelation, "Those experiences which do not destroy us make us stronger." I sat quietly and remembered with pain.

chapter 15

Storms and Prayers

The knoll upon which our house sat was about a hundred feet off the road. Across the street were the cow barn, horse barn, pig sty and chicken coops. All the bigger barn buildings had lighting rods on them. The house, even though it was set higher than the barn buildings, had none on it anywhere. Obviously, whoever installed them back then, considered the barns and animals far more important than the house and people. My father never even gave a tiny thought to putting arresters on the house when he bought it. None of us knew very much about the properties of lightning and often ignorance, by any other name, is daring.

In the event of a summer lightening storm, all the boarders would congregate in the large, main hallway. Most of them would sit on the steps of the long, wide staircase. The front door was left open (dangerous in a lightning storm!) so that everyone could watch the marvelous exhibition that nature provided. A few brave souls stood on the front porch, hair lashed by the wind yet shielded from the rain. There they would listen to the crashing, rumbling thunder and watch the torrents of water gushing down the driveway. It was a wondrous vantage point from which to view the spectacle. Great white-hot bolts of lightning danced and streaked across the sky above the valley, disappearing in brilliant flashes upon the horizon from time to time.

During the height of the storm, with all that electricity flashing and striking nearby, Mama would unhesitatingly venture out into the storm carrying a large *metal* pot filled with salt. Rain and thunder be damned! Running around the parameter of the huge house, pausing every few feet and at each corner, especially, she would reach into the pot and throw handfuls of salt on the ground close to the foundation. Each time she did so, she would make the sign of the cross while looking up to heaven and mouthing words of prayer. Hair streaming with rain-water, clothes drenched, she would continue on until all of the salt was gone. Re-entering the house, rainwater dripping and trailing after her, face glowing and triumphant, she was secure in the knowledge that she had prevailed upon God and thus had prevented lightening from hitting the house.

In retrospect, it does indeed seem miraculous that in all those years of violent thunder storms, neither the tall majestic trees which surrounded the house, nor the house itself, all higher than anything else around for miles, had ever been struck by lightning. Even more of a miracle was the fact that Mama was never struck by lightning as she engaged in her ritual and prayers, holding on to that metal pot!

The boarders were city people and though they loved to tease my family about being *"farmiole"* (a rather pejorative Italian term for farmers), I never ceased to be amazed at the ignorance displayed by the supposedly sophisticated "city folk." I often found it incomprehensible that grownups could be so stupid about the obvious. Many did not know that potatoes grew underground and expressed great surprise when they learned that watermelon and cucumbers grew not on trees, but on the ground on vines. Some children could even be convinced to drink their milk upon being told it was horse milk rather than the regular, much-hated cow milk. Many adults and children alike learned a painful lesson when they could not tell the difference between a sheep and a ram. Some were terrified in the evening when bats began to fly about at twilight. They had learned somewhere that bats would fly into one's hair and could not be extricated unless all of one's hair was cut off along with the winged intruder, of course.

The greatest fear of our "city cousins", however, was reserved for Joe, the bull. You remember him, don't you? Besides trampling mulberry trees, he occasionally pulled his stake out of the ground and "got loose." Pandemonium would break out! The lawn, filled with boarders basking in the sun or playing cards, would literally explode when someone shouted, "The bull is loose! The bull is loose!" Women and children screamed! People scattered in all directions. Most headed for the house. Those wearing red would run especially fast seeking shelter of any kind–a tree, a bush, or anything protective. Upon reaching the safety of the porch, they would run pell-mell into the house fearing that the bull would climb the stairs and charge them. Faces could be seen peering fearfully from behind windows. Soon Joe would appear at the foot of the driveway. For a little while he would stand there, pawing the ground, then he would lumber up towards the house. At that moment, close behind him, my father, brothers, and whatever hired hands had been pressed into service would be running after the bull. Some armed themselves with pitch forks. They would attempt to surround and capture poor Joe, who was probably only looking for a cool drink of water on a hot day. Joe seemed docile, but when not held by the chain attached to his nose, he could be ornery and quite dangerous (thus the pitchforks). It was a brave person who got close enough to him to grab the chain and thus gain control of the huge animal. Often it was Frankie, but Joey, even though the smallest and youngest, sometimes captured him too. Papa would beam all over when it was one of his sons who did the capturing.

I was absolutely delighted whenever the bull got loose (which was about three or four times during each summer). It was always such an exciting time, what with the bull thundering up the driveway or across the lawn and the frightened-to-death boarders screaming in fear and flying in all directions for cover. Then to watch in fascination as the men would maneuver, surround, and then capture the bull. After which they would lead him off and re-stake him somewhere! Whew! It was almost as good as the movies.

The lush green of July gave way to humid, hot, and wilting August days. It was a time when "locusts" sang their serenade to summer during the still and stifling afternoons. Everything near the barnyard seemed to be covered in a haze of brown dust. August was the height of hay season and hay season signaled the beginning of the end of summer. "Haying" was a time I looked forward to and thoroughly enjoyed. For me it was fun "work." Not so for my brothers though, who had to perform hard, physical labor. They pitched tons of hay, not only in the broiling sun, but in the dusty, semi-dark, hot interior of the barn for hours on end. However, despite the hardship, it did seem to be the one form of work on the farm that most everyone involved with appeared to relish.

Starting on the first day of haying season and always thereafter, you could find me seated beside my father in the driver's seat of the empty hay wagon. We would wait until my brothers, sister, and a handful of young male boarders climbed aboard. Papa would then hand me the reins of the two enormous horses hitched to the wagon. The most wonderful thing in the world to do, as far as I was concerned, was driving the horses out to the hay field. Each time he let me, my whole body felt as though it would explode with joy and pride. He had taught me how to hold the reins, what kind of pressure to apply to guide them left or right. How to say "giddyap" and "whoa." It all worked so well and the horses learned quickly to obey my commands.

Our "passengers" were jolted about as we bounced along over the stones and uneven ground of the rough dirt road leading down to the hay field. Before long, we arrived at a huge meadow where the dried and ripening hay lay in neat rows, cut down by the hay mower a few days before. Papa would tell me where to halt the horses. As the wagon came to a full stop those riding on the wagon bed would jump off. Pitchforks in hand, they would start spearing the hay and throwing it on to the bed of the wagon. As they pitched it on, Papa and I, taking turns, guided the wagon slowly past row after row of dried hay. Gradually the wagon filled. When the wagon was about a third full, Papa would take over the reins. Before long, the load was so high that only the strongest of my brothers could pitch the hay high enough for it to sail to the top and not slide off. That was the signal that it was time to return to the barn. Pitchforks in hand, the loaders would clamber to the top of the hay laden wagon by way of a ladder-like structure in the rear. There, they would all stretch out, exhausted, and enjoy a time of rest while the horses plodded back toward the barn, struggling up the incline from the hay field to the main road.

As Papa guided the horses, he would flick the end of the reins on their hindquarters, speak quietly to them, and make sounds out of the side of his mouth (kchk! kchk!) urging them up the long and gradual incline. The horses, directly in front of and so close to me, both intimidated and made me giggle as I watched them. You see, pulling the heavy load uphill was a real strain on them and they grunted, expelled much manure, and passed wind as they struggled to reach the top of the slope. So many odors mingled and defined those days-Papa's sweat, the dried hay, dust and seeds swirling about, the horse manure, and the sweat-soaked horses and their leather harness. The smells were rich and unforgettable. Even now, passing a field of drying hay or a horse barn can rekindle dormant memories.

From my perch on the wagon next to Papa, I used to peer up and wonder why the enormous load of hay did not slide off the wagon as we jounced wildly over the stubby fields and rock strewn road. The ground leveled out once we reached the highway (route 208). No one spoke. All that could be heard was the heavy snorting and straining of the horses pulling the heavy load and the iron clad wooden wheels squeaking and crunching over rocks and dirt as one pair rolled over the rough terrain bordering the road and the other pair clattered on the cement of the highway.

Sometimes Papa would look over at me, wink, and then start singing some Sicilian folk song, an aria from an opera, or a Neapolitan love song. At the time, I was not aware of the origin of the songs, but loved hearing all of them, especially

"O' Solo Mio." Papa's strong, clear melodious voice always filled me with a warm, pleasant feeling. When he sang, I felt a real affection for him, for only while singing did he seem much more warm and far less threatening than usual. In retrospect, I suppose it is not so strange that when I grew up and married, it was to a man, who, during courtship, always sang to me.

At this point, I must include an additional and interesting aside about Papa. Upon our return to the barnyard, while the hay was being transferred from the wagon to the hay lofts in the cow barn (an intricate and interesting project involving pulleys, horses, and much more hard work on everyone's part), Papa would send me up to the house to fetch him his customary cup of coffee. Coffee? You ask, who would drink coffee on a hot and humid day? Just listen, for Papa and I had a secret arrangement. Soon I would return from being sent to fetch his coffee-carefully carrying a large, white, St. Dennis coffee cup, walking slowly so as not to spill a drop. That coffee cup, which I adroitly handed to Papa, was actually filled with his own, bracing, home-made wine. It came straight from the barrel in the cellar. Cold and powerful, it probably did more than merely refresh him. It was filled to the brim. While others drank from and passed around a gallon jug of cold water, Papa, delighted at his little scam, blew on his "coffee" to cool it, sipping it slowly, grinning impishly at me as he did so. I grinned back.

One reason that everyone enjoyed haying season is because of what we could look forward to at the end of each day of hard work in heat and humidity. In late afternoon, when the last of the hay was loaded in the barn, my father would take over the care of the horses; water and feed them so that we could all go swimming in the creek before the sun dropped too low in the sky. Papa never accompanied us since he could not swim and never seemed very fond of water. We would gather up towels, bathing suits and a bar of Lifebuoy soap. (I loved the orange-red color and its smell.) Benny would back the pickup out of the garage and all of us would climb aboard and sit down. We were hot and sticky. As Benny sped toward the swimming-hole the cool wind blowing in our hair and against our cheeks felt good.

This particular swimming hole was located in a different part of the creek from where I had gone to gather wild flowers and where we took the boarders to swim. My first time there, much to my surprise, Benny had to drive about a mile and a half, the distance from the barn to the far edge of our property on Jenkinstown Road. When we arrived, Joey jumped off and opened the gate. Thereupon, Benny drove in and parked the truck in the pasture. Because it was where we kept the heifers, Joey always had to make sure the gate was closed. (Papa would kill us if the heifers got loose.) Eager to feel the soothing balm of the cool creek water, and scrambling to be first, the rest of us quickly jumped off the rear of the truck and headed for the woods.

A large stand of enormous evergreens grew at its edge. The sharp, delicious smell of pine and earth permeated the air as we walked under the deeply shaded canopy of branches. This pungent fragrance rose from the slippery smoothness of the forest floor as our feet crunched on the thick bed of pine needles. Hiding behind thickets and trees, we changed into our bathing suits. Each of us would then work our way down the steep embankment to that special place to swim. It was a true swimming hole, large and deep, surrounded by shallow water bubbling over rocks, boulders and small waterfalls. The shallow area was where I was allowed to "swim." Tucked into an inflated, large inner tube from a tire, I was told to stay in the shallow part of the creek while the rest of the crew dove and swam in the deep part. Unable to swim, I happily complied. I totally enjoyed bobbing about in my tube, paddling and floating past and around boulders of many sizes. Peering into the water, I sometimes caught a glimpse of fish, both large and small. The currents swirled me around and around.

After about fifteen minutes of diving and swimming, the others were both relaxed and tired. Some swam quietly, others floated. I, meanwhile, still floating in my tube, all at once felt an urgent "call from nature." Compressing the muscles in the lower part of my body to depress and control the pressure, I decided to ignore it. Perhaps the unwelcome urge would go away? It lessened a bit. Secure and comfortable in the floating embrace of the rubber inner tube, I was feeling much too lazy to leave the warm, silky water. A few moments later the urge returned, and this time, persisted. I realized I would have to "do" something very soon. Unhappy at the thought of having to walk barefoot over the stone-filled shore to the privacy of some bushes, I cast about for some easy solution to my problem. There was no time to lose, the pressure was now constant, becoming more and more insistent. That is when I decided that I would relieve myself in the water. I believed that my excretion would sink and disappear. Perhaps, I reasoned, the fish might even eat it. (Heck, I was only little, how else would I think?) Proud of myself for solving my dilemma so easily, using my hands, I rowed over to a large rock. When I had positioned myself behind it and out of sight of everyone, I pulled my bathing suit aside and after a few quick grunts, "let go." Ahh! The wonderful relief after holding it in for so long felt decidedly good. Reaching up to an overhanging branch and pulling off a large leaf, I wiped myself, dropped the leaf in the water, and complacently pulled my bathing suit back down over my "cheek." The leaf floated off slowly downstream.

I lay back in my tube, happy, and quite satisfied with myself. All at once, the delight over my solution turned to horrified incredulity. Right next to my tube, a large, cigar shaped piece of excrement popped up to the surface! It was almost touching me! Eeeks!! To evade it, I frantically paddled in one direction and then another. To no avail. Not only did it remain close by, indeed, it seemed to be following me. In desperation, I now splashed wildly, rowing every which way. Finally, with palms held flat, I tried pushing the water away from me and, somehow, thankfully, that seemed to work. The rather large, brown "shape" began to float slowly away. "Whew! What a relief!"

Within moments, however, my sigh of relief turned into a gasp of despair! The "thing" was drifting slowly, inexorably, and directly toward where the others were peacefully enjoying the water. "Oh, no!" Now frantic, and despairing, I turned my eyes up to heaven, beseeching God to intervene. "Please dear God, please! Do something quick, and make that you-know-what go away, please, please, I'll be good and pray to you every day!" then I added, " Oh please, please, dear Lord, otherwise, they'll tease me to death!" It seemed that He took pity on me. Suddenly, the object of my despair, swirled by a different current, floated off in another direction. As it went bobbing off downstream, I looked up to heaven and breathed, "Oh thank you God, thank you, thank you!" At that moment, I felt undying gratitude toward Him. He had answered my prayers and saved me from great ridicule and embarrassment.

I was positive that had my brothers and sister learned what I had done, they would never have let me forget it, even for a moment. The laughing and teasing would have been ruthless! Of this, I was certain, since I had been the object of their ridicule once or twice because of accidentally passing wind. In our family, anyone guilty of *that* was ribbed unmercifully and made the butt of many, many jokes.

It is my firm hope that I have not offended anyone with the retelling of this last tale. It is the recounting of a real and remembered time, similar in some ways, perhaps, to what some amongst you may have experienced. Childhood holds many secrets; secrets we keep hidden. Too often we believe that we, and we alone, have lived through what we perceive as sometimes shameful, sometimes trying ordeals. It can come as a great relief to know that others have had common experiences; that others have shared in that kind of misery; that you were not alone and what you did, at that time, was not as bad or as evil as you thought. In retrospect, some events are even laughable. However, the glimmer of remembrance can return us to a time long past and sometimes help erase residual pain or guilt.

chapter 16

Frankie and Cold Hands

*F*rankie was the middle one of my three brothers. He was most like me in looks since, in a family of five children, only two, Frankie and I, had straight hair like Mama. The other three were all curly heads like Papa. Frankie was also different from them in other ways besides his hair. He was rather quiet in contrast to their volatility. He rarely argued, nor answered back, nor refused to perform whatever task was assigned to him. Neither was he a complainer. Whenever Mama would ask him to do something such as take out the trash he would say, "Sure, Ma."

Four hours later, Mama would ask, "Ah, Frankie, you gonna dumpa da garbage?"

"Yeah, Ma, I'll dump the garbage."

The next day, garbage undumped, Mama again would ask, exasperated, "Frankie, no you gonna dumpa da garbage?"

"Sure, sure, Ma, you know I'll dump the garbage."

"Yeah, *ma quanno?* When, Frankie, whena you gonna dumpa da garbage?" Two days later, Mama, angry, exasperated, and somewhat bewildered would say, *"Quanto voti t'ya speyadi?* (How many times must I ask you?) When you gonna dumpa da garbage?"

In a voice still warm-hearted and compliant, Frankie would answer, "Ma, I'll do it, I tole you I'll do it and I will!"

Mama, not wanting to turn to Papa for discipline (knowing how harsh he could be and how fragile [she thought] Frankie was), would shrug her shoulders and stop asking. Eventually, of course, Frankie dumped the garbage. But he did it in his own good time and in his own way and that is how he conducted himself throughout most of his life.

He was sickly as a child, frail looking and not as strong and outgoing as the rest of us. He frequently caught colds. Mama watched him like a hawk and ministered to him with care and with many home remedies.

When Frankie was a very little boy, for some strange reason, he used to love to take off his shoes and go barefoot. Winter, summer, spring, or fall, inside or out of doors, he was always removing his shoes. Occasionally, he would even lose a pair of shoes, then a search would be instituted by the entire family. Because of his "frail constitution," Frankie was always scolded, but rarely punished for taking off his shoes. After a while, Mama decided that the reason for his frequent colds was his predisposition to going barefoot in cold weather. One day in late winter, she finally lost patience and threatened him with a severe beating should he ever again take off his shoes while out of doors.

Well, you know what happened. One gloriously windy day in March, there was little Frankie, running around happily barefoot. Mama, who had been watching from the window, raced out of the house. She ran toward him, wooden spoon in hand, eyes angry! When she reached him, towering above where he stood, she reached down to grab him and paddle his behind. He cowered, looking up at her contritely, his large, soft brown eyes begging for mercy. She was not to be deterred! In a severe voice she said, "Whera you shoes? Din' I tella you no take offa da shoes! Now I gotta give you a good lickin'. I tole you you gonna get it iffa you take offa you shoes."

Straight faced, the five-year-old Frankie replied, "I didn't take off my shoes Mama, really I didn't".

"No? *Alurra*, (then) who tooka offa da shoes?"

"The wind blew them off." His answer, so unexpected, took soft-hearted Mama off guard. Laughing, she swooped him up in her arms. Rounding up his shoes, she carried him into the house. Thereafter, she would triple knot his shoes whenever he was sent out to play. Yes, in his own gentle and unobtrusive way, Frankie always did exactly as he pleased and rarely took orders from anyone, even Papa.

Of us all in the family, he was the slowest to anger. It took an awful lot of agitation before he would respond sharply or strike out. Yet, when he finally did anger, it was a consuming kind of rage and heaven help whoever got in his way. When this level of anger finally broke through, he was utterly cruel and ruthless. So rarely did this happen, however, that the family looked upon him as one of the gentlest among us.

In a Sicilian family, sons are preferred. No matter how many come along, the first born son is the favored one. The last born son is the baby and is often deferred to. Being the middle son is not the most enviable position. It was Frankie's lot. If it bothered him, he gave no sign. He became the mechanic of the family, fixing the trucks and tractors, keeping the cars running, the spray rigs repaired, as well as anything else that needed a motor in order to run. His quiet, kind, and gentle nature made him the peacemaker.

When he reached his teens, he developed a penchant for buying wrecked cars, fixing them up, driving them about for a while, and then selling them. Unfortunately, he also was accident prone. In 1940, he bought a white 1937 Cord, a truly exotic looking car. Because it was a total wreck he paid little for it. To repair it and bring it back to its original splendor, he spent months working on it. The first Saturday night he took it out, on his way home in the a.m. on Sunday he ran off the road and into a field. The Cord traveled about sixty feet, then rolled over and over, coming to a stop wheels up. Everyone said he must have been going like a "bat out of hell." He walked away unscathed. Because that Cord was built like a tank, he figured that is what saved him. Mama, however, was convinced that it was her prayers and the candles she lit each time he left the farm in one of his "cars." After what happened with the Cord, he had at least four more accidents, yet not one single injury, not even a scratch. (Gee! Maybe those candles worked!) I never once heard Papa reprimand him in anyway about those accidents.

Since I was sort of Frankie's "favorite" and we got along so well, he was usually assigned to go with me when I needed to buy school supplies or to accompany me anytime that I had to go somewhere and needed someone to look after me. I loved it when he took me places. It wasn't too often, though when he did, he was always so caring, protective, and funny. He made me laugh a lot.

It was a raw November day, the kind of day when you can smell snow in the air and the wind is a knife-like cold, cutting through clothes and making any exposed skin tingle with pain. On that particularly cold day, Frankie and I got off the school bus in the village instead of taking it all the way to school. I was in need of paper and pencils and, being too young to go to the store alone, Frankie, as usual, accompanied me to the local Five & Ten (city people called it the five and dime) to help me buy what was needed. It always puzzled me this store was referred to as the "Five & Ten" even though one could plainly see it was called "Lane Sargent"–the big green and gold sign out front above the windows said so. I suppose stores that carried everything and that had cheap prices were all called "Five & Tens" at that time.

After buying the school supplies, Frankie was to walk me to my school, after which he would proceed to the high school to attend his own classes. We entered the store and I was totally entranced by the displays of all kinds of wonderful things. It seemed to me that everything anyone could possibly want in the whole world could probably be found somewhere in that store. Walking from aisle to aisle, I forgot my need for paper and pencils. Imagine my pleasure when I discovered that at last, I could finally see over the tops of the counters without being held up by some grownup. As a matter of fact, this was actually the first time I had been in a store without my mother or sister holding my hand the whole while, my first time all by myself (except for Frankie) and walking about alone. It was like exploring another planet, the incredible variety of objects on display left me almost dumbstruck. There were things I never knew existed and remarkable new versions of things with which I was already familiar.

"Oh, look, Frankie! Aren't these pretty? They look so nice 'n warm." I pointed, eyes luminous with longing. My brother walked over to see the object of my desire. There, on the top of a pile of assorted mittens was a pair that were made of suede. They were pale tan in color and their surface had a feathery nap. One could see how soft and supple they were without even having to touch them. The wrist bands were generous and had a green and matching tan stripe woven into them. The mittens were indeed beautiful! I shook my head and made a wry face, knowing intuitively, without even asking, that they were prohibitively expensive and thus could never be mine. Frankie nodded and made a face back at me. I knew that he agreed. Then he walked on.

Instinctively, I dug my hands deep into my coat pockets almost feeling the cold that would be gripping my fingers outside on the way to school. I had no mittens. At the start of winter, Mama had made me a pair that looked homemade, not up to her usual handiwork, from a piece of wool she had found in her rag bag. Somehow, the second time I wore them, they got lost, and she had not had time to make another pair.

Leaving the mittens, I proceeded down the aisles, now remembering, searching for the one that held the paper and pencils. After a while, Frankie was a few steps behind me. Soon he was over by another aisle. Again forgetting the paper and pencils, I found myself once more in a reverie looking at all the wonderful things I was certain I would never possess.

When Frankie called to me that we would be late, I reluctantly dragged myself away from gazing at all the fascinating displays. He was standing by the cash register getting ready to pay for my notebook and pencils which he had already picked out. The lady behind the cash register seemed to eye us both suspiciously and I felt a shiver of apprehension as the woman looked pointedly at Frankie. His guileless brown eyes gazed back at her, unperturbed and unblinking as she handed him the change. He pocketed it, picked up the bag, took my hand in his and headed for the door.

As we walked out of the door, I could almost feel the woman's eyes boring into our backs. It made me uncomfortable, but I was used to the townsfolk acting hostile. After all, they never did like "wops" and "dagos" and that's what I had learned we were from previous name calling. It still hurt whenever I heard the insults and whispers. It was not as frequent as it used to be, only because we all had learned to fight back and defend ourselves well.

Frankie took my hand as we crossed Main Street. When we reached the other side he let go. We each put our hands in our pockets because of the cold. Frankie tucked the bag under his arm. We walked along, quietly, with hands clenched in fists in our pockets to conserve warmth. Soon I looked up at my brother and said, "Frankie, why did that lady look at you so funny?"

He looked down at me and smiled a small funny smile. He did not answer.

"Come on, Frankie, she looked at me funny too! Why? Is it 'cuz we're Italian and she's like those kids on the bus that don't like us?"

Frankie, holding back a grin, stared straight ahead and said not a word. I was used to this not only from him, but from my other brothers and sister. My nickname, "chatterbox", was well earned. At home, I constantly questioned. In desperation, Mama would sometimes reply that God made all things and controlled the world and a little girl should not be so curious lest she anger Him. That would keep me quiet for a while.

"C'mon Frankie, c'mon, tell me what's happening! Why don't you answer me?"

Frankie started to grin and I was sure he was going to reply. He didn't. We walked along and I almost had to run to keep up with him. As we left the main street of the village and struck out through a deserted wooded area leading to my school, Frankie looked down at me and said, "Guess what?"

The tone of his voice made me suspect that he was going to play a joke or surprise me in someway. Warily, I paused and eyed him up and down. He too stopped and stood looking down at me. The look on his face was so full of love that I frowned in puzzlement. The funny grin from before returned

194

to his face. Then it turned into a broad smile. He had beautiful teeth. Looking up at him, I thought that he had never looked more handsome than he did at that very moment. We both stood there, smiling at each other in such a silly way. I, in anticipation, and he, happy over what was about to transpire.

Slowly, he reached into his bomber jacket into a space between two unfastened snaps. Just as slowly, he pulled out his hand and held it palm up. In it lay the beautiful tan leather mittens.

"Oh, Frankie! Thank you, thank you!." Overwhelmed with surprise, I could hardly breathe. I reached out eagerly but suddenly stopped. My hands paused in mid-air and then dropped forlornly to my sides. Suspicious and curious at the same time I asked, the words tumbling out, "Did you buy them for me as a surprise? Where did you get the money? I know they cost an awful lot, how could you afford them?"

Using his pet name for me he said, "Don't worry, Miss Prim, I got them for the 'right price.' Just shut your mouth and put them on. It's cold out. You need' em!"

Taking my hand in his, he placed the mittens on my palm. Turning away from me, he started to walk fast and looked straight ahead. I knew by the way his mouth made a thin hard line that there would be no more answers that morning to any questions. I carefully drew on the mittens while trotting after him and trying hard to keep up. The mittens were lined with real sheepskin fur and the soft warmth felt excruciatingly wonderful after the biting cold that had cracked my skin and turned my fingers red. Although I suspected that my brother had stolen the mittens, they felt so good on my hands that I wiped out of my mind any bad that was connected with them and how they were acquired. I forgot Papa's rules about stealing. I was not aware at the time that he had a double standard. I knew I could not return them, even if I wanted to. I would just get my brother in trouble. How early we learn to rationalize!

I never lost those mittens and because they were a size too big, I wore them for almost three winters. By then, they were ratty looking and no longer fit me. When that happened, I saved them, tattered and worn, in a special box of treasures

I kept hidden in my secret place in the attic. Those mittens were very special to me and I always loved Frankie in a very special way because of them.

chapter 17

Beauty and Virginity

The writing of this book has convinced me that my father had a far greater influence on my life than I had hitherto realized. Unfortunately, it was my utter fear of him that prevented me from having any affection for the man. Only now, in writing this book, have I begun to understand him. Despite that new found understanding, I find it hard to forgive him for the pain he inflicted upon us, especially my sister and mother. I suppose he did the best he could since his attitude toward women was one he inherited.

My mother, on the other hand, was so loving and kind that I adored her. Without a moment's hesitation I would have laid down my life on her behalf. Thus, in the early years of my life, whatever she said or did affected me profoundly. In truth, we are all probably far more influenced by the actions of our parents or our models, than by their words. Whether accidentally or on purpose, their reactions become our reactions. We then, so to speak, learn to run on their batteries rather than our own (sadly, some of us never develop "batteries" of our own). With that in mind, let me tell you about some of Mama's "hang ups." Hang ups which to some degree became mine and Caroline's. Both of us were influenced by our mother and each handled that influence in a different way.

It was late November of 1936, a Sunday morning, and Mama, seated on a chair in the kitchen sat staring at the picture on the cover of the *Sunday News Rotogravure* section. It was a full length color photo of the wife of the newly re-elected president of the United States. In the photo, Mrs. Roosevelt stood tall and proud, regally dressed in a long evening gown.

Mama had never learned to read but she thoroughly enjoyed looking at the photos in the papers. If a particular picture piqued her curiosity she would ask one of us to read her the caption beneath it. That particular Sunday, as I passed by, I noticed she was peering intently at the cover while frowning and muttering under her breath. Curious, I drew near and heard Mama say, *"Tallia, tallia che bruta! Ma, vero bruta! E la mogli d'lu Presidenti, e' peccato, che peccato."* (Look, look how ugly she is. I mean, truly ugly. The wife of the president, it's a sin, what a sin.) At the same time, she made little "tsk, tsk" sounds hitting her tongue against her teeth and shaking her head from side to side. I had learned early on that when Mama made those sounds and shook her head in that way, the object in question was something of which she soundly and genuinely disapproved.

I reached her chair and peered over her shoulder to see what could be eliciting such strong disapproval from a woman who rarely found fault with nor judged others. For a few moments, we both stared in fascinated silence. After taking a really good look at the photo of Mrs. Roosevelt, I nodded in agreement. Mama was absolutely right! How could President Roosevelt, such a handsome man and leader of the whole United States (and who could probably have married anyone), choose such an unattractive person as his wife? Not only would he have to look at her across the table for the rest of his life, but she would bear his children and they could inherit her looks!

For a while more, Mama sat and stared at the photo of Mrs. Roosevelt. Again shaking her head in disbelief, she commented on the poor woman's prominent overbite. Then she exclaimed over Mrs. Roosevelts weak chin and how it unflatteringly receded into a double chin. She disapproved of her somber hairdo and pitied the First Lady's unattractive mouth. Lastly she chuckled over her nose. Her greatest disappointment was saved for Mrs. Roosevelt's glasses for they indicated she had bad eyes! Head still shaking in disbelief, she held the photo at arms length, to better see it, almost to show the world and ask its opinion as well. In colorful Sicilian she said, to no one in particular, *"Tallia, non ave cindo, e pari vero laria."* (Look, no waistline at all, and so unattractive.) *"Tallia sa vesta, lu coluri di merda, di tutti li coluri, bruno!"* (Look at that dress-the color of excrement, of all the lovely colors, brown!) *"Cu tutti le sordi che avi, si putiva fare parriri ciu meglio."* (With all her money she could do something to make herself look better). *"Tallia, tallia!"* (Look at her, look at her!) *"Como po fari na cosa accussi a so marito?"* (How could she do this to her husband?) *"Non ci porta respeto?"* (Has she no respect for him?) *"E vero vergonia ca pari accusi bruta!"* (It's truly a disgrace she should look so ugly).

Of course being illiterate, Mama had no way of knowing what a truly unique, marvelous, and wonderfully kind and caring woman Mrs. Roosevelt really was, despite her lack of beauty. However, since Sicilian women were rarely called upon to use their brains, their looks were always considered their most important physical attribute next to being physically strong and able to have lots of healthy babies. It would be unthinkable for a well-off Sicilian man to choose anything less than the most beautiful and healthy woman he could find. She didn't have to be too smart. In those days, few Sicilian women ever received an education. It would have been considered a waste of time on a woman. What would she do with it? How much education did one need to be a mother or housewife? Anyway, a really intelligent woman might give her husband a hard time. Looks were of primary importance. After all, a good-looking woman would probably produce good-looking children. I quickly tired of hearing Mama addressing thin air and in such garrulous tones. Slipping out of the kitchen, I ran off to my room. The image of Mrs. Roosevelt, however, remained fixed in my brain and I never again saw a photo or movie of the woman that I did not recall how vehemently my mother felt about unattractive women in high places.

Which reminds me of another incident in a somewhat similar vein. It happened one hot summer day as I was coming down the steps of the front porch. I heard high-pitched, excited voices and drew closer to listen. The voices were those of a group of women (boarders) on the lawn. Their garrulous tones made me curious! Approaching them, I overheard my mother–who rarely raised her voice–in a heated discussion with some of her "commare." Seated in the shade of some tall maples on the front lawn, they sounded like the hens in the barnyard when the rooster was pursuing them. I smiled because of their agitated state and wondered what all the fuss was about.

The group was vehemently discussing some woman whose photo was in the newspapers. First, I heard Mama say emphatically, *"Disgratziatu, disgratziatu! 'E patsu, 'e patsu, vero patsu!"* (Dishonored man, dishonored man! He's crazy, he's crazy, really crazy!) Still speaking Sicilian, "She's not even a VIRGIN! What'sa matter with that man? Why wouldn't he marry a virgin? Not only that, she's divorced, what a disgrace! Can you imagine such a thing? God knows how long it's been since she was ever a virgin."

Next, one of her friends interjected, "Why would the King of England want soiled goods? He could have a nice pure girl or woman. A real virgin and he picks that...that... *tappinara!*" None of the conversation was in English and my ears perked up since the last word was spat out with such venom by the woman. I had heard the word *"tappinara"* before and knew it was some sort of curse word and not a very nice thing to call someone. I was surprised to hear that particular lady use such vile language since she always seemed so pious. I had heard the word "virgin" before, but only when connected to the name Mary, Christ's mother. I wondered how the women could use such a bad word while at the same time using a word that was connected to the Virgin Mother. I knew that *"tappinara"* was a word considered much worse than "hell" or "damn" and was not to be used lightly.

At the same time, from the tone of voice the women used when they said "virgin", I surmised it was a very important, very good thing for others, besides the Virgin Mary, to be. I groaned to myself and shook my head in exasperation. Here was yet another something I would have to learn! But how does one go about becoming a virgin? Anything so important must be very difficult to do, no? I tried to sort things out in my head and connect being a virgin with the Holy Mother, or being a virgin, or just being nothing. As I put it all together in my head, I surmised that being a virgin was to be pure and good, like Mother Mary. How good was good and how did one become purified?

While reading the lessons in my white Catechism book, I had noted that much was made of the virgin birth (whatever that meant? I never learned, since it was never explained) of Jesus. I also learned from my Catechism that first there had been the Annunciation and then right after that, God came down in the form of a white dove. In the book, a painting of a big, golden shining light, similar to a giant halo, was used to show what happened between the dove and Mary. The light was shown surrounding the both of them. This big shining light was called the "Immaculate Conception." Conception certainly had to be a very important thing and I puzzled over what it meant, especially if it had to be immaculate too! Of course, I didn't dare ask the priest to explain it to me. There were certain things you just KNEW you were not supposed to ask questions about and certainly conception and virginity fell into that category. The virgin birth, too, was different and also very important. Of this, I was certain, because priests seemed to talk about it a lot.

Then I wondered, "If God, in the form of a dove, came down and made Mary the mother of God, how could he do it? Ah yes, that is what conception must mean, to get pregnant. Why didn't they just tell us what it was anyway? So what did that make Joseph? Was he the stepfather? Or, since there was no visible father around, was he considered the father of Jesus? Did someone tell him before he married Mary what was going to happen? Is that why he married Mary in the first place? If God was going to be her son's father, how come she didn't marry Him?" No, I knew that was an impossible question! "Did Joseph know that Jesus was not his son? The whole thing was the opposite of what I was beginning to learn about concerning goodness and morality. Somehow the Catechism never seemed to pose or answer questions like that, or maybe I missed something. The more I thought about it, the more confusing it all became and so I resolved to ask Father O'Brian about it the next time I saw him at religious instructions. I determined I would do so no matter how much he might preach to me and act annoyed at my asking questions again. Maybe this time, if I asked properly, he might even answer my questions.

I thought back to what he had said the last time I had asked him something. It happened one day after religious instructions. He had gently scolded me for not attending church on Sundays. I replied, defensively, that I lived more than three miles from church and since no one would drive me, I couldn't walk that far. Hurt, I added, "Anyway, going to church doesn't really make you a good person. Look at Marie, she goes to church every Sunday, but she's always pickin' on little kids and always poking fun of poor kids who have holes in their clothes. I never do any of those mean things to other kids, so don't you think God sees that I try to be good, even if I don't get to church alla time? "

Father O'Brian got a funny kind of look on his face and looking down at me, said firmly, "Judge ye not, lest ye be judged." This time his tone of voice was not so gentle. In fact, it was rather unkind and then he stared at me with hard looking eyes which, of course, discouraged me from asking any more questions. At that time I looked down, ashamed, and vowed not to anger him again.

From a later point in time, I came to understand that whenever someone in authority had difficulty in answering a question, often they answered with another question, a parable, a cliche, or, as so often in the case of politicians, double talk. Many years later in a painting class at college, I often got into hot water by being too inquisitive. I recall asking one of my professors to explain what he meant by "abstract" art. He looked directly and pityingly into my eyes and in a voice drenched with sarcasm replied, "As Satchmo said when someone asked what 'jazz' was, 'If you gotta ask, you'll never know!'" He too stared hard at me, much as the priest had done so very many years ago. This time also, I looked down and felt humiliated (since I was fourteen years older than my fellow classmates and felt I should have been more knowledgeable). None of them had asked, so I assumed they "knew" and I didn't. Ashamed at being older, but stupid, I reddened with embarrassment. Later, when I became a teacher I realized his was a very good answer to an impossible question.

God was a very important part of life while growing up Sicilian, especially female Sicilian. Religious teachings were the parameters that defined ones behavior. The teachings of the church were really the "rules of life" and you were constantly measured, watched, and judged according to those rules. In my family, the men did not concern themselves with God and Church as much as their female counterparts. Curiously, and from personal observation, it appeared to me that there seemed to be two camps of belief among Sicilian men. One group were as fanatical and faithful in their belief as the women, though that group of men seemed definitely in the minority. The other, larger group, seemed to act as though they believed so as to humor their women and the community. My father fell into neither group; at least not while on the farm. Frankie told me that during the Feast of San Gennaro, on the Lower Eastside, Papa would pin a one-hundred dollar bill to the statue of the Virgin Mary, as did many other of his *"cumbari."* Men supported the church with money, women with good deeds, prayer, and example.

Upon his arrival in America, Papa had attended various churches. None of them "reached" him or convinced him. The Protestants, he decided, preached too much, the Presbyterians, probably not enough. Later, at a Catholic Church, he noted a sign that indicated seat offerings were 10 cents. He understood it to be the cost of "admission" to attend church. This angered him. That poor people would feel humiliation at not having the money in order to attend mass. It turned him off to the Catholic Church in America and probably also served as a good excuse to never again attend.

Mama, however, was deeply, sincerely, and profoundly religious. She wanted very much to go to Mass each Sunday and bring all of us. Even though she believed church would improve Papa's disposition, she wouldn't even contemplate asking him to go. He, on the other hand, said no when Mama asked for permission to take the family to church on Sundays. He insisted there was far too much work to be done (and there was). He felt we should not waste time going to church. However, as in all things great or small, there were exceptions that even Papa had no control over–Christmas Eve and Easter. They were the exceptions to the "no church" rule. The whole family (excluding Papa), got dressed up and always attended Midnight Mass and Easter Sunday morning services. One other exception was Palm Sunday. At least one person was spared to drive Mama to church in order to bring home some palms. Papa said it was one of the few times the church gave the congregation something in return instead of just taking their money. Besides, it was firmly believed that the crosses made from the palms given out at mass blessed the house and kept it safe all year. Even Papa wasn't taking any chances.

From the soft greenish-yellow palms, Mama wove the most intricate and beautiful crosses. I would watch, fascinated, as her deft hands would weave a soft, pliable palm in and out and produce the most lovely, thick, fat cross. She would tuck the ends in so cleverly that each cross appeared to have no beginning or end. I would try to emulate my mother, but try as I might, my crosses always came out crooked and skimpy. I never could master the making of the crosses and it vexed me no end. After many, many tries, I finally gave up. Mama, however, fashioned many crosses and they were then hung in almost every room in the house. As they dried out, time turned them a lovely golden brown. Each year, new crosses would be made, but the old ones were left in place since they were blessed and were not to be thrown away. The old crosses grew drier and more brittle each year. They gathered dust and eventually crumbled away.

My early childhood at my mother's side was filled with stories of God and Christ and the goodness of Mary and Joseph. As I got older and learned that people got married and then had babies, I longed to ask Mama about Mary being married to Joseph but having God's baby instead. Lacking the courage to ask the priest, I was consumed with curiosity and wondered, even if it was God's baby, just how did that all work? Yet, just as I knew there were questions that were taboo insofar as the priest was concerned, that same something told me it was not a good question to ask Mama. I had to stop asking questions and just learn to accept. I always found that very difficult to do. The WHY of everything fascinated me.

By first grade, at the age of seven (considered the age of reason), I was sent to religious instructions along with the other Catholics in my class. During that time, we prepared for communion. While taking instructions, I had no idea that at the end of the year an enormous gold cup was given to the student who excelled in learning his or her Catechism lessons. These lessons were to be found in a lovely, beautifully illustrated white book that each child was given at the beginning of the school year.

I admired the beautifully drawn and colored pictures in the book and read the dogma of the Church with great interest. Especially fascinating (and frightening) was the doctrine of mortal sin and venial sin. Mortal sin was a most terrible transgression that would send you to hell forever if it was not forgiven. The venial sin was of less consequence. As such it was not considered as bad and, therefore, was much more easily forgiven. The saving grace about all of this sinning is that one could go to confession, tell all, and be forgiven and cleansed. It didn't quite make sense to me that you could go out and do all kinds of mean or bad things and then just say a few "Hail Mary's" and "Our Father's" and be totally absolved. God had to be really good and really forgiving if He felt that way.

I often wondered if the priest ever withheld forgiveness or scolded anyone if they did something really bad like kill somebody. Then how many prayers would somebody have to say? I often felt guilty when I found myself questioning the teachings of the Church. It made me feel like I was committing a sin of some sort by merely doubting. I had an uneasy feeling that by doubting the holy teachings, I could get into trouble. I could really be punished. How? I wasn't certain. I didn't know anyone with whom I would be comfortable discussing it. After a while, getting no satisfaction from those questions that I dared to ask, I just tried to believe what I was taught. Having total faith in what I was told, however, was very hard to swallow.

What really scared me most about sinning came from the illustrations in the Catechism that accompanied some of the lessons. There was one drawing, in particular, of a very pretty black-haired girl. (I had black hair and really identified with her.) Illustrated in comic book form, the first frame was a drawing of her with a white, pure heart, showing right through her clothes. Next she was shown entering the confessional booth. As she entered, her heart had three small black dots. The captions indicated that they represented venial sins. However, in the lesson, the little girl lied to the priest and confessed to only two of her sins. Thus, when she left the confessional booth, hands folded in prayer, she now had one small black dot and one very large black dot. Besides still having a venial sin, now she had acquired a mortal sin for not confessing all. It taught, in no uncertain terms, that each time she lied, there would be a big black dot. I worried greatly that eventually if the little girl kept lying, she would have a totally black heart.

This both disturbed and frightened me and I developed a genuine fear of going into the confessional booth. On the one hand, I hated to tell the priest that I sometimes told a lie, or that I had bad thoughts about Papa, sometimes wishing him dead, or that sometimes I swore under my breath at teachers. In the semi-darkness of the confessional booth, I was certain the priest would recognize me, if only by my voice. I didn't want him to think badly of me. Thus, confession inadvertently kept me from being a "good' catholic and I never, never could bring myself to tell everything. Occasionally, I wondered if I was walking around with a black heart, full of sin, like the little girl in my Catechism.

Strangely enough, it bothered me so much that even as an adult, I never went to confession. Only the night before I got married, did I go (the priest insisted). Even then, I did not confess all and committed the worst sin of all, communion with a "black heart" filled with sin.

We had been told that at the end of the school year, when religious instructions were over, there would be a small ceremony held in church to mark the event. Seated in a front pew with my classmates, I heard people entering behind us. Imagine my surprise when I turned to look and see who was coming into church, and saw my mother enter, genuflect and then sit down in a pew. She was dressed in her best as were my sister Caroline and older brother Benny who were right behind her. Mama never left the farm or her work unless it was for a very important reason. I pondered the reason for her presence. It wasn't even Christmas or New Year's! What could they all be doing here?

Believe me, I almost fainted with surprise when my name was called and I was presented with the gold cup. I had forgotten all about it. You can be equally certain that I felt very guilty about accepting it. I knew in my heart that I really didn't believe some of that stuff in the book and now I would have to go to confession and tell *that*! Oh well, I decided I would worry about it when the time came. What really delighted me about the award was the pout on "dear", religious Maria's face as I, instead of she, carried the prize (it was at least half my size) back to my seat.

Mama swelled with pride as Benny carried the huge gold cup out of the church to our car. We could keep it for one year only, then it would be passed on to some other faithful soul with a good memory. Despite its size, Papa didn't seem to notice the gold cup on the mantle piece. When Mama proudly pointed it out to him, he raised his eyebrows, glanced at me with an amused look and said, *"Non ci'e male"* (that's not bad).

Besides being Sicilian, growing up Catholic also complicated one's life. There were only a few other Catholics in my class. On Fridays, it was quite obvious who was "one of the faithful" and who was not. The smell of tuna fish was evident. Somehow everyone else's ham and baloney sandwiches seemed to smell so much better on that day of the week. Worst yet, when the school had end-of-the-year picnics, if it fell on a Friday (which it often did), the Catholic children could not eat hot dogs. Paradoxically, nothing, absolutely nothing smells as good as a hot dog with mustard if everyone else is munching away and you can't have one. The nasty old tuna fish sandwiches were a sorry substitute. But we Catholics felt strong and above the crowd since we were sacrificing for God and learning self-control. We were certain that He would look upon us more favorably. Besides, eating a hot dog on a Friday would be one more sinful thing to have to confess.

Many of the young boarders who came to the farm in the summertime went to Catholic schools in the city. I had never heard of a Catholic school before this and was curious about them. I was told that their teachers were nuns who were very strict. Never having seen a nun, only pictures of them, I was totally fascinated and asked lots of questions. "How beautiful," I thought "to be taught by such pious and good women. They certainly would instill goodness in everyone." I automatically assumed that children who went to Catholic school would be extremely religious and well behaved. When I discovered that almost the exact opposite was true, I was surprised. It made sense to me that being brought up amongst religious surroundings would *have* to make a person better! No? (I had never heard the stories about the children of ministers either.) Most, but not all, of the religiously schooled children seemed to curse and swear and tell dirty jokes far more than their public school counterparts. I found this conduct shocking and totally incongruous. How could it be? It was years later in a psychology class that I learned about forms of rebellion as the result of severe restraints.

As a young girl growing up Sicilian, although never overtly discussed, being a "good girl" was deeply inculcated into my soul and conscience. Even before I knew exactly what the behavior was that was so taboo, whatever it was, I was aware that it was unpardonable. Once I learned, it was more so!

Besides knowing I would be "skinned alive", so to speak, by my father or brothers should I be so foolish as to disgrace my family in any way, I was also aware I could one day roast in hell for eternity if I ever "sinned." Even before I was old enough to understand, deeply instilled into my innermost being was that the worst calamity to befall any Sicilian girl was if she was so unfortunate as to lose her virginity before her wedding night. I cannot remember when or how I learned it. Maybe

I absorbed it by osmosis. I do know that the shame and guilt that went along with it degraded one beyond redemption!

An incredible fuss was made over being "pure" as opposed to being "soiled goods" which no self-respecting man would accept. Should a girl loose her virginity and bring *"vergonia"* (disgrace) upon herself, and even worse, her family, she would never be able to marry. No decent man could accept a woman or girl who had been "defiled" by someone else. I found myself worried about what would happen if, when I grew up, such a terrible thing was to happen to me. I knew I would just die! But no, I firmly believed that I would never do such a dirty disgusting thing (whatever it was). I did believe that I would be forever censured by my family and that was almost worse than being excommunicated from the Church. To be thrown out of both Church and family seemed inconceivable and too dreadful to even contemplate.

Papa was adamant. I must not talk to boys, let alone ever be in their company (unless my brothers were present, that was the exception to the rule.) After a while, I got it through my thick skull, that whatever it was that was such a bad thing had to do with what happened when a boy and a girl were alone together. I wondered mightily what it could be. As young as I was, my curiosity knew no bounds. Of course, it was only a few years later that I learned from Suzy, on that fateful boat ride, what that horrible, disgusting thing was, called sex, that could ruin your life forever.

It was hard to understand why adults made such a fuss over anything that was, in any way, concerned with sex. My father, especially! Sometimes when I would go to fetch the milk, he would come racing out of the cow barn looking like the devil himself. He would bellow at me to leave immediately. Of course, I would turn and run as fast as I could, fearing he would come after me with a pitchfork or shovel. It was years later that I realized that all those times I was chased away were the times that either a bull and cow were mating or a cow was giving birth. My father felt it was not proper or "nice" for me to see those taboo, dirty, and "sexual" activities.

Someone once told me that amongst Sicilian men there was, (perhaps still is) a certain conviction, (though men of other ethnic roots may think the same). These Sicilian males believed that if *any* man and *any* woman were left together in a room alone for any length of time, they would eventually become intimate. (family members excepted of course.) I suppose the sex drive of many of those Sicilian men was so strong that it seemed incredible to them that a man and a woman could spend idle time together and not end up having sexual intercourse. Perhaps they were right.

On the other hand, perhaps they felt that they, themselves, were such excellent lovers that no woman could resist their charms. Be that as it may, heaven help the woman relative, sister, wife or mother, who has "allowed herself" to be seduced! Heaven help them *and* the seducer. In retrospect, I realize how desperately parents in times past did all in their power to prevent illegitimate births. For good reason, I suppose, but they were not always successful.

chapter 18

Guilt and Conscience

The two front lawns of the mansion were "held up" by a marvelously crafted stone wall consisting of large squares of pinkish-white granite. (They, as well as the stones of the house foundation had come from the nearby Shawangunk Mountains, carried in 1820 by oxen that had forded the Wallkill River near Gardiner). A walk paved with large slabs of slate, edged on either side by a thick row of red barberry bushes, wound its way up the center of the lawn. It ended at the middle of the semi-circular driveway directly across from the front steps of the house. At the opposite end of the walk, down near the road, there was a five by six, two-foot high indentation in the wall, its surface also paved with slate. This formed a grand entrance into which was built a set of wide, thick slate steps leading up to the walk. To the left of the stairs a row of stepping stones through a small garden, led to an enormous, rectangular, flat stone. It measured roughly four feet by six feet and was almost six inches thick. We believed it to be a stepping stone for those in the past who arrived by horse and carriage.

Papa, somehow, using many helping hands, much sweat, horses, thick ropes, and pulleys managed to move the enormous stone slab up the drive-way to the south side of the house. Placed upon four large cement posts, it became the outdoor dining table of the family. The table was situated near the kitchen door, beneath the huge maple tree growing up past the fan-shaped window of my room on the second floor.

From that window, I could look down and sometimes see my father sitting alone, finishing his wine, or sometimes see others in the family sitting and having something to eat or drink. The table had benches on either side and heavy metal chairs at each end (they did not match one another). Papa always sat at the head of the table, furthest away from the kitchen door. Mama, always sat at the foot, closest to the kitchen.

As soon as summer approached and the days got warm, that was the signal for all meals to be served out of doors. Only a torrential rain could drive the family indoors to eat, for the canopy of the maple tree was so thick it afforded protection from light or ordinary rainfall.

Many wonderful meals were served on that oilcloth-covered stone table. There was always pasta, of all kinds. There was minestrone made from freshly picked vegetables. Most of the food we ate came directly from the farm. We enjoyed soup from freshly killed chickens, dinners of thick steaks, juicy pork chops, tender veal cutlets, fresh salads, and heaps of corn (cooked five minutes after picking). There was an abundance of homegrown peaches, pears, watermelon, apples, and grapes. All in all, good, sturdy, wholesome food was deliciously prepared and lovingly served. A certain kind of pride was evoked from eating food we had produced with our own hands and from the sweat of our brow.

Despite the drudgery and hard work, the farm was a wonderful place to grow up. While the long hours and backbreaking labor appeared unappreciated, the camaraderie, the playtimes, the laughing, joking, and love we shared with and for one another was sufficient reward. In a life of material privation, we learn to derive great pleasure from the simplest activities and objects.

Although I had few toys, I found many ways in which to keep myself occupied when not busy with chores. There were two things I enjoyed most of all. One was surely the swing which hung from the lowest branch of the huge oak tree on the front lawn. Standing on it, I would "pump" until I swung so high that the ropes would jerk when I hit the apex of the upward arc and if I had not been holding on really tight, would certainly have been thrown headfirst to the ground. As soon as I felt those ropes jerk, I "put on the brakes." Those of you who have experienced swinging the full height of a swing, while standing on the seat, will know the feeling.

My other favorite was the nearby homemade hammock (about which, enough has been said) situated on the south lawn. The other lawn, the north one, was always filled with people, most likely because that lawn was strewn with many wooden Adirondack chairs. Placed next to and among them were miscellaneous metal lawn chairs and mismatched, old, wooden chairs in great abundance so as to accommodate the many boarders. Papa became irritated when people argued over whose chair was whose. He made sure there were enough seats for everyone and cared not a whit whether the chairs matched or looked attractive.

Whatever the reason, the north lawn was the favorite gathering place. The boarders would congregate there enjoying the shade of the huge beech, maple, and pine trees, whiling away the warm, hazy afternoons. In the evening, they sat beneath the dappled glow of outdoor lights secreted in the branches of those trees. On hot days and evenings many sipped Kool Aid, lemonade, beer, or homemade wine. Others would chat, knit, or crochet. Still others played cards or checkers on a lone, long, picnic table, or on a few, old, wobbly card tables.

At the right end of the driveway encircling the lawn, was an old dirt road. It veered off from the main road directly in front of the house. A six-foot wide strip of grass separated it from the stone wall and it ran parallel to the cement covered main highway, route 208. A row of tall, ancient maple trees lined the dirt road for a distance and then gave way to meadows and shrubs. This dirt road led from the main highway in front of the house through farm property and then back to the highway about a half a mile away. Primarily, we used the unpaved road to get to the Bennett house or to the sand and gravel pit on the outer edges of the farm property.

Aside from that, the dirt road got little ordinary traffic. It was, however, much used by many and in many different ways. One use was as a riding path. Boarders took turns taking horseback rides on Billy, a former race horse. Joey was absolutely crazy about horses and Papa made him very happy when he purchased Billy at an auction. Everyone knew Billy was Joey's horse, although, of course, he had to share him with the rest of us.

Billy had beautiful lines and obviously he was not a regular work horse. Nevertheless, besides being used to ride on, he was also used for light plowing and for pulling the old fringed surrey that Papa found in the barn when he bought the place. The boarders loved riding in it. Mama longed to ride in it too. Unfortunately, every time the surrey was hitched up, Mama was always in the middle of doing something that she couldn't leave. Of course, my father would never think to hitch it up just for her (and she would never dream of asking). Such a simple pleasure-denied! I recall seeing the pain on her face and tears in her eyes one Sunday afternoon when the surrey, loaded down with boarders, took off for a ride to visit some nearby Italian neighbors. As the surrey sped off with its happy cargo, Mama turned away and I saw her lift her apron-to dry her tears. How badly she wanted to go! *Such pazienzia!*

Another use for Billy was when he was hitched up to pull the large wooden sled in winter when the roads were snow-filled and impassable with the farm pick-up. My favorite memory of Papa was of a cold winter's morning when we woke to about three feet of snow on the ground. Snow or not, the milk had to be delivered to the creamery five miles away in Gardiner. That morning, the snow was too deep for any motorized vehicle. Papa hitched up Billy to a flatbed sled, loaded the milk cans in the rear, covered them with canvas, tucked me into the front seat under some blankets and away we went, sleigh bells jingling all the way. Fat, swirling snow flakes flew past us, some melting on our noses and cheeks. He even let me hold the reins awhile. It was a delicious adventure.

The dirt road was also the place where all of us learned to ride a bike and where we learned to drive a car. But, maybe best of all, its quiet beauty and level surface made it ideal for long walks that everyone enjoyed, particularly the boarders. I know for sure it was my favorite place to walk, unlike the forest, where vines and bushes clutched at me and scratched my legs. Half way up the road, near a rather large hill, was a depression in which a pond had formed. This pond was broader than the one in the middle of the meadow in the back of the main barn. In winter, since it was quite shallow, its broad expanse would freeze over early in the season which made it perfect for skating. I tried to learn how, dreaming of gliding about like Sonia Heinie. How I tried! But try as I might, I never did get the hang of it. My feet would freeze, the laces would be too loose, the skates (old, and second hand) would be dull, and besides–I hated the falling down part.

During my long walks, young as I was, it became obvious to me that other people beside the Bennetts, the boarders, and my family used that old, dirt road, especially at night. Many a morning, I would find men's handkerchiefs discarded on the ground next to fresh tire tracks. This told me that maybe at night, when no one else was around, cars had driven into and parked on the wide, secluded, flat space next to the pond.

The handkerchiefs would usually be all crumpled, stiff, and have stains on them that were sometimes pink, sometimes pale yellow, or sometimes both. Occasionally, my curiosity would overcome my sense of revulsion. Gingerly, I would pick up one of the handkerchiefs by the very tip of one corner. Holding it at arm's length, to examine it, I wondered why people would, after blowing their noses so much, throw them away. The handkerchiefs, for the most part, looked perfectly good and almost new, I wondered why their owners did not take them home and launder them. I somehow realized it would not be a good idea to take one home. Our teachers at school talked a lot about germs!

215

Just as often as I found handkerchiefs, I also found many funny-shaped, weird- looking "balloons." They all looked alike and all were the same strange, powdery looking opaque, off-white color. I thought it odd that they were not red, blue, or yellow like those familiar birthday and party balloons. What was even more odd was that these "balloons" looked like small, really skinny doughnuts with a very thin, rubber membrane across the hole. Sometimes the "balloons" were unrolled and convoluted or crumpled and stuck in a mass. I would stand and stare in wonder and try mightily to figure out what possible use these strange looking rubber "balloons" could be to anyone.

Once I found one that looked pretty clean and new. My curious nature got the best of me. I unrolled it and then tried to blow it up. What seemed most curious is that opening into which I had to blow was much larger than most balloons. I wondered why? As I tried and tried, it was difficult to keep the air from escaping from the sides of the opening. It was so much larger than my pursed lips. Finally, I figured out how to squeeze the opening smaller by compressing it against my lips inside a circle I made with my thumb and forefinger. After a few tries, the "balloon" blew up into a long, straight, large, funny-looking, deeply ridged sausage shape. When it reached its maximum size, I held it out at arms length to examine it. Immediately, it started to droop. Consumed with curiosity and fascination, I decided to bring that particular balloon home to show Mama. Maybe she would know what kind of balloon it was and why it was such a funny shape.

As I entered the kitchen, my mother was busy at the stove. She was whistling merrily as she poured coal from the scuttle into one of the stove openings. *"Mama, Mama, tallia che auio trovato. Ci'e sta cosa?"* ("Mama, mama, look what I found. What is it?") Running toward her, I happily waved the deflated, flapping "balloon." Mama turned, still whistling, eyebrows raised in curiosity. The whistling stopped and a strangled gasp took its place. The pleasant look of expectancy on Mama's face turned to disgust and incredulity as she whispered, *"Bedda Matri!"* (Beautiful Mother!) Plunking the coal scuttle quickly on the side of the stove, in a flash, with two fingers of one hand (pinky extended), my mother snatched the condom out of my hand and swiftly threw the "rubber" into the hot coals.

All of this took place so fast that for a moment I believed I had entered empty-handed. She said nothing more. Reaching over, she picked up the coal scuttle and continued to fill the stove. I knew that the moment Mama had turned her back, I had been dismissed. I also knew I had done some despicable thing. What it was, I did not know. A sense of shame engulfed me. "Well, I better not ever touch one of THOSE things again, whatever it was!" I thought to myself with a shiver.

My mother's silence and the stiffness of her shoulders as she poked at the coals, and raked them smooth, told me that the "balloon" I had brought into the house was something unspeakably disgusting. It was something that was not to be brought up or even mentioned! On my way out of the kitchen door, totally confused, I wondered, "Boy-o-boy! Will I ever learn all the things I want to know about what's happening in this world? There are so many questions I want to ask. How am I ever going to find out about all the 'stuff' that's goin' on, or how to be grown up? An' who can I even ask? If I ask my brothers or sister, they'll probably smack me. If I ask my teacher, she'll just say what she always says, 'Look it up in the dictionary.' I sure can't ask Papa, unless I want my head handed to me. An' Mama never talks about what I really want to know." I shook my head in bewilderment, "Well, I'm not too sure I want to grow up and learn about all that 'junk' anyway!"

Thereafter, whenever I went walking down the old dirt road, for a long time I refrained from picking up strange objects to take home. Do you think that for one moment that the "balloon" lesson would have cured me forever of picking up things along the highway or in the fields? Right, I never learned!

One day, on my way to visit Mrs. Bennett with the possibility of maybe making some cookies, I caught sight of a small pamphlet lying on the side of the road near the pond. It was partly opened, lying there engulfed by weeds and wild flowers, its pages crumpled, but still in readable condition. Since learning to read I had devoured whatever written materials

I could find. There were few books (only Maceo's) and no magazines in my house. The only current reading matter was the Sunday News, of which the comics and the Rotogravure section were the only parts that I could understand or found interesting.

Fairy tales and myths were what interested me most. That is, until one summer, down by the garbage heap I found some *True Confession* and *True Story* magazines. So much more exciting were the stories about girls kissing, falling in love, and having babies out of wedlock (whatever that meant). Thoroughly engrossed, I did not notice my sister Caroline approach. First, I felt a good solid cuff on the side of my head. Then Caroline berated me soundly for reading such "dirty" things. I sat, head bowed. Those shameful feelings surfaced again! I eschewed magazines for a long time thereafter.

You can understand my hesitation when I saw what looked like a magazine lying in the weeds. I recalled Caroline's tirade. From a cursory look (it was black and white), the pamphlet looked more like a bulletin of some sort, not some "forbidden" magazine. "Yes, but maybe it's a magazine, then what?" My conscience suggested I should pass it by. "Well?" I argued with myself for a full minute or two. Nobody was around to see me look at it. "Heck, why not?" I bent over and picked it up. When I saw what was on the opened page, I felt my eyes widen in disbelief and almost pop out of my head. I gasped in surprise at the photo. Holding the booklet at arms length and staring, I stood rooted to the spot. I felt almost paralyzed with shock.

"Oh my God! Caroline will KILL me if she knows I was even looking at this, let alone planning to read what's inside." The photo "screamed" at me. It was a close up of a naked girl directly facing the camera. Her legs were spreadeagled and at right angles to her body. She was peering seductively through the 'V' formed by her legs, while at the same time her forearms were clasped around the front of her thighs, helping to hold them up. At the same time, she was using her forefingers to hold, wide open, the outer lips of her vagina. I can still remember feeling mesmerized and revolted by what I *knew* was a "dirty" picture. However, I could not stop staring at it! Suddenly, a warmth began to flood my body and I felt a hot flush coursing through me. It started at the back of my knees and rose until it reached my neck. My cheeks felt like they were on fire. Beads of sweat formed on my temples and forehead. I continued to stare intently at the photo.

Suddenly, totally revulsed, I flung the booklet into the bushes and started to walk quickly away from it. After walking a few feet, I stopped. My body still felt on fire and my curiosity was overpowering. I wanted so much to look through the pages and see whatever else there was to see. I stood and again argued with myself. "No! No! It's a "dirty" book! Far, far worse than *True Stories* or *True Confessions*. No, I mustn't! If Caroline knew I was looking at such stuff, she would be so disappointed in me. And Mama? Mama would DIE of shame if she knew I was such a pig that I wanted to look at such things. And PAPA!" Just the thought of what he would do made me want to run home immediately. "Don't read this thing! No! No! No!. And what about confession? What would I ever tell the priest? He, too, would think me a pig." I paused. I felt so mixed up.

By now, you know what happened next–my curiosity got the better of me. I went quickly back to where I had thrown the book. Not even the poison ivy, close by, deterred me. Searching carefully in the bushes, I retrieved the booklet, rolled it up, stuck it securely into the waistband of my slacks, pulled out my shirt to cover it, and started for home. As I strode homeward, I could feel my heart pounding and strange feelings washed over me. "So that's what 'it' looks like inside! Why would anybody want to take a PICTURE of 'it?' And that girl, she must be a real *'butana'* to do such a dirty, filthy, disgusting thing." My brain whirled with pictures and thoughts of naked women and men with cameras. "I mean, probably a *man* took that picture. HOW COULD SHE? YUK!!! She should be ashamed of herself." I tried to imagine from what kind of family she came, from what kind of neglectful upbringing? "To do such a thing! Doesn't she care about her family? What if her father or mother ever saw that picture of her? Wouldn't they feel terrible?" I remembered Papa's admonition about losing your good name. "Didn't she care what people thought?

What would neighbors and friends think? Boy! Isn't she afraid that her whole family might see it?" An awful thought struck me! "Her brothers would see her naked!" My God, what a bad girl she must be, doing all those horrid things–and letting someone take pictures!!! Papa would boil me in oil if I ever did anything like that!"

Still, I couldn't wait to get home so I could look at the rest of the book and read whatever it had to say about that pig of a girl. Excited at the thought of what I would find in the remainder of the book, I started to run, my thoughts racing. There were so many questions in my head that it felt like it might burst. Who could I possibly show this book to? And who could answer my questions about it? I wouldn't dare take it to school. The thought of a teacher finding me with something so repugnant made me almost nauseous with shame.

I ran faster and faster and very soon was bounding up the front steps of the house, two at a time. Racing to the hallway stairs, I climbed them in a similar manner. Reaching the top, I ran to the end of that hall, darted into the bathroom located over the porch pediment, and, breathing hard, closed and locked the door. Then, leaning my back against the closed door, I tried to catch my breath. Suddenly, I was aware of a dull ache in the lower part of my body. I mistook it for a strong urge to urinate. Placing the booklet under my arm, I quickly pulled down my pants. Holding the book with both hands, I sat down on the toilet. Keeping my eyes on the ceiling until I finished, I clutched the book to my chest, still open to the same page. Unexpectedly, the dull ache was still there. Even after I had finished peeing! Slowly, I lowered the booklet, placing it on my lap, smoothing out the first page so I could study the photo. As my eyes devoured the gross and unfamiliar sight, I shook my head in disbelief and wonder. The girl looked so "nice." She had curly blonde hair and blue eyes. Angels had blue eyes and blonde hair, thus, I could not equate this pretty and normal-looking person with the "monster" I believed her to be; this creature who was such a "bad girl."

Then I turned the wrinkled, dirty pages, smoothing out and brushing off each one, until I found the front of the book.

The cover was gone, but the first page began with a story about a man and a woman watching some horses in a field. Mating. At first, I was baffled and could not make a connection to horses and those awful pictures in the rest of the book. However, as I read on, intrigued, piqued, shocked, disgusted, and, (most of all) apprehensive, I began to see the connection. The pictures of naked men and women doing strange things to one another made my "private" parts start to quiver. The dull "ache" had turned into a hot and throbbing sensation!

I couldn't understand what was happening. Never in my whole nine years of life had I felt *anything* like this before. I actually felt hot, *very hot*, all over, but especially between my legs. I felt "that" part of my body pulsating and worst of all, it actually felt pleasant! I felt excited! Because of these feelings, I was certain that somehow I was sinning. Then I felt deeply ashamed. So there I was, feeling so very good and so very bad, both at the very same time! What a dilemma!!!

Engrossed in the story and overwhelmed by the new feelings in my body, I did not hear my mother approach. Mama's gentle tap on the door made me jump! I was frightened half out of my wits by guilt. Guilty?? I felt so guilty that I was sure Mama could see right through the door and could tell that I was reading dirty things and having all those sinful feelings. What if she found me with this...this...whatever it was. I was so ashamed, I wanted to die right then and there. And she thought I was such a good girl!!

"*Seri? Doccu se? Che fa? Perche' non ma respondato quanto t'chiamavo? Che ti succede? È cosi male?*" (Sadie, are you in there? Why didn't you answer when I called you? What has happened? Is anything wrong?")

"*No Mama, no, tutti cosi sono buono. Ora neshu. Veniu subito!*" (No, Mama, no, everything is OK. I'll come out now. I'll come out right away!)

"*Bene.*" (Good.) "*Veni subito, ca me serb'aiuto 'nda la cucchina.*" (Come quickly, I need help in the kitchen.) I breathed an enormous sigh of relief as I heard the sound of her footsteps retreat and then disappear. Quickly, I wrenched off some toilet paper, reached down to dry myself, and was surprised to find a great deal of moisture. I had been sitting there quite a while after relieving myself and assumed I would be almost dry. Pulling up my slacks, I walked to the door and after opening it part way, peeked out surreptitiously to see if anyone was about. I tiptoed over to the attic door, stealthily climbed the stairs, walked noiselessly to my "secret" place and slipped the pamphlet beneath some loose attic floor boards. Descending the attic steps, I sprinted down the hall, bounded down the two sets of stairs, ran through the rest of the house, and arrived, almost out of breath, in the kitchen.

"*S'onio ca Mama, che ti pozo fari?*" (Here I am, Mama, what can I do for you?)

It seemed to me that Mama first eyed me strangely then said, "*Ca. Primo che tu m'auito, porta st'aqua a tuo patri 'nda la vinia. Cammora iddu ave situ.*" (Here, before you help me, bring this water to you father in the vineyard. He is thirsty by now.)

Relieved that my mother did not question me further, I dutifully took the quart of icy cold water and raced out the door. I covered the quarter of a mile over to the vineyard in no time flat. There, at the far end of one of the rows, papa could be heard singing "La Donna e' Mobile" in a clear, rich baritone.

It was a while before I worked up the courage to look again at my "dirty" pamphlet. Retrieving it from beneath the boards, I sat near the attic window one rainy Saturday and read it through. Twice! Then my conscience made me burn it, oh so surreptitiously, in one of the garbage cans down by the dirt road. I never told anyone about it, nor showed it to any of my friends. Neither did I mention it during confession.

Such are the "bits" and "pieces" of information; bits and pieces much like parts of a giant puzzle. A puzzle which we, in childhood, put together in order to make sense of the world around us. The myriad, diverse ways that we are introduced to knowledge in those primary years exerts a tremendous influence upon the shape of the child. The child still trapped in each of us at maturity and beyond.

It is my earnest belief that the shock and guilt of that day was far more indelibly etched on my psyche than I realized. After that experience, rarely did seeing "dirty" pictures or "dirty" movies arouse me. In fact, nothing that I can remember since then has set me on fire as deeply as that first encounter with the hot, raw, feelings experienced in that long, long ago, pre-adolescent moment.

chapter 19

Caroline

My sister, Caroline, had almost as much influence on shaping me as did my father. Yes, my mother's *"pazienzia figlia mia"* did influence me, but I believe that she was less of a role model in my life than the others. (On second thought, some of my best traits are those few I retained from Mama.) When she brought me home from the hospital, much of my care fell to Caroline. This, because my mother often had to help my father tend to their fruit and vegetable stand.

To Caroline, I was some kind of doll to play with, since she was only eight years old when I was born. She carefully fed me, bathed me, and put me to bed. (Once I caught pnumonia and the doctor said I would die–mama prayed five hours straight, and I lived.) It was Caroline who heard my first full word *"perico"* (apricot), which I repeated over and over on the day that I took my first steps at nine months of age. (Why didn't I say "ma-ma?" Please don't ask, I am only telling you what she said I said and did.) Because of my early care by my sister, to a great degree, I am her child and she, my mother. Her's (along with Mama's), was probably the first face that

I learned to love and equate with nurture (my mother nursed me for two years).

Caroline was, and still is, a complex and incredibly charismatic person. Of all of us, she was the favorite of the boarders; they were all crazy about her. She alone had the courage to "march to a different drum." She alone embodied more of my father's best traits, charm, wit, and courage. Unfortunately, she also had his black temper, and I for one, although I adored her, was intimidated by it.

A real tomboy, she could take a car motor apart and put it back together again. She could herd and milk cows and do just about anything that our brothers could do–even drive the tractor! Somehow, somewhere, she had learned to whistle very loudly through her teeth. It was a sharp piercing whistle; the kind people use to call a cab. It was so loud that she could summon the cows to the barn and never have to walk all the way out to the fields for them. No one else in the family could whistle that loudly, no matter how hard they tried.

On those days when my brothers were exhausted from working very hard or if it was intensely hot, to avoid walking out to bring in the cows at milking time, they would offer Caroline a quarter if she would "whistle" the cows in for them. She just gloated when they did that! Delighted, she would run down to the gate in the meadow, and let loose a few long, piercingly loud whistles. About five minutes later, as the cows filed slowly through the open gate and into the barnyard, she would grin wickedly as she collected the quarter. It was a rare occurrence in a Sicilian household for a female to excel over the males in any way outside of the kitchen. One had to enjoy the moment, and she did.

As each year passed, the family was growing and changing. Caroline was at an age where she was visiting friend's homes. She talked about making the house we lived in prettier and so she started to try to make our austere surroundings more attractive. Our big, beautiful house was a place we occupied rather than lived in–really it was just a place to eat and sleep. From the day Papa bought it, it was put to absolute utilitarian use. There was little inside that made the house beautiful or decorative. Furniture was an amalgam of unmatched pieces bought at auction by Benny. Nothing had ever been attempted to make our home comfortable or appealing. Sad to say, the house was as dreary and dull on the inside as it was beautiful and elegant on the outside.

The only redeeming room in the entire house was the front room, otherwise known as the living room. It was furnished with an old overstuffed living room set brought up from our apartment in the city. The set consisted of (what else?) a sofa and two matching chairs. There was also a large console Philco radio, the kind with the little green "eye" in the center. Two mismatched end tables completed the decor. The lovely oak floors were bare and there were paper "drapes" at the window. Drapes that were only a dollar a pair. Our windows were so enormous that the cost of real drapes was prohibitive. The printed design on them was a colorful paisley in blues, whites, and reds with a touch of yellow here and there. They matched *nothing* else in the room.

The overstuffed furniture was a shade of deep yellow-green, upholstered in what appeared to be very short bristly "fur." It sort of itched when you sat on it for any length of time. I remember how I used to run my fingers over the "fur" and watch the small bristly hairs pop up behind my slowly moving fingers.

Each Saturday, in that bleak living room, Caroline would sweep and clean the floor and I would help dust the furniture, window sills, and woodwork. Caroline could not work unless the radio was playing and it was *always* tuned to WNEW and the *Make Believe Ballroom*. I do believe that the first music I ever heard was from that program. Even as a very little girl, I loved their music. I was especially taken by the host's deep, melodious, and beautiful voice. His name was Martin Block. Because of his voice, I imagined him to be extremely handsome; somewhat on the order of Tyrone Power or Clark Gable. Mr. Block's format was to play the music of one particular singer or band for fifteen minutes at a time. Thus, during that segment you would get to hear three or more songs by either Bing Crosby, the Andrew Sisters, Glenn Miller, or any of the other music "greats" of the day. (Frank Sinatra had not yet come on the scene.) Some of my favorites and top hits were

"Tea for Two", "I'm Gonna Sit Right Down and Write Myself a Letter", "My Blue Heaven", and "Talk of the Town."

Years later, when in my teens, I got to see a photo of Martin Block. I was hugely disappointed. The photo pictured him with a bald head, a walrus mustache, baggy eyes and droopy eyelids. His smile was broad and pleasant, but he was far from what I had imagined. It almost destroyed my memories of a time irrevocably past that had seemed, back then, romantic and beautiful. After a while, I came to understand that I had stupidly equated anything that sounded good with looking good. Unfortunately, it took a long time before I realized how wrong that premise was. It took me almost as long to eventually accept the fact that beauty, while important, was not the most important criterion in judging others. It was a lesson for which I eventually paid a high price.

The search for beauty inspires many and Caroline, cleaning the living room was, in truth, seeking just that. She had matured to a level where it was important for her to have our house look as nice as others. Almost overnight, it seems, she developed an overwhelming urge to clean, scrub, and dust. And not just on Saturday, cleaning day. Caroline would spend time after school and every other spare moment cleaning one room after the other; dusting, mopping, and changing bed linens. Although I followed my sister around and tried to help, I was probably more underfoot than helpful.

One cold, snowy Saturday just before Christmas, Caroline decided that the "middle" living room (the room the family used the most and which held the pot-bellied stove) would look better if the floor was scrubbed and the furniture, however meager, was polished. She wanted to make the house more pleasing for the holidays. It was a very large room and no simple task to clean. To begin with, she had to move all the furniture to one side in order to scrub the floor. After scrubbing a section, as it dried, she would immediately replace the furniture. In doing so, she inadvertently rearranged the pieces so that some of the chairs where not exactly where they were before. Moved from its usual spot, for instance, was Papa's favorite chair. It was a foot or so away from its normal position and turned in a slightly different direction.

Caroline had been working for hours. Now, only a small portion of the room remained to be cleaned. The crisp smell of furniture polish and pine cleaner hung in the air and the room fairly sparkled. Down on her knees, barefoot, in order not to mar the cleanly scrubbed floor, she was whistling and scrubbing the last, small section near the narrow back stairs. Wiping the sweat from her brow with the back of her hand, she looked around and was quite pleased with the results of her labors. It was late afternoon and the sun was glinting through the huge windows. The slanted beams bathed the room in a golden light. The room appeared different from before and she was very pleased with how much nicer everything looked.

Because of the bitter cold on that particular day, Papa came in earlier than usual from the fields. As he entered the room, he took note of his elder daughter down on her knees, surprised she was barefoot (the house was not that warm), while scrubbing the floor. Her back was toward him. She was still whistling and there was a pail of warm soapy water next to her. In another corner of the room, I was folding towels. As Papa entered, I watched him, smiling in anticipation, eager to see his face light-up upon seeing the immaculate room. He was always pleased when we worked "extra" hard.

A sharp sliver of fear slid up my back when I saw the dark look that came over his face as he glanced about. Petrified, I watched as he strode quickly across the room. I wanted to look away but couldn't. Without a word, he took aim and brutally kicked Caroline squarely and solidly on her upturned rear! His aim was perfect and she went flying, face forward. Her elbow hit the bucket and warm, soapy water spilled everywhere. Sliding on the wet, slippery floor, her head banged against the bottom of the staircase stunning her momentarily.

At that point, Papa sprang to where she lay. Bending over, he began to pummel her, all the while shouting in Sicilian, *"Disonorata! Perche', perche' a moffatto la furnitura? Specialimenti la seggia mia! Perche' non m'aspiato primo? Cu'ti lu dissi per fare sta cos'accussi? Ti'nsegniu di fare cosi con senzo spiadi primo 'mia! Con senza permisso mio!!"* (Dishonored one! Why, why did you move the furniture? Especially *my* chair! Why didn't you ask me first? Who told you that you could do this? I'll teach you to do things without first asking me. Without my permission!!)

Mama, drawn by the shouting, came running from the kitchen. Seeing Papa beating Caroline, she screamed at him to stop, grabbed his shoulders, and began pulling him away from her. Caroline, thereupon crawled quickly out of his reach and jumped up! Sobbing, she ran to the kitchen door, pulled it open and raced out, wet and barefoot, onto the snow-covered ground.

Before I could comprehend what was happening, I heard Mama shout some terrible things at Papa. He shouted back! The highly emotional scene made the remainder a blur. The next thing I remember was leaving the house with Mama. Coats and boots on, we were loaded down with a blanket, shoes, galoshes, warm socks, and Caroline's coat. We left the house in haste and peered down at the ground, finding and then following Caroline's bare footprints in the snow.

They led us down a steep incline to the apple orchard in the rear of the house. We tracked her through the orchard and out to the other side. From there, we ran on as we followed the sometimes faint, then suddenly bloody prints over what, to bare feet, had to be terribly painful: the frozen stubble of a large hay field. Finally, the bloody footprints led up to the door of Maceo's house, now a deserted tenant shack. It was more than a quarter of a mile from the main house.

Mama pushed open the door and peering into the gloom of the front room called out, "Carolina?" (Caroline?)

There was no answer. We entered the frigidly cold and stale smelling house. The drawn shades made it dark and musty. By now it was close to sundown which added an eerie darkness and bleakness to the place. I was frightened and looked up at Mama's face. Her eyes, straining in the semi-darkness, seemed to be popping out of her head. They were filled with such anguish that it made me want to weep; to reach out and comfort her. Again Mama called, "Carolina?" (Caroline?) This time Mama's voice trembled with fear and held the hint of tears, ready to spill. Also, the call this time was much louder, almost shrill. It bounced off the cracked, peeling walls and echoed through the empty house. We paused a moment and waited. No sound could be heard aside from our own heavy breathing. The quick puffs of our breath made white wisps that hung, then vanished, in the cold, still air.

I could feel my heart pounding a wild staccato, a painful dirge. My mother peered down at the floor, where smudged, bloody foot prints were visible in the dust. Swiftly, she followed them across the room and up the stairs. I followed very close behind. It was a spooky place! As we climbed the stairs and approached the second floor, faint and muffled sobs could be heard. At the sound of my sister crying, my heart almost burst with pain and tears filled my eyes. Caroline and I were close and I loved her so much that for a moment I actually felt her hurt, her misery. Even now, I can still remember that bone-chilling instant, as if I was actually experiencing the cold and the rage felt by my sister.

That feeling of empathy, suspended in the raw, frigid air, intensified my anger and resentment toward my father. So overpowering was my sense of injustice that had he been present, my instincts decreed that I could have killed him with my bare hands. If pressed in later years, I would have to admit it was from that very instant that I really began to hate my father. As terrible as it sounds to admit it, when a very serious illness befell him later in life, I constantly wished it would prove fatal. When it did so I felt no guilt, only relief.

The muffled sobs had come from somewhere on the second floor. We reached the top of the stairs and raced toward the now barely audible moans. Bloody footprints led to a bedroom. Entering the room, we followed the prints. The faint sounds led us to a closet under the eves. Reaching it, Mama wrenched open the door. There was Caroline, huddled on the closet floor, her arms covering her face and head, her knees drawn up to her chin. Even in the gloom, it was apparent that her toes were blue from the cold and covered with blood. Crumpled, wet, and freezing, she looked like some wounded, hunted animal.

"*Carolina, povera figlia mia!*" (Caroline, poor daughter of mine!) Mama's voice was soft and filled with love and compassion. Caroline peeked at us through the crook of her elbow as we stood silhouetted in the doorway of the closet. Then she looked past us to see if Papa was anywhere in sight.

The look of fear in my sister's eyes was something I shall never forget. Neither will I forget how long Mama begged, comforted, and cajoled before Caroline would consent to put on the things we had brought. God, she was stubborn! Through chattering teeth in an angry voice she said, "Go home, ll-l-leave me alone! I w-w-want to d-d-die!! D-ddd-dd-do you hear me? I ww-w-want to die! If I die, mmm-m-maybe then he'll bb-bb-be ss-s-sorry." She turned her head away, dismissing us. Mama reached out and stroked her arm. We waited. After a moment she faced us again, eyes red and swollen "Any-w-w-way, what g-good is ll-l-living? He's horrible! M-m-mmean 'n horrible. I hate 'im, d-d-do you hear me? I hate 'im!!" Again she looked away. Then, "W-w-why should I go home? S-s-sso he can b-b-bbeat me again? Is that what you want for me? To get b-b-b-beaten again?" Bowing her head against her knees, she sobbed bitterly.

Now Mama knelt down and reached out for her. Caroline retreated even further into the closet. She seemed to shrink into herself. In an angry, strong, loud voice she said, "Better to stay here and freeze to death, better than to give him any satisfaction." Her voice suddenly changed, it broke into a tiny, small pitch, almost a whine. "I only tried to make the house look nice, Mama. T-t-t-hat's all I wanted. T-t-to make the house look nice and look what he does!" Now she was wailing, "Oh, Mama! M-m-mama, how d-do you stand him?"

By now Mama had scooped Caroline into her arms, her warm, ample body pressed against the solid, but cold shivering one of her daughter. *"Coraggio, figlia mia, coraggio."* (Courage, my daughter, courage.) "You no can stay here. *Si tu mori, io moro.*" (If you die, I die.) She put her cheek against Caroline's tear soaked face and held her tightly. In a voice strong and defiant, she said, "You coma home an I maka SURE he no toucha you! He toucha you, I killa him. Yes! I killa him! Put ona the coat 'n a you shoes ana we go home now. Iffa he toucha you o' say anyting, *l'ammazzu, lio 'mmazzare!*" (I'll kill him, I will kill him!) *"S'io ti diccu na cosa, tu saui ca lu fazo!!"* (You know when I say a thing, you know that I'll do it!!)

Still hesitating, the shivering, half-frozen Caroline let Mama help her put on the socks, shoes, galoshes, and coat. Mama covered Caroline's head and shoulders with the blanket and put one arm around her hugging her close to give her warmth. We left the desolate, tenant shack and trudged slowly through lightly falling snow back to the main house. Caroline truly had wanted to die right then and there (and could have)! She wanted to freeze to death and make her father sorry for what he had done.

Upon our return to the warmth of the house, Mama ministered to Caroline's needs, gave her steaming cups of Ovaltine and tucked her into bed with a hot-water bottle. After that, as usual, nothing was said. Papa said nothing and so Mama said nothing. It actually seemed that the whole thing had not really happened, that it was all some nightmare we had only dreamed.

Peace would reign for awhile, but then Papa would go off again on another tantrum or rampage. Again we would all pretend that nothing had happened. You see, ignoring it prevented further pain and antagonism. It kept the "peace." The mystery of the man is that he never once showed remorse for any of this cruelty toward his very own blood. Perhaps he believed that somehow his actions showed strength and kept him in control. Despite his heartless actions, paradoxically, my brothers seemed to know that to Papa, in his own enigmatic way, we were all very precious.

To my sister and me, however, he seemed a cruel and unloving person who took pleasure in our unhappiness. In the course of writing this tome, I have learned otherwise. My father's youth was filled with unremitting poverty. Who knows what kind of childhood he had and what, if any, love or affection was shown him as a child. There is a saying that perhaps captures the essence of Papa's behavior toward us, "We are victims of victims."

chapter 20

Papa

At this point, one must wonder about Papa's behavior toward those he was supposed to love. He certainly seems a brutal and unfeeling man. Where and how did he develop this attitude? Some possible explanations have come from Frankie, who, apparently was closest to him. My brother did much to enlighten me during discussions and notations concerning this book. He pointed out many things. Above all, he has now made me understand that those times in the past were times that I was then too young to fully comprehend. Nor did I realize what was actually happening, since perception and reality can be poles apart.

It seems that during the years that this story takes place, (from 1937 to 1943) there were periods, especially during the earlier years, when times were critical and the farm was almost lost. Surely, foreclosure would have taken place had not Papa's "friends" from New York City come to his aid and helped monetarily. This would also explain his letting members of the "Black Hand" use his farm occasionally as a hide-a-way or as a place to escape to when "on the lam." The Black Hand was the precursor to what is now known as the Mafia. It touched much of the Sicilian community at that time.

It was (to stretch a point) a Robin Hood type of thing. As Joey explained it to me, in those early days, one needed protection from theft. Since the police seemed unable to supply it satisfactorily, there were others who did. Those who supplied the much needed protection were often looked upon with a degree of appreciation. The protection money was normally not exorbitant and it guaranteed that robbers would not empty out one's store during the night.

Each morning when a vendor opened his store, he would find a small "ticket" stuck in the door jamb. It was proof that the property had been under surveillance the night before. Let not romance blind one. There probably were members of the Black Hand who preyed upon their own as well as others for unfair amounts of "protection" money. Nonetheless, there were a great number who were fair and honorable. These same members also gave aid to those who were helpless, who needed justice, and who had nowhere else to turn (the first few pages of Mario Puzzo's *The Godfather* covers that far better than anything I could add). Although threats and bluffing were commonplace, it was never personal, it was business.

For instance, my mother had in her possession for many years, a crudely written note penned on blue-lined paper. Jagged at one end, it had been carelessly torn out of a pad. The message it conveyed threatened the kidnapping of my brother Benny unless a rather large sum of money was delivered to a specific place at a specific time. A primitive drawing of a smoking gun at the bottom of the page exacerbated the warning. Benny was an infant at the time and the light of my father's life.

Papa suspected a close acquaintance of sending the note. Soon he invited the person in question, named Turridu, to ride to market with him on board his wagon. It was on a day when Papa was on his way to purchase a load of bananas. The horse clip-clopped along the streets of New York as the two of them, seated on the front seat of the banana wagon, smoked "DiNobili" cigars and chatted. Casually, between quick, short, puffs of smoke, my father told Turridu about the note he had received. Turridu grunted with surprise but made no answer. After a short pause, Papa said that he had definite suspicions about who had sent it. At this, his companion stiffened a little and said, *"Vero? Tu credo ca sa cu e?"* (Truly? You believe you know who it is?) Eyes like slits, my father nodded. *"Si, si. Lu sacci'o."* (Yes, yes, I know.) The horse clip-clopped along. The two men were silent.

Suddenly, in one swift move, while holding the reins in one hand, with his other, Papa reached down. From somewhere on the side of the seat he pulled out a Sicilian stiletto (a round bladed knife, about eight inches long). Touching its razor sharp tip to the breast of his companion he said, *"Iddu cu mi manna la lettera, l'o ammazzari! Che taglio lu cuore si 'li figli miei che venu qualungi danno!"* (The one who sent me the letter, I'll kill him! I will cut out his heart should harm come to any of my children!)

"Adagio, adagio, Pippino! Io non saccio perche' tu mi dice sti cosi. Io ti respecto a non voglio ca male ti veni. Ora si fa tardo, m'nia gairri. Ti vithu!" (Take it easy, take it easy Joe I don't know why you are telling me these things. I respect you and I don't want to see any harm come to you. It's getting late now and I have to go. I'll see you!) With that, the man leaped off the wagon while it was still moving, stumbled a little, then disappeared into the crowd. There were no further threats and none of us ever came to any harm.

Another memory of the Black Hand took place when I was very, very young. I recall arriving with my parents one morning when they opened the vegetable store on Scamel Street. Next door, at the barber shop, a large group of highly agitated people were milling about. Expressions of fear and anger could be heard. Apprehension hung over the group like a storm cloud. My father questioned a few people. Holding me in his arms, mine wrapped around his neck, my father and mother peered into the shop. The image of what we saw is still fresh. High on the mirror that lined one wall was the imprint of a hand. It was black and drips of paint had trickled down from it and dried in place. It was "la mano nigra" an ominous sign and meant that the barber had refused to cooperate in some way. The handprint was a warning. Needless to say, the barber was scared (for want of a better word), shitless! The poor man, seated in one of his barber chairs was hyperventilating, his face a grayish-white.

Accustomed to the mantle of "protection" of the Black Hand in Sicily, it is probable that most people stoically accepted "protection" (extortion), good or bad, as the price to be paid for success. The victims reasoned that the carribonari in Sicily did little to protect them, so why should American police be any different?

To my knowledge, my father was never a member of the Black Hand. Neither was he their enemy. If their demands were within reason, he was willing to help them when asked. Especially those times when they made him an offer he couldn't refuse. My view of Papa was of a man who would not knowingly break the law. His good name was far too important to him. As a matter of fact, I firmly believed that only dire circumstances would have made my father ever stray from strict adherence to the laws of his adopted land. He not only loved, but also cherished America, constantly praising both the country and its choice of opportunities. He was adamant about being a law-abiding citizen, always preaching to us about the importance of honesty and the disgrace of being a liar or a thief. At least that is what he preached over and over to me and to my sister. Frankie, on the other hand, when I read him the above, laughed and said, "Whoa, what did you say Papa said?" I repeated the part about never lying or stealing.

"Well, you're right about lying, but Papa always told me, 'Iffa you gotta steal, maka sure you no getta caught.'"

"No. No! Papa wouldn't say that! He was totally and completely honest. I can't believe Papa told you that."

"Believe it!" said Frankie, staring at me with eyes dark and somber, totally serious for a change. Joey on the other hand, when recounted the above, also laughed. However he pointed out that to him, Papa had said, " Iffa you gotta steal, no steala less thana fifty thousa dollars." (An incredible sum at that time.) Perhaps Frankie misunderstood and took him seriously, while Joey thought it was his way of telling them not to bother. In retrospect, I suppose he sent us all mixed messages.

I only know that Frankie and Joey's words came as a total surprised to me: that in relation to honesty and one's good name, Papa told the females in the family one thing and the males another? It caught me completely unaware. I had assumed he taught us all the same things. Perhaps he surmised that as females, we would always have some male around to take care of us and would have no need to steal. He was also probably well aware of the temptation to steal in a land of such abundance. His constant threats and reminders were his hedge against that time when we might be truly tempted. Above all, he did not want his...or our good name tarnished.

Papa bought the farm in 1934 knowing absolutely nothing about farming or animal husbandry. My brothers were quite young; Benny was thirteen, Frankie was eleven, and Joey was nine. Caroline was twelve, and I a mere four. Mama knew little of farm life, of baking bread, or gardening. The economy was a disaster. The world was a mess. Besides all that, Papa was a sick man. He was told, by his doctor, that if he did not move to the country, he would die. Thus, the move to the farm in upstate New York, to the small WASP town of New Paltz was a necessity, not a whim. (The term WASP does not really describe the makeup of the village, but it seemed to us that the majority were *White Anglo-Saxon Protestants*, many of whom could trace their families back hundreds of years. Others had families who had been in the area for at least fifty years or more. The remainder were a mix of lots of things, including "foreigners." (Of course, there were Catholics, mostly Irish, but not great in number.)

Insofar as Papa's illness, there is nothing I can relate to you about it since I do not recall hearing it mentioned nor discussed. I was only peripherally aware of the fact that he had been operated on and that he did occasionally visit a doctor. Only now have I learned that before moving to New Paltz, he had undergone three or four operations. To me, he always seemed strong, healthy and impervious to stress. The large growth on his forefinger (mentioned elsewhere) probably did indicate some sort of tumor. In the 1930s, cancer was never mentioned (that I knew of) either on the farm or in the village.

Not until years later, when Papa got sick and died, did I learn about the word and its meaning.

New Paltz was not like the other small towns that surrounded it. New Paltz was an inordinately proud town. It was a "college" town. It was proud of its Normal School which trained teachers. Proud of the Van den Burg School of Practice, a school of recognized excellence and a part of the Normal school. Proud of its unusually colorful history, its growth, and its remarkable Huguenot ancestry. It was proud of its people and its utterly beautiful setting.

Into this town, set in the middle of a broad and spacious valley that seemed miles from any place, came our Sicilian family. In those early years, I was aware that there were only about six or seven Italian families. I could not know all of them. I'm sure there were more. The ones my family were most aware of in those earliest years were named Tantillo, Zannucci, Badami, Cina, Schiero, Ligotino and Lagatuta, most of whom were store or business connections. They helped one another.

I heard people say that Mr. Carroll, who owned the only department store in town was Jewish. I had no idea what "Jewish" meant, only that the term, as conveyed to me, had pejorative connotations. I thought Mr. Carroll was a delightful man and wondered what all the fuss was about. There were other Jewish families in the area; the Cohens and the Ackermans, who were also in the apple business, come to mind. My father got to know them and certainly appeared to like and respect them. There might have also been other "outsiders." I was too young to know them all. However, it was a small town and everyone (grownups), knew almost everyone else. The village natives, especially those of Huguenot descent, had a proprietary air about their village and I am certain wanted to maintain the status-quo. It *was* their town! Their ancestors had bought it, settled it, developed it. With hindsight, I can understand why, when we arrived, they were not at all happy about this additional influx of foreign, dark-looking, outsiders invading their community.

As a matter of fact, when I reached my teens, my first boyfriend's mother did not want him to date me since she thought that my brothers looked like "gangsters." Indeed they did, since they dressed like city people and preferred to look "sharp", not like "farmers." When dressed in suits and ties, they did resemble the gangsters in the movies. Back then, and sad to say, even today, the "gangster look" was, and is, definitely Italian; sharply dressed, dark-haired, dark-eyed, slick-looking, young men. (Think of *Godfather III*) How many curly-haired, blonde, blue-eyed gangsters have you seen lately in the movies?

Apparently, many viewed our foreign family, and others who were different, as unwelcome intruders. The New Paltz natives probably had the same fears and trepidations about the arrival of Jews, Italians, and Sicilians as the Jews, Italians, and Sicilians felt when their sections of Brooklyn, the Bronx, and Manhattan saw an influx of Blacks and Hispanics.

The reason for all of this background is to give you a picture of why Papa moved to the farm, why he seemed so merciless at times, and why the community reacted toward us in the way that it did. That Papa was operating under difficult and trying times might help to explain, but certainly does not excuse, his behavior. On the surface, his actions would undoubtedly appear to be not only cruel, but almost depraved. Certainly, there must have been many times when he was desperate, under pressure, and in great pain. He never let it show. This would have been considered a sign of weakness. If a Sicilian man is anything, he is not to be seen as a weakling. Better to be dead!

His background and upbringing as a young Sicilian male definitely shaped his attitude toward women. In those times past it was common and accepted that many, if not all Sicilian men, mistreated their families. Be aware that they did not consider their actions "mistreatment." Maintaining control by dominance or by whatever other means was what they had learned by word and example. Obviously, there were enough of those who went beyond the pale, who were so cruel that their actions are still remembered by many. They are the ones who gave birth to the reputation Sicilian men have concerning the total domination and utterly callous treatment of females. Some of the stories that my ninety-year-old aunt in Sicily related to me about Sicilian fathers and husbands would curl your hair! In defense of modern day Sicilian men (those that I am familiar with), be assured, they do not fit the old stereotype. This includes my brothers and cousin, who are warm and caring individuals.

To onlookers, Papa always appeared strong, supremely confident, and in control. He seemed to fear nothing and no one. We, his children, sincerely believed this and while we feared him, we knew we had nothing else to fear since he would always protect us from any form of danger, adversity, or want.

Although illiterate, he was intelligent, brave, and faced adversity without flinching. In addition, he was a charming, handsome man who made friends easily and instilled in others respect for himself and his integrity. He had class and style. Eventually, he enjoyed a fine reputation in the community as an honest, hardworking, and honorable person. His name was as "good as gold" in our town until the day he died. Of this, he was most proud.

As a departure from this side of him, sometimes honesty works in strange ways. Because Papa stated in his will that all debts should be paid upon his death, after he died, the farm had to be sold to satisfy them and our family lost everything. My mother had nothing to show for her lifetime of labor. (Cheerful to the end, she immediately started working in a dress factory. Years later, when she began to collect her social security pension, she felt that losing the farm had, perhaps, been a blessing.) Besides the enormous costs of my father's lingering illness, serious frosts had destroyed the apple crop for three years in a row and mounting debts far outstripped earnings. My brothers were desperate and worked very hard. They could not overcome a run of solid bad luck. Had my father foreseen what his honesty eventually wrought, perhaps he would have decreed otherwise in his last will and testament.

Another aside is a really amusing story about Papa that I must insert somewhere and this is as good a place as any. Shortly after his arrival in America, seeking work, he was sent to Chicago to help build the railroad. While there, he was assigned to labor with a group of husky, blue-eyed, blond young men. Papa decided that during lunch would be a good time to learn to speak English. Each day, he would hold up and item or two and give "his" word for it in Italian. They would laugh and give him "their" word for it. Before long, my father could carry on a valid, if halting, conversation with all in his group. Soon, he was quite proficient in their speech. Upon his return to Manhattan he decided to try out his "English" on some friends who spoke the language. Imagine his chagrin when he discovered that he had learned to speak *Polish* rather well!

To pick up again on Papa as father: as protective of us as he was while we were growing up, it appeared that he was unmoved and unfeeling when it came to what we wanted: as opposed to what he wanted, or thought was best for us. Like most, he was shaped by his time and place. The place was a small town high in the mountains in central Sicily, in the Province of Agrigento, an area colonized by the early Greeks.

The time, one hundred years ago. Papa's ancient and dusty farming village was probably as far from civilization as one could get. I'm not positive about the date, but I believe that sometime during (or close to), the tenth century the Normans invaded the town and occupied it for a long, long time. They built a magnificent church there. Today, the remnants of one of its ornate and beautiful arches is the town logo and called "*Il archi Normani.*" The Norman occupation had to have had some sort of affect on the local culture. Of what or how I am unaware. Their physical affect on the populace, however, was long lasting and is still obvious. Many Bivonese (including quite a few of my cousins) are blonde, some are red-haired, while others are light-eyed and fair-skinned. It almost seems that the darker Sicilians were the ones who immigrated in larger numbers. Upon visiting Sicily, I was surprised at the preponderance of fair people as opposed to the preponderance of their darker counterparts in America. In America when one thinks..."Sicilian"...one thinks black hair, dark eyes, olive skin. (The movies again!) Not truly so.

Bivona, Bivona! It was the hometown of both of my parents. For many years it was only a word to me. However, years later when I arrived in Sicily, I went in search of my roots. I found "their" Bivona and it was no longer just a word; it became a place. A marvelously warm, friendly, intriguing place. A place filled with cousins both immediate and distant. A place filled with people curious about me and the purpose of my visit. A place of picturesque hovels and high-rise modern apartment houses. A place where *sciccareddi* (jackasses) and *pecori* (sheep) shared the highway with trucks and sleek cars. A place drenched in antiquity.

Curious about everything, after visiting the house my mother had lived in (a nephew and his family still occupy it), I went in search of my father's house. It was a hot, sunny day in May and I walked with my newly found cousin, Nini (in Sicily *everybody* has a nickname) down a narrow, dusty street. It had steps leading from one level to another and was not as nice a section of town as where my mother had lived. Pointing ahead, down the street, Nini said we were nearing my father's house. It was the house he had been born in and lived in until the day he left for America.

A few more steps and we were there. I stood across the street staring. For a long time, I looked at the archaic, stucco-covered, stone walls, cracked and bleached white from the sun. Large pieces of stucco were missing, exposing the rough bricks beneath. I stared at the thick, wooden front door, worn and scarred, sagging from years of use. I admired its rusting, antique hardware. The windows were few, small, and unkempt. The contrast of a modern dumpster parked against the wall of the house made me aware of the contrast in times. It looked so incongruous.

Looking up, I noticed an old woman leaning out of a second story window. Most houses in the village had a small balcony where one could sit, but this house had none. Thus, the old woman sat, elbows on the window sill, white hair pulled back in a bun, wisps of hair hanging about her deeply wrinkled face. She peered down at me with great curiosity: an obvious stranger in their midst, "na 'Mericana." Looking up, and shielding my eyes with one hand, in Sicilian I called to her.

"Signora, quest e' la casa uini mio padre nasci. Pozo tracidi 'cussi pozo talliadi un'iddu stette?" (Madam, this is the house where my

father was born. Can I enter so I can see where he lived?) To this request, my cousin added a few shouted words of introduction. The old woman grinned wide, exposing one, yellow tooth. Motioning with her hand she said, *"Si, si, traci, traci, veniti 'nda la casa."* (Yes, yes, enter, enter, come in the house.)

With that we approached the door and pushed it open. Cool darkness greeted us. Entering from bright sunshine intensified the darkness. As our eyes adjusted, the form of the woman descending a dimly lit set of stairs could be seen. We waited for her in what seemed to be a small foyer. Immediately to the right of the entry was a room: its doorway had only hinges left on it. Peering in, we saw a litter filled room that was barn-like and that seemed as large as the whole house. Diluted sunlight beamed through windows opaque with dust. The woman explained to me that, in the past, the animals were kept on the first floor in that room and that the family occupied the second floor. *Now* I understood what my mother had meant when she told me that in Bivona, in many instances, people and their animals occupied the same house. I never said so, but I had found that disgusting! As a little girl I believed she meant they shared the living room, the kitchen, bedrooms and others. I smiled at my misconception.

We climbed the worn stairs, stained, and soiled from years of use. While ascending them, many feelings flooded my heart and mind. I realized that my feet were treading where my father's feet had once trod. I sensed that he had inhabited this same space in some far off time and that now I, in some unfathomable way, was sharing it with him. It was eerie! I could almost feel him climbing there ahead of me, showing me the way. I could feel my heart beating faster as I drew nearer and nearer to the top of the stairs.

When we reached the landing we were led into a room about 12 by 15 feet. The vaulted ceiling looked low, only about seven feet high. At one end was a fairly good-sized alcove within an archway from which hung a rather tattered curtain. Beyond that a bed could be seen. The curtain formed a make-shift door. I was told that my grandfather and grandmother had probably slept there. She believed that my father and his siblings shared the rest of the main room as a bed chamber.

Off to the right was the kitchen. It was small. In its center was a beehive oven. Its surface was made of some sort of stucco-like clay, encasing handmade bricks. Black from years of accumulated soot and dust, it looked positively ancient, hundreds of years old. The oven opening was in the shape of an arch. At the top of the beehive shape was a hole positioned directly below a chimney-like aperture in the ceiling. I asked, *"Stu forno angora po fari lu pane?"* (Can this oven still make bread?)

"Si! Perche no? Angora travaglia, l'uso sempre." (Yes, why not? It still works and I use it all the time.)

I nodded in amazement. It seemed incredible that such an ancient form of open-hearth oven was still being used to bake bread. This, in the latter part of the twentieth century, in a village that had electricity and running water. Many of the houses even had dishwashers. (Later on, I found the same kind of beehive oven in the home of one of my farm cousins. From it, I was served baked ziti, cooked next to the open fire.)

On one wall of the kitchen, near the oven, set on an old, decrepit dresser, was a two burner gas plate. It appeared so ancient that I decided it was probably one of the first ones ever manufactured. Next to it was a stained, battered, kitchen sink held up precariously on rusted metal legs. On the opposite wall was another dilapidated old dresser. Off in one corner was a small, shabby table with a few mismatched chairs. On this table was a tall glass holding some spoons and forks. Next to it sat a sugar bowl, cracked and missing its lid. A shabby piece of oil cloth of orange, yellow, and white flowers covered the table.

Continuing to gaze around the room, I noted a small, dirty window which shed little light. From the center of the ceiling, a bare light bulb hung from a tattered wire. It all looked so austere, so grim, and *so* poor. I could almost see my father and his family seated around the table eating their evening meal by candlelight or perhaps an oil lamp. Olive oil, of course.

This! This is where I came from, I reflected. The reflection made me shiver. Then a thought struck me. I hit my forehead

246

with the palm of my hand, "Stupid woman! How could I forget my camera! Of all times!" I walked back into the main room. The old woman watched me with great curiosity. I continued to study the house, to engrave on my mind what it looked like in order to describe it in detail to my family when I returned to America. The whitewashed walls were worn and discolored. Years of wear had made the wooden floors uneven. Cobwebs and layers of dust were everywhere. A sense of emptiness pervaded the room. Neither was it warm or inviting in any way. The old lady, however, unaware of her bleak surroundings, seemed quite cheerful. She questioned me extensively about my background and about America.

What puzzled her the most was the fact that although I was born in America, I spoke Sicilian like a native of old. A majority of the Bivonese, both young and old, now spoke "Italian." Because education had become so universal in Sicily, the ancient tongue was almost lost. Many, especially the elders in the village, were unhappy that the use of the true and ancient tongue was outmoded. During my travels in Italy and Sicily, I was surprised to discover that I spoke Sicilian much as a one-hundred-year-old woman would speak it. This I learned from a conversation with a young person. *"Ma como va che tu parli coumo una veccia di cent' anni."* (So, how come you talk like an old lady of a hundred years?) We both laughed and then I explained that I had learned to speak Sicilian as a child from parents born in the late nineteenth century. To some degree, I had become a sort of "time capsule" in maintaining the authenticity of the ancient tongue.

My language was so accurately Sicilian that my cousin, Nini, who is an elementary school teacher, took me to class one day, so that I might give the students a lesson using original Sicilian words. They had never heard *"scribacchi"* (upside down, topsi turvy), *"picchilida"* (little child), *"sciffiusu"* (dirty man), and many other words. They laughed and clapped when I spoke the "funny" words. My cousin told me that in order to preserve the island's heritage, the elementary school curriculum in Sicily had been redesigned. This in order to support a weekly session devoted to teaching Sicilian customs and traditions of the past. It was hoped that child-

247

ren in modern Sicily would, through study, keep alive their ancient heritage.

After I finished explaining my ability to speak "her" language, I questioned the old woman about my father and his family. She could give me no direct information having lived there for only the past twenty years. Papa, had he still been alive at that moment, would have been ninety-seven years old.

My cousin, Nini, and I slowly and carefully descended the shadowy staircase and went out into the bright, hot Sicilian sunshine. As I did so, thoughts of Papa returned. My mind once more traveled back to an interval long gone, that time that my father had descended these very stairs on the day that he left for America. I tried to imagine his feelings. I couldn't.

Originally, I thought he had never returned to Sicily. Again, my brother Frankie enlightened me. He said Papa did indeed return to Sicily. Dressed nattily in a dark handmade suit and a thick, white, turtle neck sweater he arrived in his home town, pockets filled with money. While there, he spent generously and gave some cash to those of his relatives and friends who were in need. This one time, he was generous almost to a fault and had a great time "showing off" his new found wealth and success in America. This visit occurred before he married.

In all my years of growing up, I had never heard my father express a desire to return to Sicily. Seeing the meanness of his early life and the poverty he had experienced, I could now understand why. I also sensed other things about him. Above all, I could finally comprehend his obsessive love affair with America. Now, even his penuriousness was also comprehensible. Despite his lack of schooling and desperately poor background, in America he was able to work and not only collect wages, he was able to save money. He sincerely believed America to be the land of opportunity and plenty. (It was and still is!)

When he left Bivona, headed for America, he was eighteen and had only a bit more than enough money for steerage class. By scrimping on board, he managed to have ten dollars in his pocket when he disembarked at Ellis Island. The ship that carried him to America had a side paddle wheel and was positively ancient (at least that is what he told Frankie). How Papa parlayed that landing and that ten dollars into a fruitful, successful life seemed a miracle to him. Yet, in America such stories are commonplace.

All these thoughts about my father made his presence palpable to me. I felt a part of and closer to him than when he had been alive. Inwardly, I lamented my resentment toward him, my angry memories. Now, only regrets remained. My cousin and I slowly climbed the steep and dusty streets of Bivona. Thirsty and hot we sweltered in the sunshine of the Sicilian afternoon making our way back to my aunt's house. All at once, as we walked those archaic streets, I felt tears well up and then spill. They streamed slowly down my face. (My cousin Nini glanced at me, but said not a word.) I kept wiping them away with the back of my hand. They continued for a while and it was not until we arrived back at the house and they had dried, that we spoke again.

chapter 21

The Twenty Cent Career

When Caroline was about fifteen, she and my brothers attended a block dance. Only seven, I was too young to go. Blissfully unaware of how much fun I was missing, I never questioned being left behind. It had been made very clear to me early on that these dances were for "grown ups" only. At the block dance, there were other entertainments, one of which was a bingo game. After wandering about, sampling ice cream and soda and playing some of the other games of chance, Benny and Caroline decided to try bingo. It was 10 cents a game. Benny won bingo on the first try. He chose a lamp for Mama. After four tries, Caroline won. As she surveyed the prizes, Benny urged her to choose a clock. He was certain a clock would please Mama very much.

She said, "No, Benny, I don't want the clock. We already have a clock. No, I think I'll take that Charlie McCarthy dummy up there", pointing and motioning to the person handing out the prizes. "The one on the top shelf. No, not that one, the one next to it. He has shinier eyes, I think."

Benny insisted she choose the clock. "What'sa matter with you? You crazy? You're a grown girl! What the dickens

are you gonna do with a dummy? A boy dummy at that."
He clenched his hands into fists, at his side and rolled his
eyes upward in impatience. "Somp'in wrong with you? Why
do ya' want a dummy? Get the clock, I tell you, get the
clock!"

Caroline was not to be swayed. "No! I want the dummy.
A few weeks ago I sent for a booklet on how to throw your
voice and I wanna try it out!"

"So? Try it out on the chickens or the pigs, but don't waste
yer time with that dummy. Get the clock I tell ya or, at least,
another lamp. We can always use another lamp."

"Lissen Benny, I won this game and I can pick whatever
I want for a prize. Nobody told you what to pick, so leave
me alone." Turning her back on Benny and facing the
attendant, in a strong voice she said, "Yes! I want that Charlie
McCarthy dummy! The one I pointed out to you on the top
shelf, please."

The attendant grinned broadly, having listened to the heated
exchange and having "rooted" for Caroline. Using a prong
on a stick, he reached up to the top shelf and retrieved the
wooden doll. "Thank you. Thank you. Oh, he's lovely!"

"I should give 'er a shot in the head, that'd wake 'er up!"
Benny mumbled.

Caroline, ignoring Benny's annoyance, smiled as she reached
out and took the dummy from the outstretched hands of the
attendant. Holding the Charlie Mccarthy at arms length, she
stared at him. Then slowly she drew him closer and examined
him more carefully. Turning him this way and that, she found
a slit in the back of his jacket. Intrigued, she slipped her hand
into the opening and felt some levers attached to a wooden
pole connected to the dummy's head. Jiggling, them she found
that not only could she make his mouth open and close, she
could also turn his head from side to side and also back and
forth. Now, all else at the block dance had paled. She was
impatient to get home so that she could practice with him
in the privacy of her own room. Annoyed that the block dance
would not be over for a few hours, she resigned herself to
the fact that she would have to wait until Benny, Frankie,
and Joey were ready to go home.

As she mingled with the festive crowd, people commented on her dummy and were curious about why she chose it. She replied to all of their questions telling them about the book she had sent for a few weeks before and which had cost her only a dime. It had instructions on how to "throw your voice" and wasn't it a coincidence that she should win the game and have a dummy to choose as a prize?

Each time she repeated her story, her smile seemed to get wider and wider. She became more and more elated as the evening wore on. Glad she had chosen the dummy, she was certain her Charlie McCarthy was so much better than some stupid old lamp or clock! Besides, it seemed like fate had planned it all since months before, Caroline had seen an ad in one of my comic books. It read: "Learn how to throw your voice. Astound and mystify your friends. Only 10 cents!" She sent for the book and weeks later, received a small green pamphlet. Joey and Frankie teased her and asked her if she was going to make the cows or chickens talk. She just smiled.

After she won the dummy, I could hear her practice nightly, since our rooms were adjacent to one another. Caroline practiced and practiced. Each night when we got ready for bed, she would talk to me about the dummy. As she combed and braided my hair, she wondered aloud if it could really be only coincidence that when she won at bingo, how odd that she would have a dummy to choose as a prize; a Charlie McCarthy dummy at that! He was her favorite radio character.

About a month after the block dance, Benny came home one day and announced that he had signed up Caroline for the talent show at the high school. We all knew that she spent every spare moment playing with her dummy, although she tried to hide the fact. When Benny made his announcement, Caroline was mortified. She had not consciously planned to have to perform in public with her dummy, whom she had named Tommy. Actually, she really thought of it more as a hobby or play thing. Benny, however, finally shamed her into saying yes.

For the next few weeks, she was a wreck, mumbling to herself constantly, trying to memorize a routine. The night of the talent show, Caroline's friend, Louis Schaffert, who was going to play his violin and was favored by everyone to be first place winner, was backstage encouraging her.

"Don't be so nervous, Caroline. They'll probably really like you. Why you might even win second or third place. I'm sure you'll do OK." Louis ran his fingers through his short-cropped red hair. "Jeez! I mean, all those jokes you wrote down from Edgar Bergen, Bob Hope, and Jack Benny, heck, you'll be real funny and you're sure to win *something*! Be calm." Then he had a new thought. He put one hand on each of her shoulders, his blue eyes looking deeply and sincerely into her brown ones, he said, "I know it's tough when you're on last, but sometimes that's the best place of all. Lissen, I have to go on now. Promise you won't be nervous and you won't feel too bad if you don't win."

Caroline waved her hand up and down, motioning him to leave, "Go on Louis. Heck, don't worry so much about me. I'll be OK. Really I will. I don't care about winning. I just gotta prove to Benny that I can do it." Then she stamped her foot and said, "Get out there and play that violin and win first place again! You win every year, so go ahead, I'm really rooting for you."

Waiting and listening to all the contestants made Caroline more and more nervous. When it was finally her turn, she almost threw up. She steeled herself and tried to remember her lines. Her stomach was one big knot when she heard her name announced. As she strode out on the stage, our brothers and all of their friends, seated in the front row, clapped loudly and hooted and hollered. They made so much noise shouting her name that they distracted her. Frazzled, she completely forgot the routine she had spent so much time memorizing. Standing center stage, Tommy seated on the palm of one hand, her other hand at the controls in his back, she peered out over the audience. Tiny beads of sweat covered her upper lip. Her stomach twisted even more. It was agony. The lights from the stage enabled her to see only the people seated in the middle of the first row. She noted her school principal, the president of the local bank, the police chief, her history teacher, and her gym teacher.

She was not aware of it, but they were the judges. She could also just about make out Benny and his friends at the very end of the same row. She made the dummy slowly scan the first row. There was absolute silence. Then Caroline began. First she had Tommy say a few choice words about her principal. "Hey, who's that funny looking man in the front row with the bald head and the big nose in the ugly brown suit?"

"Tommy, you must apologize, that's the principal!"

"The principal? He looks more like the janitor!" The crowd roared! The principal laughed louder than anyone else. Then the little dummy, looking squarely at the chief of police, declared he looked like a vagrant and should be arrested. The crowd cheered. She didn't even hear them. Sharp tongued and quick, she just said whatever came to her head. She found herself making the dummy insult and tease the bank president, the history teacher, and the gym teacher. The audience went wild with clapping and shouting.

Oddly enough, those who were the brunt of her jokes clapped the loudest of all. She had been on only seven minutes, but in that seven minutes she had unknowingly "wowed" them. Unsure of what she had done, certain she had been laughed "at" because she had forgotten her routine, she rushed backstage, still sweating, her heart banging against her ribs. Quickly stuffing her dummy in a large, brown paper shopping bag, she ran for the door. She had almost reached it when her friend Louis came running after her. Reaching out, he said, "You won! You won, Caroline! You won first place! Quick, come with me, they're waiting for you!" He grabbed her hand. Caroline was dumbstruck. So engrossed in her own effort at overcoming her memory lapse, she had not really heard the ovation at the end of her act. Trembling, she let him take her hand and lead her back in.

She reemerged on stage to a boisterous ovation. As she was being presented with an envelope holding the prize money of ten dollars, she heard Benny proclaim loudly to his friends that he had taught her everything she knew. This infuriated her. Later, when they all went for sodas at the "College Inn," she bought ice cream sodas for everyone except Benny. That was also repayment for his giving her a hard time about choosing the Charlie McCarthy dummy rather than a lamp or a clock at the bingo game.

The next week, the phone started ringing off the wall. It seemed every organization in town wanted her to perform at their monthly meetings. "The Ladies's Home Sewing Circle," "The Great Books Club," "The Firemen's Annual Minstrel Show," just about everybody wanted the little dummy and his "friend" to come and insult everyone. In the beginning, in lieu of payment, Caroline was often given a gift. Strangely, it always turned out to be a size 48, 46, or 50 slip or an oversized cardigan sweater. This was rather mysterious, since Caroline was a diminutive size 10. She reasoned that people got extra slips or sweaters as birthday or Christmas gifts and this was a good way to get rid of them. She also received a really weird assortment of perfumes and talcum powder.

That year, as Christmas time approached, an orphanage somewhere near Poughkeepsie called and asked if Caroline would be so kind as to donate her time and entertain the little orphans for Christmas. Caroline said yes, she would be happy to do so. Right after that, one day in early December, Caroline called down to me from her room and asked me to come up. When I entered the room, she said, "Guess what?"

I hated to guess at anything, so I said, "Aw, don't make me 'guess what.' You know I stink at trying to guess anything. Just tell me! Please?"

"I have a surprise for you."

"A surprise? Oh, Caroline, quick, what?"

Grinning, Caroline answered, "Guess!"

"Aw..."

"No. Just one guess."

" Well, OK." (after much thought.) That you'll bring me some candy or cake from the party at the orphanage?"

"Nope, guess again."

I was puzzled. If she wasn't going to bring me something from the party, I couldn't imagine what the surprise would be. "Gee, Caroline, what else can there be?"

"How would you like to come to the party with me?"

"What? Wow!! Would I! Could I! Boy-o-Boy, would I ever love to! Caroline, you mean it? I can really come with you? Nobody will get mad if you bring somebody extra?" By now, I was jumping up and down, thoroughly excited at the thought of going to a Christmas party. I grabbed my sister around the waist and hugged her as hard I could. Caroline then picked me up, hugged me tight, and whirled around and around, the two of us laughing and laughing. After a while, we calmed down and Caroline said, "How would you like to be part of my act?"

I almost stopped breathing! "Oh! Oh! Could I? Could I? Sure, sure I would! Gee! Gee, Caroline, you know I would love to!" Gleefully, I whirled around and around the room a few times. Returning, breathless, I said, "Heck, not only to finally see you 'n Tommy on stage, but, oh my God, to be on stage too! Wow! I'll do anything you say. I'll remember anything you tell me. Oh, thank you, thank you!" Again I threw my arms around her waist and again hugged her as hard as I could.

"Hey! You wanna break my ribs? Take it easy, it's only a little show, and you won't really have that much to say."

"I don't care if it's only two words, I'll love doing it."

A few days later Caroline approached me. "OK, I've got your routine, are you ready?"

"You wrote it already? Sure. Sure I'm ready. What is it?"

"Well, while I'm on stage with Tommy, when Tommy says 'Where's Stooge,' you walk out."

"Stooge? Y'er gonna call me 'Stooge?' It sounds like a dirty word! Stooge? (In Sicilian, the word for human excrement is *stroonzu*. To my young ears, "stooge" and *"stroonzu"* sounded very similar). I actually whined. "Can'cha call me something else?"

"No. And "Stooge" is not a dirty word! It just means somebody who's not too bright and does silly things. And you are going to say silly things so people will laugh."

"Silly things?"

"Look, you wanna be in this or don't you. Don't be a pain in the neck. You do what I say or you can just stay home."

"OK. OK. What do I say when I come out?"

"Well, you come out holding a blank piece of paper. You wave it at me and Tommy and say, 'Look at this picture I just drew of a cow eating grass.' We look at the paper and then I ask you where the grass is. Then you say ' The cow ate it.' Then Tommy asks you 'Where's the cow?' and you say 'You don't think the cow is gonna stay around after it ate all the grass, do you?' "

I waited. I didn't get it. Perplexed by my silence, Caroline asked, "Well, what do you think? "

"Yeah! Yeah, then what?

"Then what? That's it!"

"That's it? It is?" Annoyed, Caroline repeated the last line again. After a moment's thought I said, "Yeah, well, I guess that's funny. Yeah, that's pretty funny, no cow, no drawing. Gee, you know how much I love to draw! (Then, wistfully.) I wish instead that, that I, that I could draw... a really good picture of a cow an' show it to everybody. But I guess you're right. We got to be funny and make those poor little orphans laugh." I was none too pleased to have to act stupid and I would have preferred to show off my drawing ability. However, since I wanted very much to be part of it all and having no choice in the matter, I agreed to everything.

The days passed by and soon it was time for the show at the orphanage. I had become quite enthusiastic about the whole thing and could hardly sleep the night before. After days of reciting my "part" over and over to myself, I was certain that I had memorized every intonation. Besides being my first time "on stage", this was also to be the first time I had been to a children's party at night and with only my sister. The ride to the orphanage was exciting, especially when we drove on board the ferry boat that took us from Highland to Poughkeepsie. The lights from the city seen from the prow of the ferry; their reflection in the waters of the Hudson River, the Christmas decorations everywhere, all combined to make the trip almost magical and completely unforgettable.

On our way to the orphanage, Caroline kept telling me how very unhappy all the orphans were because they had no mothers or fathers. (I thought to myself that maybe they were lucky they didn't have a father.) Caroline went on and on about the fact that orphans had so little and that those lucky children who were not orphaned and had "everything" should be grateful and maybe even think about someday helping and sharing what they had with "others." I had only a dime in my possession. My "Zia," Aunt Jenny, had put it in the small pocketbook I carried which she had given to me as a gift. Always the frugal one, the dime was still in the purse. Now, guilt ridden, I was ready to give it to the first "poor little orphan" I met.

Soon we pulled into a long driveway leading to a very large, somber looking, brick building. It was, of course, the orphanage. When we entered the lobby, we were met by some nuns and priests and led to a large auditorium. In a far corner, to the right of the stage, was the most enormous and beautifully decorated Christmas tree that I had ever seen. Placed all around the bottom of it, were piles and piles of wrapped presents. Never had I seen so many beneath one tree before. I decided there must be hundreds of orphans in the place.

Soon Caroline and I found ourselves offstage and waiting to go on. After a clown and then a magician, Caroline performed. She did about ten minutes. There was much laughter and clapping. Those "poor little orphans" were really enjoying themselves. My palms were wet and my heart started to beat very fast as I knew the time for me to go on stage was approaching. Then I heard it, "Where's Stooge?"

My heart was beating so wildly I was sure the whole world could hear it. Shyly, awkwardly, I walked across the stage. It seemed to take an eternity before I reached my sister and Tommy. Pausing, I looked at them. Reaching into my pocket I drew out my piece of paper: holding it out proudly for them to see. Swallowing hard, I said, in a clear, loud voice, "See the grass I drew eating a cow?" The audience exploded with laughter and Caroline got a funny look on her face. Puzzled, I looked at her and frowned. Why was everyone laughing? They were only supposed to laugh at the end. From looking at me, Tommy's head slowly turned, mouth open, and looked at the audience. He paused, staring at them. They howled. Then, turning back to me he said, "What did you say you drew?"

Facing the audience and holding up the blank paper, I said, "I drew a cow eating grass." They waited expectantly.

"So? Where is the grass?" asked Tommy.

"The cow ate it." A few people snickered.

"So? Where is the cow?"

"You don't think...uh, you don't think, um..." I froze! My mind went completely blank. In a panic, I turned, face red, eyes filled with distress, and looked at Caroline. Quietly she mouthed a few, cue words. Relieved but upset, I turned back to the audience. Stiffly and mechanically I said, "Well, you don't think the cow is going to stick around once she ate the grass do you?" Humiliated over "messing up" I ran off the stage as fast as I could. The audience, charmed by someone their own age being on stage and "erring," gave me such a big hand that Caroline had to call me back. I reemerged, flushed and happy that they seemed to like me and that they had finally laughed in the right place. That incident, however, cured me of ever wanting to be an entertainer.

After the show, everyone mingled and had ice cream and cake. The children got to open some of their presents and saved others for Christmas Morning. It seemed to me each orphan got a lot of presents. On the way home that night, I wondered aloud if one could live at an orphanage without becoming an orphan. It seemed to me that they had it "pretty good." They lived in a nice, big, warm place with plenty of other kids to play with. They got lots of presents for Christmas and even had ice cream and cake. Best of all, there weren't saddled with any mean fathers. Besides that, they didn't have a whole bunch of brothers and sisters always telling them what to do or bossing them around! It seemed like an ideal place to live. Maybe my family could even come and visit me once in a while.

While answering me, Caroline explained that to be an orphan BOTH your mother and father have to die and you could not live there under any other circumstances. I choked over that. The thought of Mama dying made me feel I too would want to die. I could not imagine a life without my mother to love and hold me and make me feel precious and wanted. So? Perhaps being an orphan was not such a good deal after all. What good was all that other stuff without a mother around to help you and love you and just BE there.

After that orphan show, Caroline's career really took off.

Despite the fact that she entertained three or four evenings per week, and despite the fact that she gave Papa a part of her earnings, she was still expected to rise early in the morning and to perform all of her chores as usual. Somehow she managed to complete them, plus practice her routines, plus do her school work, plus entertain during the evenings. She not only did it all, she even made it look easy. It took its toll however. A bit short tempered to begin with, all the pressures made her temper even shorter. There were more arguments with Papa than usual. Working and earning money made her extremely independent, a trait that did not jibe with being female and Sicilian.

Caroline received more and more requests to entertain. She became quite famous within the community. So much so that to this day, when I meet certain people in New Paltz, they always ask me about Caroline and what she is currently doing.

My sister went on to make a successful and lucrative forty-five-year career of being a ventriloquist. Her twenty cent investment at age fifteen served her well throughout her life and eventually took her all over the world. Not only did she travel world-wide while with the USO during WW II, she also went on world tours and cruises afterward. In addition her work took her all over the United States. Besides lots of small cities she entertained in Hollywood, Las Vegas, New York City, Miami, Chicago and the "Borscht Belt." She delights in the fact that in the final analysis, that 20 cent investment allowed her to live very comfortably in her well-deserved retirement.

She eventually moved back to this area, near to where it all began and close to where almost all the members of our family still reside. Her success has enabled her to help make all our lives more comfortable. Contrary to Mr. Goodman's claim, "You CAN go home again" and, if you are lucky, it's better the second time round.

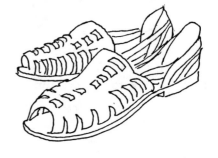

chapter 22

The Red Huaraches

In our family, as in many Sicilian and Italian families, girls of dating age could not even think of dating. Quite frequently, marriages were arranged by parents, although often surreptitiously. Sicilian females, especially the young, were not allowed to wear lipstick or makeup. Short skirts were absolutely out of the question. Incredibly, even the kind of shoes one wore were proscribed although it seems ludicrous in today's permissive society. Believe me, it was serious business. How serious, I found out one day in early fall.

The boarders would leave on or, right after, Labor Day. There would be tearful farewells, much hugging and crying, promises to write, and to see one another again next year. Caroline always disappeared on those Sunday afternoons that signaled the departure of the boarders. Everyone would be searching for her in order to say goodby. Five minutes after the last car pulled away, Caroline would appear. She would never tell us where she had been. Only now have I learned that she used to hide in the attic because she could not bear goodbys. To this day she says only *Ciao* (by-by or so-long, in Italian.) Bonding can take place rather quickly!

All the rooms which the boarders had occupied would then be cleaned and aired out in preparation for the next group of visitors, the hunters. Each autumn, groups of men would come up from New Jersey, Brooklyn, the Bronx, or the lower east side of Manhattan. Some came for a week, others just for the weekend. They would roam far and near over the 212 acre farm, shooting everything in sight. These men did observe the law by each purchasing a legal hunting license. However, once armed with rifles and shotguns, they took aim at and killed whatever crossed their paths–foxes, woodchucks, cranes, ducks, large and small birds of all kinds (they even shot Chico's pet crow), and, sometimes, even chickens (they would pay my outraged father whatever the price of the chicken when he confronted them). Of course, rabbits, deer, and squirrels were brought back proudly and in great quantity from the woods. These men were a virile and noisy group and only years later did I learn that some of them had belonged to the Black Hand, later known as the Mafia.

One man in particular, Saro Colletti, was a silver-haired older man, very handsome and distinguished looking. I became very fond of him. He was always friendly. A real gentleman who often teased me playfully and sometimes would look at me in the same way my father did. His eyes would take on a warm look...I don't know...I just felt that he liked me. Since he had never had any children of his own, I probably represented the daughter he knew he could never have. (I was told years later that he was believed to be one of the top men of the then Black Hand.)

When the hunters prepared to depart for home, they would always tip me just before leaving. It was I who brought them their wine and fetched for them while they were there. Mr. Colletti was especially generous. Often, he would tip me five dollars, which was an enormous amount of money in those days. Others would give me two or three dollars. A genuine miser at heart, I hoarded all my tips and spent very little of my money. I kept it hidden in a secret place in the attic under a loose board. The same place where I kept all my secret, favorite things stored safely out of sight.

Each fall, I managed to collect fifteen or twenty dollars in tips. Occasionally, my brothers or sister would try to convince me to part with a dollar or two. They usually succeeded since they knew I was a sucker for a touching story. Being all of nine years old that particular autumn, I decided to use some of my money to buy new clothes for school. Approaching my sister, I asked if she would take me shopping sometime. Caroline had purchased a splendid, used, little red English Austin Convertible with her earnings from entertaining with Tommy.

Thus, one sun-filled Saturday in late September, the two of us climbed into the Austin and took off for Newburgh, a large city nearly twenty miles away. I had never before been there. My family usually shopped in the "farmer's" city, Kingston, also large and a bit closer. This time, because she felt it was a more sophisticated place, this time Caroline decided on Newburgh.

In the 1930s Newburgh was a magnificent city. I may be wrong, but I believe it was referred to as "The Pearl of the Hudson". The view of that river from the unusually wide avenue called Broadway was breathtaking. (I read somewhere that it is the second or third widest main street of any city in America.) The Victorian homes were stunning and the stores were in greater number and were much more grandly stocked than those in Kingston. Caroline was right. It was a much more sophisticated place to shop.

I remember being especially delighted with the little metal "money cars" that could be found in J.C. Penny. Even the store in Kingston had them. They were shiny, oval shaped, flat on top and bottom. The salesgirl put your money in them, pressed something, and away the little tiny "cars" would whiz on long "tracks" up and down and across the ceiling to some magic place in the sky, or so it seemed to me. Soon it would come whizzing back down with the change and a receipt. It was all so intriguing and I never stopped wondering where they went and who sent them back.

We went from store to store. It was a heady experience to be free to choose and then pay for one's own clothes. When we finished shopping, I took stock of what Caroline had helped me buy. Of all the purchases, my favorite was a pair of red leather Huaraches made in Mexico. To me, they were the nicest shoes (I know now they are sandals, but they were shoes to me) that I had ever owned and I could hardly wait to wear them to school. Before finally choosing them, I had tried on so many different pairs that the salesman looked like he was ready to choke me. Caroline kept saying "No. No." to all of them. Then he brought out the red Huaraches. We both fell in love with them and since we had the same shoe size, my practical side figured we could take turns wearing them. (Besides, they were probably on sale.) I had never owned anything but ugly brown oxford ties. The purchase of the red shoes made me ecstatic. They were opened toed and made me feel so grown up when I put them on.

After shopping, we stopped at the Highland Ice Cream factory and Caroline bought each of us a pint. She then drove to and parked the car near the edge of large, clear pond in the middle of a lovely park. I was amazed. Never before had I seen a park, although I had read about them. The manicured grass and the wide variety of trees, the small footbridge, the pathways, the lovely rolling lawns, and the huge beds of day lilies were a revelation. Used to the tangle of farmlands, meadows, woods, and overgrown brush, I thought the park the largest and loveliest "garden" I had ever seen (outside of the movies). It reminded me, just a little, of the grounds at Suzy's house.

We sat and ate slowly, enjoying the view of the pond as we savored each delicious spoonful of ice cream. It was not often that we got any and a whole pint all at once was pure bliss. As I devoured the ice cream, quickly scooping out the soft, melted part on the outer edges with a small, flat wooden spoon, I contemplated my surroundings. It was all so enchanting and peaceful that I did not want to leave. After we finished the ice cream we licked the empty containers clean, tearing the sides apart in order to get to the bottom (we always did the same thing to Dixie Cups). Ice cream on the tips of our noses and chins, we laughed and giggled.

"We're just pigs!" said Caroline.

"Yes, and what fun. Umm, that was good!" I licked my lips and wiped my chin. Caroline wiped the tip of my nose with her napkin. We put the empty containers in a nearby waste can and then started home.

Mama made a real fuss over the lovely things that had been purchased and I immediately put on the red, opened-toed Huaraches. She admired them, but had reservations since she thought they were too "old" and too brightly colored for me. Then she noted how happy I was and said little more. However, as I pranced about, both Mama and Caroline admonished me to take off my new shoes and "save" them for school. I did so reluctantly. The next day was Sunday and when I rose that morning I simply could not wait until Monday to wear my new Huaraches. I decided to use them that morning, just for a little while. Putting them on slowly, I savored each moment. I couldn't believe how good they made me feel; not only grownup, but rich too! After I washed my face and combed my hair, I went down to help with breakfast. Soon I was busy setting the table and assisting Mama who was frantically frying eggs and making heaps of pancakes, trying to keep up to the voracious appetites of my brothers and hired hands.

I was totally preoccupied and had forgotten that I was wearing my new red Huaraches. Papa entered the room, sat down at the head of the table, and waited to be served his breakfast. I brought him his coffee and as I turned to walk back to the stove for the pancakes, I heard an awful bellow and the sound of a chair hitting the floor. It was Papa! Terrified, I turned and looked at him. I wondered to myself, "Now what?"

Papa, standing, eyes black and glaring, looking like a tornado about to explode, had gotten up so quickly that his chair fell over!. He was glaring directly at ME! I felt paralyzed. Numb with fear! I had never seen him look at me like that before. His face registered both rage and alarm...mostly rage.

"Butana, tappinara, disgraziata! Scarpi rossi! Scarpi cu le gieti di ped'aperto, vergogna! Vergogna! Figlia di butana!" (Whore, slut, disgraced one! Red shoes! Shoes with open toes, shame! Shame! Daughter of a whore!) He started toward me, arm raised to strike. Seeing Papa coming at me, I darted for the kitchen door. In a flash, I was on the porch and flying down the steps, papa close behind! Running, heart beating wildly, fear, adrenalin pumping, I ran like the wind. Papa knew he could not outrun me, so when he reached the porch and a big pile of cut firewood, he stopped. Picking up log after log, one after the other, he flung them at me. I continued running, fearing for my life. The split logs showered down around me as I ran. Some, so close, I felt them whiz past my head! Luckily, the pieces all missed and soon I was out of range. I continued to run fast, not even daring to look behind. I imagined Papa close on my heels.

Barely pausing to watch for cars, I zipped across the highway. Making an instant decision, I decided to run through the yard of the cow barn (the gate was open, the cows were out to pasture) instead of across the meadow that bordered the road. I chose to run through the mud and fresh cow manure rather than have to pause to climb under the barbed wire fence. I feared any pause would help Papa catch up to me. Frightened beyond reason, once out of the barnyard and on solid ground, I continued running at top speed and was starting to breath very hard. Swiftly, I crossed the meadow and approached the pond, not from the wet, swampy side!

Now for the first time, I felt it was safe to look back. There was no one behind me nor was anyone, anywhere in sight. I stopped abruptly and tried to catch my breath, dropping to the ground, my heart was beating so hard that it actually hurt. There was a sharp throbbing pain in my lower left side. Taking bigger breaths, I inhaled and exhaled slowly, deeply, and tried to get my breathing back to a normal rhythm. Sweat ran profusely down my neck, down my brow, and into my eyes. It plastered my hair against my cheeks and forehead. I could even smell my own body odor; it was a kind of sweet-sour smell and made me slightly nauseous. My still thudding heart made the blood pound against my temples. Reclining into a flat-out position on the ground, my arms and legs spread-eagled, I rested a bit while keeping a sharp look out. My face turned toward, my eyes practically glued, to the rear of the barnyard where Papa would appear, should he decide to pursue me.

I was afraid to stay where I was since I knew he could spot me should he look out over the field from the upper door of the cow barn. Certain that if he saw me he would come after me and beat me to death, I decided to continue on. My heart had stopped thudding and now had resumed a quieter beat. Feeling less pain, I rose and trotted slowly toward the large hill that rose from the woods through which flowed the creek. I knew that at the top of that hill was a thick, old, dead tree lying on the ground. It would be a good place behind which to hide and, at the same time, keep watch on both the house and the barn. From this elevated point at the very top of the hill, if I spied my father coming after me, I could quickly escape down to the woods where he would be unable to find me.

Quivering with apprehension and fear, I stayed all day behind that tree, first squatting then kneeling, cautiously watching the house and barn, waiting fearfully for my angry father to come looking for me. He had been so furious! Never before had I seen him that angry with me. Never before had he called me those horrible names. I surmised that perhaps now I was starting to grow up and would have to go through what I had seen my sister endure. The thought of growing up was disconcerting. I enjoyed being the "baby" of the family, in many ways it was quite nice. Having to exchange that for an unknown quantity called "adulthood" was a frightening thought I did not relish.

While I waited, still fearing that my father was yet intent on finding and punishing me for being so "bad", I wrung my hands, scratched my head nervously, and picked my nose. It bled a little. After a while, I rubbed my eyes, yawned and stretched. My mouth was dry so I pulled, then chewed on the grass by my feet. After that, I tore small twigs off the trunk of the tree and peeled them down to the bare, moist wood. Lining them up on the dark bark of the downed tree, I made patterns with their white forms.

By mid-morning, I felt the urge to pee and looked about for a safe place to squat. Nearby was a large patch of moss. (First I checked it out to be sure there was no poison ivy or oak near by. Once, when I was about seven years old, I had peed in a patch of poison oak. The memory of the agony and pain of that itching has *never* left me.) Finding it clear, I prepared to relieved myself.

Whenever I peed out of doors, while squatting, I always giggled to myself and found it very amusing. It usually struck me as very funny; all that "water" spraying out between my legs and especially the force with which the stream of yellow liquid hit the ground. If it hit a small stone or rock, it would sometimes splash back. You also had to be very careful and hold your panties up from your knees, so they wouldn't get wet. If you accidentally hit them (knees *or* panties), that "nasty yellow stuff" could dribble down into your socks. Sometimes I would tip my hips up to see how far I could aim it.

As I peed, it sank immediately into the moss. I could smell the warm earthiness of its odor rising like a strangely perfumed mist, enveloping me. Combining with the pungent smell of earth, it was familiar and comforting, almost pleasant! This came as a surprise since I had always been taught that bodily functions were "dirty" and "smelly." After I emptied my bladder, I found some broad, soft leaves with which to wipe myself. The leaves had some tiny little hairs on them and at first they made me itch. I scratched, but I still itched. I was getting more and more uncomfortable and unhappy but still I kept a vigilant eye on the barn and house. After a while the itching stopped.

Noontime was signaled by hunger pangs, insistent and vexing. Still too frightened to go home, I had no idea what to do. "Why didn't someone come and find me? Didn't anyone care? What if I died out here?" I started to cry. Maybe because there was no one around to hear, I soon stopped. Keeping my eyes on the barnyard, I knelt on the ground, my body against the fallen trunk, my arms akimbo on top of it, cradling my chin. Staying in that one position for a long time caused me to doze off. I don't know how long I slept, but after a while I woke. The sun was much lower in the sky. Anxiously, I looked towards the barn. There was no sign of anyone in the barnyard, but the cows had been brought in to drink at the trough. I waited, bored and miserable, still uncertain about my next move.

As the sun set lower and lower in the sky, the air took on a chill. My arms felt cold. I glanced about. For the first time, my friendly woods seemed ominous. I peered down toward the creek. The shadows, purple-black beneath the trees, seemed forbiddingly dark and spooky. As much as I feared my father, spending the night in or near the woods was something I suddenly feared even more. I could almost hear coyotes howling and feared that wolves would come out of the forest and chew me to pieces. I had to do something!

I gathered my thoughts. Maybe by now Papa had eaten supper and had drunk some wine and was feeling mellow. Maybe, if I took them off and never wore them again, he would forget the red Huaraches. I looked down ruefully at them and noticed that some of the leather straps had broken. My hasty departure from the house and running over the rocky and uneven ground of the meadow, had probably torn them loose. There was also dried cow manure on the opened-toed part of the shoes and I looked in disgust at my poor feet covered with dried mud and cow dung.

I sighed. Once again, tears fell. I licked at them as they trickled past my mouth. My nose was full and having no hankie, I snuffed long and deep to clear it. At home, when I snuffed like that, Papa would sharply reprimand me.

Thinking of him made me wish things were different. I wished I could be free of him, free to wear whatever pleased me, free to do whatever I wanted to do, whenever I wanted to do it. But I knew it was an idle wish. I knew I was still just a little kid and that, especially because I was female, I would always be constrained by certain rules and regulations. Ordered about, whether by male or female, young or old, if it wasn't by Papa, it would be my brothers or sister or the teachers or the bus driver or sometimes bigger kids at school. There was always someone bigger or stronger or older telling you what to do. And worst of all, you always had to listen and do as you were told...or else!!!

I got up slowly, a little stiff from kneeling on the ground in place for such a long time. Taking a few deep breaths to give me courage, I started walking back to the house. It was twilight and I picked my way carefully across the field; realizing that if I tripped on a rock, or if my foot got caught in a woodchuck or rabbit hole, I could be seriously hurt. Thinking about injuries as I walked, I sighed again, remembering Papa's "cardinal rule" and resigning myself. You see, in our house, none of us had ever had an accident and none of us had ever even broken a bone. Imagine five children living and working on a farm for fourteen years and not one of us was ever seriously injured? The reason for this was quite evident. If any of us ever did get hurt, we knew we would be hurt twice: once when we accidentally injured ourselves, then once again when Papa would beat the hell out of us for being so careless.

Sounds simplistic? It was! It was also highly effective.

We were probably the most careful children ever to grow up on a farm. The boarders were forever falling out of the hayloft or twisting an ankle, getting a pitchfork in a foot, getting butted and knocked down by a ram, or a dozen other silly things that can happen to the unwary on a farm. My father's brood, however (aside from a scraped knee or shin, which illicited a beating rather than sympathy), somehow escaped all kinds of serious accidents that frequently occur to those who live on farms. Looking back now, I can see that maybe Papa had the right formula. Somehow it worked.

As I got closer to the house, my heart again started to beat very fast. Fear was beginning to squeeze in on me again. I took deep, gulping breaths. Crossing the highway, stealthily, I crept up the long winding driveway to the house, hiding behind trees as I went. I felt like an Indian, sneaking up on the troops. It was dusk by now and the warm, inviting lights of the kitchen beckoned me. However, this time I chose to enter through the front door since, this time of year, it was rarely used and I probably would not run into Papa in that part of the house. It was also a way to bypass the kitchen where I was certain he would be.

I climbed the stairs of the great front porch. Crossing it, I slowly pushed open the front door. The faint sounds of talking could be heard. Sounds that echoed through the darkened hallway, thick with the mouth-watering smells of cooking wafting from the kitchen at the far end of the house. I was starved. No matter. I slipped down the long expanse of hallway and up the staircase. Automatically, I avoided those steps which I knew squeaked. Reaching the top, I tip-toed quickly and quietly to my room and crawled under the bed. It felt so good to be home again despite the pounding of my heart and despite the fear of Papa so strong that I tingled all over. I curled up listening to the sounds below. Soon I was fast asleep.

My family went on about its business, unconcerned about me since one of my brothers had seen me sneak into the house. They all knew I was safely home. Later that night, when Caroline came up, she woke me and made me get into bed. This I did, fully clothed. The next morning I got up early, dressed carefully and went off to school, sans the red Huaraches. I was happy to still be alive. What became of them? Caroline refused when I offered to give them to her. She didn't dare wear them either. Besides, now they were broken and soiled. I stored them in the back of my closet. Eventually they disappeared and were never mentioned again, until now.

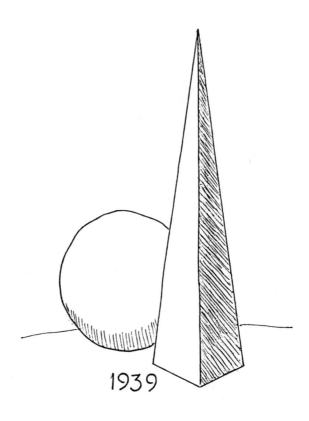

1939

chapter 23

World's Fair and Bowery Bums

Time heals. It also civilizes. Only as people grow and experience do they learn. While real learning takes place over great lengths of time, adaptation seems more quickly achieved. City-bred, but growing up Sicilian in small town involved enormous changes and levels of acculturation. Yet, in only a few short years, we learned to meld into the "American" way. Remember, despite the fact that we were born in America, before moving to the farm, our early years were spent in an Italian Ghetto. There, the language and customs were anything but American. Thus, confronted in New Paltz with different customs and beliefs, we had to adapt. However, we still retained the roots from whence we came despite the change of "plant and flower." The ability of human beings to understand and to conform to their surroundings is remarkable. A great deal depends upon how rigid or flexible are the customs and beliefs of the newcomers, how ready they are to accept adjustment and change. Social success, especially, depends on their willingness and ability to adopt new attitudes and mores. I guess the term I am striving for is "integration." It is this ability which has made this land of America, this land of enormous diversity, such a success. (No, it is not a perfect land, but there is no where else on earth that I would rather live.)

The negative experiences which my family experienced have probably been repeated in various forms by just about all of those who came to these shores as strangers. The will to survive, to succeed in the face of adversity were important qualities inherent in those who took their chances in the new world. Whatever instincts or personality traits that made them dare to, and then depart for the unknown, were probably what made so many succeed once they arrived. Great personal sacrifice and very hard work on the part of my mother and father for many years was what brought us finally to the farm and to, in my father's eyes, success.

The years passed by and as we grew up on the farm and attended school in New Paltz, we were developing both mentally and emotionally. We gained new and different insights. So, too, our parents were experiencing changes, but of much lesser proportions than we, their offspring. We were being molded by the dual and often conflicting information from home and school. They, meanwhile, had already been molded, their convictions hardened in trials by fire and pain. They had already made progress and learned to cope long before any of us had been born. Until now, all of it had been experienced in "old world" surroundings.

As one year led into the next, life on the farm continued and things improved financially. Prosperity brought even greater changes in our lives. Gradually, although steeped in things Sicilian, we were learning to be less so and more American. As such, we were interested in behaving the way our peers behaved. We dressed, talked, and even ate, "cosi 'Mericani" (things American). Our social life was more in tune with the "outside" world. When not under Papa's watchful eye, we often did not adhere totally to the restricted strata of Sicilian beliefs and mores (especially those we found meaningless and confining).

Of course, to a great degree, Papa still decided who, what, when, and how, but my siblings were maturing and were beginning to have definite ideas of their own. There were times he had to acquiesce to their requests. He did so grudgingly. My brothers and sister attended many outside activities and were interested in what took place in the community. At that particular time, in 1937, what was on everyone's tongue was, of course, the New York World's Fair. It was under construction somewhere in a place called Queens and it seemed to be the major topic of conversation of everyone, everywhere. The Fair was to open in 1939 with something called the Trylon and Perisphere as its logo and theme. "Such weird-looking shapes," crossed my mind the first time I saw a picture of the logo. I was seven years old at the time and highly impressionable. To me, from all the hoopla going on in newspapers, radio and newsreels, it appeared that the World's Fair was destined to be the most extraordinary and unique occurrence in the history of the world. Most incredible was its global premise. All the nations of the world would be gathered in one place to be viewed by the public. It seemed a difficult yet glorious achievement.

Years later, I learned that world fairs were not particularly uncommon, having occurred many times in Europe during earlier centuries. Thinking about it now, I realize how very much I had been influence by media hype. (Even then, it was pervasive!) Photos in newspapers of the "World of Tomorrow" depicted all sorts of highways sprouting up over other highways with streamlined bullet-shaped vehicles zooming about and planes soaring overhead! Those images made a lasting impression on me. That particular World's Fair will always be the one I most wanted to see. That I never got the chance to attend was one of the great disappointments of my early childhood. I promised myself that if and when the next fair arrived in New York City I would not miss it. Twenty-four years later, when the next world's fair arrived in New York City, I fulfilled that promise. In the second year of the fair, I packed up my mother (she, too, had missed the fair in 1939) and my two children, and took off. I was surprised and a bit disappointed at how commercial the whole thing appeared to me. My mother and my children thoroughly enjoyed it. Unfortunately, I suffered from a lasting sense of expectation from my childhood memories and probably no world's fair could ever satisfy what my imagination had conjured up and created those many years ago.

In 1939, World's Fair or no, life went on. And as it did each fall, apple picking season arrived. It was my favorite time of year, that time when summer seems reluctant to leave and crisply cool autumn nights give apples their blush. It was the time when the hot September sun plumps and forms the small, hard, green apples into large, juicy, luscious red or yellow fruit.

Early in September, as he did each year, my oldest brother Benny, drove down to the Bowery in Manhattan to pick up a load (sadly, that is how we referred to them) of "Bowery Bums" (today, lumped into a group, we call them "homeless"). Late in the afternoon he would return, the truck filled with about twenty men, of assorted ages and backgrounds. They would help harvest the apple crop. They were always white men. Never Black or Hispanic, ever. (Why? Perhaps there were none in the Bowery. I know that we felt no prejudice concerning race. Who knows?) The men had agreed to be paid a dollar a day (no work, no pay on Sunday) plus three meals a day with a clean bed to sleep in each night.

Even from this distant point in time, the memory still lingers of watching from behind one of the Greek columns of the front porch as my brother returned from the city. Across the street from the house, the large truck, enclosed on three sides, pulled into the barnyard and stopped. The men started jumping off the back even before it came to a complete halt. They had been riding for more than two hours on winding roads, in a cramped, hot, crowded space, probably seated on apple boxes. Many walked about stiffly at first. Some shook their legs or did deep knee bends. Others stretched or swung their arms. I tried to count them as they were hopping off, two and three at a time. I soon lost count as they milled about. Besides, they all looked alike and I became confused. Sighing, I shrugged my shoulders and thought, " More work! Phooie! Work, work, work!" For almost a week, Mama, Caroline, and I had been dusting beds, cleaning out, and airing the rooms in the two-story shack in the rear of the main house. It was some sort of house/barnlike building, but not like the huge cow barn, horse barn, or the chicken coops across the street.

Neither was it as big as the tenant house, down back (the one that Caroline had run to barefoot in the snow.)

Upstairs in this "barn" was a loft that could be reached by ladder-like stairs from the first floor. The loft had a wonderful smell of wood, pungent and rich that almost "attacked" my nostrils each time I clambered up to its warm and friendly space. To this day, I still enjoy the smell of old wood in attics, barns, or wherever. It was a delicious odor!

This barn was as much fun to play in and to explore as the woodshed had been. Somehow, I was always discovering what were, to me, extraordinary treasures: a tiny book tucked behind a beam, a small toy teacup in the corner of the room, or a torn coloring book, the pages brown with age. I surmised that this barn must have been the playhouse for the children of the former owner. The dimensions of the barn were modest, about fourteen by twenty feet and no more than sixteen feet to the peak of the roof.

There was even a small porch attached to the north side of the building; it was rustic and unpainted, just like the barn. The porch overlooked the valley and afforded a beautiful view of the mountains. It was a good place from which to view sunsets. Both the porch and barn shared one of the walls of the wide, thick, stone foundation which supported the building. Around back (the shack was on a steep slope), the stone foundation was open and formed a garage-like storage area.

Thus my favorite "play house" was now to serve as the sleeping quarters for the men who were, at this point, crossing the highway that separated house and barnyard. Watching from the porch of the main house, I stared at the men coming up the driveway. Benny was leading them. As they walked to the right of the house, heading toward the back building, some of them glanced up at the house and at me watching from the front porch. What they saw was the "boss's daughter"; a small, rather thin little girl with shoulder length black hair and large dark eyes, wearing a shirt that was much too big, with sleeves rolled up at the wrists. My shirt and baggy pants were those of my brother Joey. To keep the pants up, I had threaded a piece of clothes line through the belt loops and tied it in a simple knot. The legs of the pants were rolled up as well. Droopy socks and scruffy-looking sneakers completed my outfit. Certainly, I did not look like the daughter of the owner of this large and prosperous-looking farm.

I, in turn, saw a group of wretchedly dressed, unshaven, uncombed, scruffy-looking men. Most were carrying a small rag-covered bundle which I assumed held their only possessions. As I watched them file past, one man seemed to stand out from the crowd. He was taller than the others and, unlike the others, held his head high. His shoulders were straight and square and he walked with a spring to his step. The others seemed to just shuffle along, heads down.

His hair was a silvery white, thick, and straight. He looked directly at me as he passed. Our eyes met and locked briefly. I felt my face flush and looked away quickly. Rarely did I have the opportunity to look into the eyes of a strange man. It felt odd! I turned and ran into the house.

That night, Mama let me cook the main part of the apple pickers' first meal, hot dogs and beans. All I had to do was open many large cans of Campbell's pork and beans and cut up about four pounds of hot dogs into bite-sized pieces. Spreading them over the surface of the beans, which had filled three or four pans, they were then baked in a hot oven until the hot dogs were plump and brown. I was delighted to be cooking for so many people. It made me feel proud and very grownup. While the hot dogs cooked, a big kettle of potatoes simmered on the stove. When cooked, the potatoes would be mashed with lots of sweet butter and fresh whole milk and then laced with salt and pepper. A large salad plus many loaves of homemade Italian bread and gallons of cold, fresh milk completed the meal. You can be certain that the men consumed every morsel with gusto. Dessert was, what else? Jello! And apples, of course.

Lunch and dinner were cooked in the kitchen of the main house and then carried down to the summer kitchen. That is where the men were assigned to eat their meals. I noticed right away that the place had a very different "smell" when the apple pickers used it as compared to when the boarders were there. Each time I helped carry the food down to the kitchen, I was struck by this unusual and acrid smell. It was made up of stale cigarette smoke, mingled with fresh smoke, and the smell of beer emanating from discarded beer bottles sometimes strewn about the kitchen. Of course, there were also body odors, we supplied no showers or bathtubs.

The men were to cook their own breakfasts. The refrigerator and cabinets were generously stocked with food. We supplied them with eggs, bacon, coffee, milk, and, each day, freshly baked loaves of Italian bread. There were also boxes and boxes of Kellogg's Corn Flakes and Rice Crispies (I believe they were only 10 cents a box at that time. We purchased them by the case.)

The men took care of their personal grooming by taking turns washing at the kitchen sinks. They shaved there, as well, peering into an old cracked mirror. They used the back outhouse for a toilet. After a few weeks, the summer kitchen took on an even stronger smell. A combination not only of their usual smells, but also of poor housekeeping. (We cleaned and fumigated when they left.)

Although beer was kept in the refrigerator, Papa was adamant about drunkenness during work. Once, I saw my father smack the daylights out of one of the men who reported for work drunk. I remember feeling very sorry for the man. He must have felt totally humiliated to be slapped about in front of everyone. Those who drank, knew that if they broke the rules, they would be banished and would have to find their own way back to the city. Most of the men followed the rules in earnest.

On Saturday night, each man would be paid six dollars. They could then choose to ride into town in the back of the truck, with Benny at the wheel, or stay home. In town, they would wander at will, spending money as they saw fit. The *Daily News* was 2 cents, the Sunday newspaper 5 cents, a pack of cigarettes a nickel, spaghetti 10 cents a pound, steak 25 cents a pound. Candy bars were a nickel apiece. I have no idea how much a bottle of wine or whiskey was, but I am certain that six dollars could buy a lot of things.

Whether the men decided to shop, go to the movies, or visit a tavern, they would be picked up by Benny with the truck at a certain, designated hour and place and then returned to the farm. If they were not there on time, they would have to walk the three miles home. Few were ever late more than once.

Some men spent their entire pay at the bars in town; others hoarded their money and returned to the city at the end of the season with a nice sum. Occasionally, they stole from one another. Fights broke out and my father would verbally, sometimes physically, chastise the antagonists. The men feared him and rarely did those so chastised ever repeat their negative behavior.

After a week or so, I got to know all of the "bums" and discovered they were a pretty decent lot. From talking to my brothers, I found out that some of the men had been doctors, lawyers, teachers, cowboys, all sorts of exciting areas of work. After a while, some of them would come over after supper and sit around in the evening on the back porch and spin yarns. They would try to out-do one another telling tall tales. We children would all listen, mesmerized by them and their stories of far off places and adventures. One old man said he was once an Indian fighter and told us of his adventures as a cowboy and of encounters with Indians. From others, I learned about riddles and what the "comics" were. I had never known about *Dick Tracy*, *Little Orphan Annie* and *Blondie*, to name just a few. The "bums" were the first to introduce my family to newspapers and to brown coffee, we knew only black. The white-haired man I mentioned earlier was called Doc because at one time he had actually been a doctor. He was well-educated and spoke impeccably. He became my "favorite", mainly because often he would read the Sunday comics to me. Some Sunday mornings, he would have a bad hangover from the night before. Those times I sorely missed the readings. On sober Sundays, he would sometimes bring me candy bars-a double delight when combined with reading the comics. I found that I liked Doc better than my own father. It made me wonder if I was sinning by feeling this way and it filled me with guilt.

Almost all of our "Bowery bums" were alcoholics, of varying degrees, who had ended up on Skid Row. Happily for many, their stint on the farm picking apples was their road to recovery. Some actually "dried out" while they were with us.

Now and then, one or two would stay on after apple picking season ended. They would become permanent hired hands. While most turned out well, one, named Slim, did not. Close to my brothers in age, he was befriended by them. Having no kin, he had traveled a lot in his teens. His worldliness fascinated my brothers, who, at that age, had never been further than New York City. When apple season ended, Slim was invited to move into the big house; we "sort of" adopted him. He became a part of our family, sharing my brothers' bedroom, eating with us and going everywhere that we went. For two years he was an important part of our lives. Just before Christmas, one crystal-clear winter night he took off, never to be seen again. With him went $180, stolen from a dresser drawer in my brothers' room. Money they had earned, on their own time off, packing apples at 10 cents a box. They were devastated and not just from the loss of money. It was an early and dramatic lesson on human frailty and deviousness.

I never could take to Slim and disliked him from the moment he entered our lives. Over six feet tall, he was extremely thin, and had stringy, dirty-blonde hair. Although he had pleasant features and could even be called good-looking, those of his teeth that were not brown with rot, were green. When he stooped over in order to talk to me, his face close to mine, I could smell him; reeking of cigarettes and that same strange smell, like that of the "bums." Some of his fingers were brown with nicotine stains and his fingernails were bitten down to the quick. As I write this, I can still see those hands, soft looking, flabby white hands, disfigured ridges where his nails should be. Long, boneless-looking fingers. Ugly red palms. When he smiled and looked into my eyes, it made me uncomfortable. Despite my fondness for blue eyes, his did nothing for me.

I avoided him and made sure that I was never alone in his company. Once, when I had finished feeding the chickens, he called to me from inside the horse-barn. "Hey, Sadie. C'mon in here. I got somthin' I wanna show ya'." The barnyard was deserted. I remembered Mama's warnings.

"I gotta set the table!" I hollered. Dropping the empty chicken feed pail near the coop, I ran home as fast as I could.

Our house was about a half mile from the tracks of a freight train. Hobos, riding the rails, often hopped off the train and making their way up the hill to our farm, would ask for a day's work in exchange for a meal. My father always accommodated them. One cold winter's night, just after Christmas, there was a firm, loud knock on our kitchen door. The pot-bellied coal stove was glowing, its belly part a soft, dull, red. We were all seated around it, eating baked sweet potatoes, out of hand, which had been cooked on the top section of the stove. The radio was tuned to *Jack Benny*. He was arguing with "Rochester" and we were roaring with laughter. Since it was well after nine o'clock, Papa answered the knock.

The light from the open kitchen door fell on a tall, well-built man, standing on the stoop. He had straight black hair. It fell over one eye like the wing of a raven. Dressed in clean but shabby clothes, he stood straight and proud looking squarely at Papa. Papa, taken back a bit at the man's dignified stance asked, "Yessa! Watta you want?"

Through chattering teeth he said, "G-G-Good evening, sir. Here's mm-my pipe, t-t-tobacco, and matches. C-C-Could I p-p-please sleep in your b-b-barn tonight? It's m-mighty c-c-cold out."

My father stood a moment, carefully sizing up the man. "No. No! You no canna sleep ina my barn. (a pause ensued) No. Buta you canna come ina da house ana we talk. Iffa you gonna sleep enyplace, thena you canna sleep witha my sons in they bedaroom. It'sa too colda fa you to be inna da barn. You no animale. *Traci, traci, che troppo freddo.*" (Enter, enter, it is too cold.) Thus, did our family meet Joe Landis, the most fondly remembered of all our hired hands (aside from Carl). To be sure, when papa told him in Italian that it was cold, the man did not understand. That didn't bother Papa, it's just that sometimes he forgot, and spoke "half and half."

Joe was knowledgeable and a hard worker who stayed on with us for more than a year. From him, we learned even more "American" ways; buttered toast, buttered bread, gravy and pot roasts, aftershave lotion and Brilliantine, Band-Aids, peroxide and Kleenex, Campbell's tomato soup, poker and craps, *Life Magazine, The Saturday Evening Post,* and lots of other "neat" things. He could also chew razor blades and shards of broken light bulbs and swallow them! (He had been a carnival worker.) A fascinating man, he left us only to rejoin the Army Air Corps when the war broke out. He had once been an air force pilot and because, on a dare, he had flown his plane beneath the George Washington Bridge, he had been dishonorably discharged from the service. From then on, it was all downhill until he came to our farm. Because of the war, the army reinstated him. Since he was older than the accepted age of pilots, he became a flight instructor.

One bright fall day, when the war was over, a bus stopped on the highway in front of the farm. A smart-looking man in a uniform with a trench coat over his arm alighted. It was our Joe, back to see us and thank us for giving him another chance. His life had finally turned out well and we were all happy for him.

Those men who stopped by our farm for food or work and those men from the Bowery, all shared in shaping our view of the world. Everything does, I guess. I remember reading somewhere: "We are the sum total of all we experience." Looking back, it is clear that besides the hobos and bums, the teachers, the Yankees, the boarders, the hunters, and much of the other hired help that came into our lives, all of them, in one way or another, enriched, changed and increased our understanding. They added to our appreciation not only of ourselves but of the human condition. Remembering the pain and prejudice we had experienced as outsiders, we learned to treat others as decently as possible, regardless of color, age, or position in life. Those early years on the farm were a rich texture of experiences that were woven into a cloth of life; one that covered us, shielded us, and comforted us for many, many years to come.

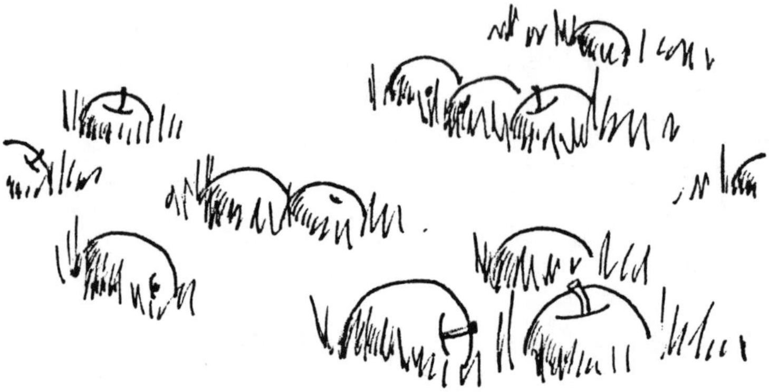

chapter 24

The Prom

Caroline suffered more of the pain and frustration of growing up Sicilian and female than I. She, for whatever reason, bore more of the brunt of Papa's wrath and anger. Maybe it was the result of her, his second born, being a girl instead of the boy he wanted. Perhaps she, more strong-headed than I, invited his wrath more often. Perhaps it was because he had less control over my teen years (he died in my seventeenth year after a three year illness.) Regardless of the reasons, my sister was a classic example of the ordeal of growing up Sicilian and female.

It was May, prom time in high schools across the country. Caroline was now a sophomore. One day, her friend, Louie Schaffert asked her to go to the prom with him (the prom was not limited to Juniors only in our school). She was delighted and elated, but at the same time apprehensive. Knowing Papa, she was certain that he would not allow her to go. However, she decided to risk asking him anyway. That evening she waited until he had finished supper and was having the last of his bottle of wine. We children had learned a long time ago that he was most mellow at that time and more amenable to suggestions or requests.

She went to where he sat and said quietly, "Papa?" She waited, eyes downcast, trembling with apprehension and waiting to be acknowledged. Papa, slouched comfortably in his chair, puffing on a DiNobili cigar, looked at her suspiciously through squinting eyes.

"Si, che voi?" (Yes, what do you want?)

She took a deep breath and swallowed nervously. It took much courage to ask for permission to go to a dance. Doing so indicated that she had talked to a boy, and for this alone she could be punished. Further, she could incur a beating for merely *asking* to go to a dance accompanied by a boy. This, despite the fact that she was in her mid-teens.

She stared directly at him. Their eyes were almost level with each other. He, being seated, had to look up ever so slightly. The words came pouring out in Sicilian. (She wanted to be sure he understood perfectly!) She had rehearsed what she was about to say and it all came out in a rush. "Papa, in school they have a big dance every year. It's a very special dance and all the teachers and the principal and some of the parents, even, are there and everybody wears really pretty clothes and the girls wear long dresses and a corsage of flowers and there's music and it's all decorated so pretty and oh, Papa, can I go?" Heart beating, she paused to take a breath. Swallowing hard, she took another deep breath and continued, " Louis Schaffert asked me to go. YOU know Mr. Schaffert? Louis' father? Remember him? The short man with red hair and a moustache. He came and bought apples and grapes last fall and you talked to him a long time, remember? Oh, Papa, please, I'll work extra hard and do anything you ask me, but please, oh Papa, please can I go?"

Papa's large brown eyes, no longer merely squinting, now looked almost like slits. Peering at his elder daughter standing there, he could see that she was trembling. Smiling a tiny smile, he thought of how very much like himself she was- tough and quick to anger, seemingly afraid of no one. She accepted discipline or direction only from him. Although it sometimes bothered him to be so, he learned that he had to be very hard on her because she was so strong willed. She had to learn discipline and only harsh measures could contain her.

Although suffering numerous beatings, never would she yield or be compliant if her principles were challenged. In many ways stronger than her brothers, she was just the opposite of her baby sister who was totally obedient.

Yes, his Caroline was strong and willful, but she was a good daughter and a hard worker. He paused, relishing this moment of power. He stared directly into her eyes, his no longer narrowed. Now they were wide-open and questioning. Knowing she was nervously waiting for his answer and that her happiness or disappointment lay solely in his hands, with no show of emotion on his face he said, *"Io non saccio stu picchot'o maccarri so patre. Justu perch'iddu s'acatatu la fruita mia, Io l'o fare gierri a nu ballo cu te?"* (I do not know this boy, or even his father. Just because he come an' buy fruit from me, I gotta let you go to a dance with his son?) *"Che si, pazza?"* (What are you, crazy?) *"Per quanto tempo la'conoscutu?"* (How long have you known him?) *"Idd' ave nu carru?"* (Has he got a car?) *"Dimi, cu uave cacciarri lu carru, idd'o so papa?"* (Who will drive the car, him or his father?)

Answering strongly in Sicilian, Caroline said *"Iddu e 'nda la classa mia. E uno picchoto cuieto. Siamo amici. Non av' altri amici femini. Percisso m'aspiatt' a mia. Perch'io non aiuo un amico. Non sachio cu ave cacciari lo carru, ma iddu av' uno."* (He's in my class, Papa, and he's a nice quiet boy. We're friends. He doesn't have a girlfriend and so he asked me since I don't have a boyfriend and I don't know who'll drive, but he does have a car.)

Papa gazed down into his wine glass. It was almost empty. He motioned to her and she quickly reached over and refilled it, using the last of the wine to do so. He picked up the full glass, took a long sip and then put the glass down. Arms akimbo, still slouched in his chair, again he stared directly into her eyes. His deep, brown eyes suddenly looked black to Caroline and she could never before remember seeing them look so dark and piercing. For a moment, she did not know whether he was going to jump up from the chair and slap her for daring to make such a request or if he would simply nod and smile and say yes.

Papa, sensing her uneasiness, was enjoying his little game. It was not often that this daughter came before him with a request of such obvious importance to her. "Whatta you say ifa I say yes?"

"Oh, Papa, I would be so happy..." she started toward him to hug him and thank him but he put up his hand to stop her.

"Whoa! Whatta if I say no?" She froze in place just a few inches away from him. Their eyes were locked together almost in combat, her brown eyes now almost as black as his. She said not a word, but her eyes never wavered. She continued to stare at him. It was only for a few moments, but it seemed an eternity as they both stared intently at one another, signals and feelings flashing back and forth.

Looking up and away for a moment, Papa grinned, shook his head and said, *"Basta! Si! Che po gierri."* (Enough! Yes, you may go) "Ana no hugga me o' tanka me, justa, *va, vatinni, lasciami.*" (Go, get going, leave me) "Go 'way 'n no bodder me no more!" Caroline grinned a broad grin of happiness and triumph. Papa grinned back. Teeth flashing, she turned quickly to run off and share the good news with Mama.

With that hurdle cleared, now the important part began. The making of the prom dress. The prom was a month away. Soon it seemed to me that every free waking moment of the women in our house was spent on "THE DRESS." Designing it, making a pattern, choosing the material, cutting, fitting it, and finally, sewing it.

My part in the project was to make drawings of one design after another. Caroline described and I drew, amazed and delighted over the variations she ceaselessly invented. After many sketches, adjustments, and changes of sleeves, bodice, neckline, and belt, at last, she was satisfied.

The final design was a floor-length, white organdy gown, printed all over with tiny navy blue polka dots. It would have a sweetheart neckline, shirred at the bosom, full, but short puffed sleeves, and a three-inch flounce at the bottom hem of the skirt. A one inch, navy blue velvet ribbon would serve as a belt. It would be tied in the back, in a bow with long streamers, ending halfway down the skirt. A matching, thin, shoestring velvet ribbon tied around her neck, ending in a tiny bow at her throat, would take the place of a necklace. Caroline decided that since she owned no jewelry and did not want to wear Mama's fake pearl necklace, the ribbon around her neck would be just fine. She decided also there would be no earrings.

Just two days before the prom, the dress was finally completed. It was beautiful! Mama had outdone herself in this labor of love and we were certain that this dress would be the loveliest at the prom. A born romantic, Mama seemed more excited about the prom than Caroline. In Mama's small village in Sicily, there had never been anything like a prom. Even if there had been, there was no money to waste on such foolishness. To Mama, it seemed almost a royal affair, what with floor-length dresses and corsages. She whistled constantly as she fitted and sewed the dress to fit my sister's sturdy frame.

The day of the prom finally arrived. There was a feeling of electricity in the air. An air of expectancy lay so strongly over the house that it was palpable. As Caroline did her chores that day they seemed endless. She couldn't wait until 4:30 to arrive so she could leave her work and start getting ready. Louis was to pick her up at 6 o'clock. I was every bit as excited about the prom as Caroline and Mama. The dress had turned out even more beautifully than I had imagined. I couldn't wait to see my sister in it. Caroline was taking hours to bathe and do her nails and get ready.

Finally, it came time for Louis to arrive. He would fetch Caroline and whisk her off to that magical place–the prom. The family gathered at the foot of the long, beautiful stairway and waited for her to descend. Barely able to contain my excitement, I was hopping up and down. My father told me, in rich Sicilian, to cut it out or he'd smack me. It took me a moment to calm down, but I stopped completely when I heard the floor boards of the upstairs hall creak as Caroline walked out of her room and headed for the stairs. We all stood waiting, almost transfixed, listening as we heard her footsteps descending the first set of stairs. Soon, they could be heard on the rose-window landing. She rounded the corner and started down the main staircase. There was utter silence.

With one beautifully manicured hand she was holding up the front of her gown slightly. The lace of her petticoat peeped out from beneath the flounce. Her other hand was on the bannister to help her balance on the unfamiliar and delicate high heels that matched the white of her dress. Slowly, she descended, smiling at all of us waiting below.

Who was this lovely person? Could it possibly be that tough tomboy who wore her brother's clothing? Clothing that was miles too big for her and that made her look like a vagrant as she ran about the farm. Could it be that tomboy who shoveled manure and milked cows and took cars apart. It couldn't be that rough, sharp-tongued person who would not hesitate to argue or fight with anyone twice her size. Somehow, something magical had to have happened to transform that rough, unyielding person into this exquisite, soft, feminine creature floating down the stairs of the huge hallway. She was so lovely! When she paused, a few steps up from the bottom of the stairs, everyone held their breath.

Suddenly, from the silence came the sound of someone clearing his throat. Now, all eyes were on Papa! It was he who had cleared his throat, not once but twice. We all watched as a strange expression came over his face, one his family had never before seen. He stared at his daughter. His eyes glistened and he swallowed hard a few times. Now, there was even more of a hush. Caroline and Papa stared at one another. Time seemed to stop. Then Caroline, still looking directly at Papa, smiled a heart-breaking and beautiful smile. She felt so grateful that he was allowing her to go to the prom. At that moment, she was filled with happiness and love for everyone. She felt especially warm toward Papa.

Upon seeing her smile, a soft, red flush started at his neck and slowly crept up past his cheeks. Soon his whole face had turned red. The veins in his temple stood out. The day-old stubble of beard made his face look almost malevolent. At the same time, he appeared anguished. Gazing at his daughter, he gasped as if in pain... then he blurted out, "*YOU NO GO!*"

There was a collective gasp, then stunned silence as his words fell upon us. No longer flushed, his face had turned an ashen color. He looked about and there was thunder in his eyes. The stubble of his beard now looked blue-black and ominous. He stamped his foot and repeated, "YOU NO GO!" Turning quickly, he stalked out of the hall, headed for the familiar comfort of his favorite chair on the back porch. The same chair from which he had given Caroline permission to go.

Dazed, those of us left behind could neither move nor speak. Papa had done some really cruel things in the past, but nothing seemed as heartless, as unfair as this. It was unreal. We were stunned! Looking in disbelief at each other, we knew we were helpless to change anything. Papa had spoken and his word was law. There was no recourse. Tears and imprecations did not move him. This outburst had been like no other. Therefore, no one dared approach him to try to change his mind.

Caroline stood frozen and expressionless. It was almost as if she had expected this to happen. It was just one more terribly unjust thing over which she had no control and which she had to accept. She accepted it stoically. She had listened all her life to "*Coraggio, figlia mia.*" (Courage, my daughter.) It is what Mama had drummed into her head, just as she had drummed into mine "*Pazienzia, figlia mia.*" (Patience, my daughter.)

Caroline and I have puzzled over why Mama drummed two such different phrases into our heads. I suppose Mama, because of our personality differences, was intuitively preparing us for what she assumed each of us would have to cope with in the future. As I look back now, how very right she was!

My father's actions that night crushed me. Me? All of us!! Nothing he had done before seemed so totally unjust. It was my first major experience with gross, inexplicable inequity and while..."I was not," at that moment, "standing at the end of the world, I felt that I could surely see it." It yawned wide and deep. An abyss.

Caroline was devastated. Utterly so! Especially when Louis arrived and she had to explain what had happened. She was utterly mortified to know that he, too, now had to suffer her disappointment. That Papa had punished him also, for no reason. At first, he could not believe what had happened. The tuxedo, the corsage, the expectancy of a joyous, fun-filled evening was all for naught. The capricious actions of the father of this strange family was alien to him. He could not, in his wildest imaginings, see his father acting this way. No explanation. Nothing!!

Caroline shed not a tear. However, her face was a deep pink and she had two bright red spots on her cheeks as she explained to Louis the futility of trying to talk to Papa or to change his mind.

"No, Louis, even if your father came to talk to him, it would do no good. I'm so very, very sorry that I have spoiled your evening. I'll never forgive myself for saying yes when you asked me." A long pause ensued. "*I should have known better!*"

This last sentence was spat out with such venom and rage that Louis reddened, surprised at the ferociousness of her anger. He, however, was almost as angry as she was concerning her father's unfair stance.

Late that night, I was awakened by muffled, heart wrenching sobs coming from Caroline's room next door. It sounded like she was crying into a pillow so no one would hear her. I lay in the darkness, wide awake, listening, eyes wide open. My heart was thumping and seemed to turn over inside of my chest as I heard my sister, always so strong and brave, now crying as if her heart would break. Hearing her cry, made me cry too. I cried not only over my sister's heartache, but because I was certain that I, too, would have to experience the same kind of anguish; the same kind of cruelty as I grew older and entered my teen years.

Again, and as usual, the next day, life resumed as if nothing had happened. No tears, no recriminations. No one dared! Now, however, I noticed there seemed to be a new set to Caroline's mouth and jaw. The young-girl softness of her face gave way almost overnight. There was a different look, imperceptible to most, but obvious to my loving eyes. My big sister had changed and somehow I felt she would never again be the same.

In the days that followed, Caroline seemed to have some hidden agenda moving her. Actually, she was making plans. She was planning and working toward the day when she could run away from home. Anything, she felt, would be better than to stay under the roof of that cruel, uncompromising, unfeeling person we called Papa.

All of us have our dreams and they often shape our perceptions far more than reality. Caroline was no different. Her dreams of a family were shaped by the "Andy Hardy" series of movies with Mickey Rooney and Judy Garland. Those movies seduced her and made her long for the dream world depicted on the screen. Reality was far too treacherous and, unfortunately, infinitely more disappointing than if those dreams had not seduced her in the first place. Growing up Sicilian and female was difficult enough without having to compare everyday reality with make believe. Certainly, the pain Caroline endured from the disappointment of prom night cannot be excused away. It was cruel and unfair and Caroline had every right to be bitter and angry about it. However, life hands us many situations and how we cope with them, determines the quality of our life and our state of mental health. Somewhere, I have read that sociologists believe that the younger we are when we learn to cope with problems, the better we can handle them when we reach maturity. I don't know if that is so, but I like to believe it is.

So, perhaps before we judge this particular Sicilian father too harshly, we must keep in mind his perceptions as well. Upon seeing the womanly beauty of his daughter for the first time, he suddenly feared for her. He might have found it difficult to believe that she could leave the house looking so beautiful and not have some awful encounter with some savage man who could not help himself. No, I am not making excuses for him, but I think that now I know where he was coming from. It was from a different place, alien from that of the rest of us. We must also keep in sight the result of his harsh disciplinary measures and actions. In his own odd way, accidentally or on purpose, he was giving his children strength of character. You laugh? "But at what cost?" you say. Who can say? Inadvertently, it just might be that his firm, disciplinary measures helped us develop strength of character. A strength that enabled us to adjust to and face the reality of life in a strong, healthy, and honest way. "Those experiences that do not destroy us, make us strong." *Vero!* (True!) Papa did his best. It was the only thing he could do.

chapter 25

War and Leaving

*I*t was September of 1941. That September day in 1937 when I had started school now seemed a million years away. There was no more pejorative name calling. The war in Europe, though I did not understand why, helped the farm to prosper. There was lots of money for new, store-bought clothes, fancier indoor plumbing, and even central heating. We had cars and trucks and all kinds of farm machinery. The horses were gone, except for Billy who was kept on only for horseback riding.

Civilization or, more probably, "Americanization" had arrived almost with a vengeance and had engulfed my Sicilian family. In reality, we had finally learned to emulate what we saw, thereby adapting to and enjoying a better life-style. Autumn came and went, as did apple picking season. So many things had happened since last winter. It had been an exciting and different kind of year. I could not remember another even remotely like it.

Winter was settling in and the house was readied for that pale, cold time of year when the earth was naked and exposed. Soon winter winds would howl over the empty meadows. The snow would be piled so high, that I would walk through what

seemed to me cavernous tunnels, formed as my brothers
shoveled paths to the barn and to the wood shed. I looked
forward to Christmas, but little else about the coming season.

It was a Sunday evening early in December and the family
had been working at full throttle for the entire day. Animals
take no time out from eating and drinking. Eggs had to be
gathered, barns shoveled clean, and cows had to be milked.
Farming is a seven-day-a-week job with no vacations or days
off. Papa always refused to recognize Sunday as a day of rest;
but what choice did he have?

The supper dishes had been washed and put away and
Caroline and I wearily headed up the stairs to our rooms.
It was my sister's custom on Sunday night to tune into "The
Edgar Bergen, Charlie McCarthy Show" and to write down
some of Charlie's jokes. She incorporated them into her routine
with her dummy, Tommy.

Caroline listened to the radio while sitting up in bed, so
she could write on her pad, her head and shoulders propped
up comfortably on two pillows. I sat on the floor, on a throw
rug, my back leaning against the bed. To my immediate right
was a night stand, on top of which was a small radio. We
listened and laughed heartily as Charlie McCarthy and
Mortimer Snerd, his loutish cousin from the farm, traded
insults. Chuckling at the humor, Caroline was writing away
as fast as she could. During a commercial for Chase and
Sanborn coffee, she said, "Sadie, go get me some grapes and
apples."

"Gee whiz, do I have to? You know how much I hate to
go down to the cellar. 'N anyway, it's three flights down. Can't
I getcha something from the kitchen instead?"

Caroline fixed me with a stare, frowning. Her eyebrows
drawn together, her eyes narrowed. With an edge of annoyance
in her voice she said, "You heard me! GIT!"

When Caroline looked at me like that and used that particular
tone, I knew enough to quickly obey and not argue. I raised
myself up off the floor and ran to do her bidding. In no time
at all, I was back. The dark cellar still gave me creepy feelings
even though I was older and knew there was nothing hiding
down there that would attack me. Still, the gloomy darkness

of the place always made me want to avoid it as much as possible.

Since there were no apple storage "coolers" in the area, Papa stockpiled apples and grapes in the enormous cellar. I presume that the cool, damp air down there helped to preserve them. Being able to store freshly picked fruit for a while meant that it would not all have to be taken to market at the same time. If a farmer could store some or all of his crop for a few weeks longer than others who took their produce to market at its peak, often the prices improved. Any farmer who had viable fruit, when others did not, was bound to improve his profits.

Returning from the cellar, I reached the top of the stairs and was approaching Caroline's room when I heard her shout outloud and in great surprise, "What? What? It can't be!" From the tone of her voice, I was sure something terrible had just been reported. I rushed in carrying the apples and grapes, my mouth open and ready to ask "What happened?" My sister, frowning in deep concentration, put her forefinger to her lips, "SHHHHH!" motioning to me to be quiet and listen. An announcer was saying, "We repeat this emergency bulletin. The Japanese have bombed Pearl Harbor! Please stay tuned for further information."

Caroline had her ear close to the radio. She was breathing hard and listening intently. It scared me to see the look on her face. She looked pale, stunned, and devoid of all expression. Somehow I got the feeling that someone had taken a magic cloth and wiped all the feelings off my sister's face. As the announcer gave out more information, suddenly, as if someone had pulled a chain and the lights went on, her face changed again. She flushed a deep rose color and then said in a very strange, low voice, almost a whisper, "WAR, we're at WAR! OH MY GOD! We're at WAR!"

I could feel a puzzled frown on my own face as I squinted at Caroline, my brow wrinkled, my eyes almost slits with trying to concentrate and make sense of what was going on. Caroline's face was a study in consternation. Her eyebrows were drawn together and her eyes shifted from side to side. Never before had I seen my sister so agitated. I looked around for a place to put the fruit and then decided to put them on the night stand, next to the radio. She did not notice.

From time to time in my young life, I had often heard adults mention something called "World War I." But it always sounded more like a story someone made up, one that had happened a very long time ago. It seemed far fetched, not real. I always got the feeling that war was actually like what happened in the movies. And war movies were awful. It seemed difficult to believe that grown men would actually go around shooting, killing, and bombing each other in such great numbers. Mama had tried to explain to me what the First World War was, but obviously had not succeeded in making me understand. (It all seemed so far away and not of any concern to me). But for now, I was worrying about my sister. Her face was still very pale and she was listening intently to the radio. Within a very short while, another urgent announcement was heard. We each held our breath so as not to miss a word.

"For those of you who have not heard the announcement, we repeat that early this morning, Pacific Time, the Japanese bombed Pearl Harbor. Many aircraft carriers and planes have been destroyed by this sneak attack and hundreds of American soldiers have been killed and wounded. Numbers are not available at this time. Please stay tuned for further information."

I do not recall whether or not the Charlie McCarthy show resumed. After we had heard the first announcements we stayed glued to the radio afraid we might miss something. During the first commercial (and there were far, far fewer in those days) Caroline hopped off the bed and ran downstairs to see if the rest of the family had heard the news. Frightened, I followed quickly behind. Heck, maybe those Japanese would come over tonight and bomb us too! When we reached the living room, we found the rest of the family gathered closely around the floor model Philco radio; the one with the magic green eye in the middle. So intent were they on what was being announced, that they did not even notice us when we entered. I cannot remember precisely when, but sometime during that evening, or maybe even the next day, we heard the familiar clipped syllables of President Roosevelt. Most of his speech was incomprehensible to me. However, I distinctly remember his opening words, "Today is a day that will live in infamy!"

"What's infamy?"

"SHHHHH!!!" Angry looks of annoyance were sent my way. This speech was definitely not one of his famous "fireside chats."

During that moment, with the fear of impending doom practically smothering us, the entire family huddled close to the radio, listening intently. Not only could we hear better, it probably made us all feel connected to something. It gave us something to hold on to–a feeling of oneness with the rest of the nation. Our country was seriously threatened, but we knew we were not alone. We were all in this together, sharing surprise and anguish, sharing fear and frustration. Just as television has made the world, in our time (to quote McLuhan), a "global village", so too radio, at that time, had the capability of binding the entire country together from east to west and from north to south.

Each person in the room was reacting to the news in basically the same way, surprise and shock. And why not? To face so abruptly the stark reality of war, perpetrated in such an unexpected, devious, and destructive way during a time of beginning prosperity and peace in America must have been devastating. (The war that was raging in Europe did not concern us much. It seemed removed from everyday life. Now, however, WE were at WAR!)

Very little was said. Just hushed "My Gods!" "Ohs?" and "Whews" during the announcements. Much later that night, silently, one by one and two by two, we all went off to bed. The enormity of it all took a while to be absorbed and as I followed my sister back up the stairs to the bedroom, the pit of my stomach felt funny. Fleetingly, I wondered why my stomach and not my heart or head should feel so very bad over war.

After the initial shock, life resumed as usual. Meanwhile, "who would go off to war and when" was the topic of concern and of much discussion. Of the boys, only Benny was of draft age. Papa was deeply concerned about him. Despite all the concern, the declaration of war did not really change our lives. At least not right away.

Actually, the first noticeable change was that for the first time, there seemed to be much more news on the radio. Miles from the battles, safe on the farm, to my siblings and me, after a while, the steady stream of news presentations became a boring interruption, an annoyance. Prior to war-time, uninterrupted music could be heard on the radio for hours on end. Now there were many bulletins and announcements about the war stressing that now the entire world was embroiled. Most of the reports concerned battles on land and sea, aerial dog fights, and bombings of cities and islands. War seemed to be the only topic of conversation when adults got together. The newspapers were filled with big screaming headlines about what was happening, not only in Europe, but in the Far East, the Near East, and Russia. Since I was so young, to me it was all just words; words from which I could not escape. I heard them say that prior to this attack, the war had been confined to only Europe. But now, America was at war too and the "Allies" were pitted against the "Nazis", the "Fascists", and the "Japs." It was a terrible time.

So many men were dying on land, on sea, and in the air. So many innocent children and adults were being killed in the bombings. There was mass slaughter, or so it seemed. There was hunger and privation. Here, in America, children were told endlessly to clean their plates since the children of Europe had no food and we should not waste what we had. At the movies, during the newsreel portion and *The March of Time*, the depiction of starving people and the battles overseas made it all more real. Besides newspaper photos and reports, *Life Magazine* had a great impact with its photos of the war dead and the devastation of the bombing raids. It was all too terrible to even think about. A blanket of sorrow covered the earth and only its edges touched America.

What I recall personally and most about the war was that we had black-outs, rationing of food and gas, and people searching the skies at night for enemy aircraft. Caroline became an "air-raid warden" and spent a few evenings a week watching the skies during those black-outs. It was all very scary for a ten year old child, who didn't really understand what was really happening.

A few months after the war had started, I began to notice more of a change in Caroline. She had turned eighteen in April. To my knowing eyes, she now seemed different in a way I could not explain. Her face had taken on an inscrutable expression and there was frequently a strange kind of look in her eyes. On many a warm April evening, while a chorus of peepers rose up from the meadow, Caroline, sitting on the stairs of the back porch, would stare for hours at the far off, deep-purple Shawangunk Mountains. I, seated at her feet on a lower step of the porch, staring at the same mountains, wondered where her thoughts were taking her.

Ever since the ill-fated incident with the Junior Prom, she had not been the same. She seemed to be biding her time, waiting. For what? I could only guess. Somehow, the start of the war had accelerated change. I had the distinct feeling that my sister was getting herself ready to make a final move of some sort. I was reminded that for almost as long as I could remember, Caroline had always spoken of "running away." Each time she talked about it, it upset me. The thought of not having my sister around was painful and whenever the possibility of it entered my mind, I tried to push it away. Anyhow, to me, running away seemed like an absurd thing to do. Whenever I gave it any thought at all, I would wonder to myself, "Where would I run to?" I only knew of New Paltz, Kingston, Newburgh, and New York City. I could not imagine being in those places or ANYWHERE without Mama or my family around me. No! "Running away" was something I could not even contemplate. Besides, I figured, if I ever ran away, it would be such a "disgrace" that Papa would never forgive me. I could never come home again. Not being able to come home again was the most awful thing I could imagine! Even at his worst, Papa was better than the mysterious unknown "out there."

I was unaware of it, but time and nature were at work. Both of them would soon be changing my life. Most of us follow a certain day-by-day pattern. Usually it is a comfortable, if not always pleasant groove. We get used to a certain way of living, attuned to some internal schedule. Life then slips by, minute by minute, hour upon hour, day in, day out. So imperceptibly, we are hardly aware of it. The same things happen over and over, with just enough small, sometimes big surprises to make life interesting. Then, one day, or year, or month when a monumental event takes place, it makes you ponder life and those experiences that alter and transform the way you perceive the world.

One of those "monumental" events happened on a Sunday about a month after I had noticed the obvious change in my sister. I was coming out of the front door of the house when I heard loud, angry voices outside and a car motor running. The voices were those of Caroline and my father. I ran down the steps, looked down the driveway, and there they were, standing next to Caroline's English Austin. Papa was obviously furious and was shouting and cursing very loudly. He was raising his hands in a threatening way. By the tone of his voice and by his actions, he looked and sounded like he was getting ready to assault Caroline. It looked like she was in for the beating of her life! But when I looked to see her response, to my complete astonishment, she was shouting back! (My God, she was brave!) Her shouts were equally loud and her raised hands were equally threatening. Raised hands?? I was dumbstruck!! It was unheard of to answer Papa back. To raise your hands to him was suicidal!

In the midst of the argument, Caroline leaned over and picked up a suitcase that was on the ground next to her. Quickly, she opened her car door, threw in the suitcase and jumped in. Papa, shouting invectives and livid with rage, jumped on the running board and was reaching through the open window. (Trying to turn off the key, I suppose.) He was seething with anger and wanted desperately to stop her. She was not to be stopped! With Papa clinging to the door and balancing on the running board, the car took off, careening down the driveway. Papa, still raging at Caroline, hung on precariously with one hand and was desperately trying to turn off the key with the other.

Halfway down the driveway, Caroline's hand darted out of the open window. She gave Papa a strong push. He went flying off the car, rolled over a few times and then came to an ignominious and sudden halt on the lawn. The car sped on down the driveway, paused at the state road, turned right and drove off at full speed, southbound toward New York City.

At first, I stood petrified with fear, appalled at what had just taken place. Where *did* Caroline get all that courage? I trembled with fear, positive that Papa would NEVER forgive Caroline for pushing him off of her car. He would NEVER forgive her for disobeying him. She would probably NEVER be able to come home again for as long as she lived. Tears filled my eyes as I thought about the fact that I might never see my sister again for as long as I lived. I didn't even get to say goodbye!

First the war, now this! I was filled with apprehension, not sure how to respond to what had just happened. I knew, however, that I had better keep out of Papa's way. He was probably in such a rage because of what Caroline had just done, that he might now vent his anger on me! I watched as he slowly started to get up off the ground. He looked somewhat dazed. Before he could see me, however, I turned and ran as quickly as possible back into the house and up to the sanctuary of my room. The moment I got there, I wanted to run and hide under the bed, to feel the comfort of the dark intimacy beneath the dusty springs and the mattress. The thought struck me that I was too big to do that anymore. So, instead, I threw myself on top of the bed and stared up at the ceiling, waiting fearfully for the sound of Papa summoning me.

I lay there and waited. And waited. Many thoughts crowded my mind. Over and over, I reminded myself that now my sister was gone and I would never, never see her again. I cried as I thought of how very much I would miss her. A heavy leaden feeling enveloped me. I felt as if someone had just told me that she was dead. I was in mourning. Life without my sister seemed inconceivable to me. I ran to the bathroom for a towel. (We could not afford kleenex back then) I sobbed and sobbed. Somehow, the longer I cried, the harder I cried. Some of those tears were tears of self-pity, for now I would have that much more work to do. There would be no big sister to help me when I needed help. No big sister around to treat me like the much loved kid sister in the family. Now I was even going to have to take my sister's place, to some degree. I knew in my bones that I could never be, for the family, what my sister had been. I also felt strongly that my world would never again be the same. I had a lot more work ahead of me and a lot of growing up to do. After a while, I calmed down somewhat, but I sat on my bed and cried quietly for a long time that day. Papa never did call me down.

During supper time that night, he ranted and raved and carried on. He blamed Caroline's behavior on Mama, on Benny, on Frankie and Joey, on the war, on the boarders, on school! He even pointed his finger at me and raged. We sat and ate quietly and let him vent his anger and frustration. He consumed an extra bottle of wine that evening and went to bed earlier than usual, kicking a wall and some chairs on the way. We all were very sad. Mama cried a lot.

The seasons changed and the pattern of life continued. In early winter, Mama heard from Caroline. She telephoned and said she had gotten a basement apartment in Queens, in the home of the Ciccarellos (one of the families who had boarded at the farm during past summers). She was working some small night clubs in New York City with Tommy and was making enough money to pay her rent and still have enough left over to live rather nicely. She even sent money home to Mama. Whenever my mother asked her over the telephone when she was coming home, Caroline was adamant. She swore she never would and wanted nothing to do with Papa. She declared she never wanted to see him again. He, in turn, felt the same way, or so it seemed to everyone.

More and more I missed my sister. Things just were not the same since she had gone. Now there was nobody to scratch my back at night just before going to bed, no one to kneel down with to say evening prayers, no one to share jokes and stories, no one to help me wash and dry the dishes, and, above all, one less person to look at me with eyes shining with love and pride whenever I brought home a nice drawing or a report card full of A's. Of course, my brothers showed care and concern and there was still Mama around to love me and who thought I was wonderful, but my sister Caroline was special. We missed her terribly. She made us laugh a lot. It was like a light had gone out somewhere in the house and we were always trying to find it and turn it back on. Nobody talked about it very much. Gradually, we learned to accommodate ourselves to the big empty space she left. I eagerly looked forward to the day when I could go and visit her where she lived, but I had no idea when that would ever be. Thanksgiving and Christmas were especially trying for me since Caroline, more than anyone else, had always made those holidays, especially Christmas, really beautiful and memorable. We adjusted and life went on.

It seemed to take forever, but spring came again. I heard Papa say that some of the boarders who had come to the farm for many years were now going elsewhere, to fancier places, like the Catskills, on their vacations. Their rooms, therefore, would be available for others. Strangely enough, we adjusted quickly to the fact that fewer and different boarders were planning to summer on the farm. Though we missed our "regulars", the changes were not as sharply felt as we expected. Somehow, the world did not end, though I felt it would, if the same boarders were not coming up in droves any longer.

Since we were now into the 1940s, times were different and life on the farm was different, perhaps because the revenue the boarders had provided was no longer as necessary for survival, perhaps because all of us were growing up and growing older, perhaps because times had altered drastically, and attitudes had changed along with them. The war had caused the price of apples and other agricultural products to skyrocket! Thus, the farm prospered even more. The negative aspects of the war had not affected us in any painful or personal way. Benny had been granted a deferment because he was a farmer. That ended our fears of his going off to battle and being killed. Rationing was no great sacrifice since we had lots of meat and eggs and could even make our own butter. Sugar and gas were a small problem, but our farm had gas stamps for the farm machinery and, sometimes, in a pinch, they were used for personal travel. Joey, the youngest of my brothers, kept threatening to join the Navy but was too young when the war started. He eventually did join, despite Papa's objections.

Less than a year after leaving the farm, Caroline joined the USO and was immediately sent overseas to entertain our troops. She traveled to Europe, Africa, and the Middle East. While entertaining, she was often very close to the front lines. She even survived two plane crashes. We were very proud of her and, much to our surprise and delight, the people in the village of New Paltz were proud of her. They gave her a parade when she came home from overseas for a family visit. You wonder how Papa responded to her return? He welcomed his "hero" daughter with open arms and they embraced. He was so pleased and proud of her accomplishments, and well he should be. It was a relief to have Caroline back as part of the family. It was also my first real experience with the fact that people do not always mean what they say, no matter how vehemently they say it!

chapter 26

The Last Summer

That first summer without my sister seemed even more strange than not having her around for the holidays. My earlier concerns about her absence were proven correct. I had to take on even more chores now that there was only Mama and me. All of the "female" work on the farm fell on our shoulders. And there was more than enough to go around. We worked sunrise to sunset.

The summer that I was twelve, strange, ominous feelings pervaded my being. They made me feel that nameless changes were about to take place. I was suddenly more aware of things I had not heeded as keenly as before. Fussing with my hair a lot more, I even suffered sleeping on metal curlers! Using some perfume my sister had left behind I started dousing myself with it, each time I left for school. After bathing, I reveled in patting dusting powder all over my body with a big powder puff. (I actually spent some of my hoarded money on a large round box of talcum powder that had a big lamb's wool puff.) Much of my time was spent decorating my bedroom, often painting and repainting the furniture. I read *Seventeen Magazine* which saw publication the year I was twelve.

It was my favorite reading matter despite the fact that its influence on me was not always positive. It did nothing for my self-image since 99% of the models were tall, blue-eyed, and light-haired. I wondered where I fit in, only five feet tall, with jet black hair, olive skin, and dark-brown eyes. I cannot remember ever seeing a raven-haired girl in the important, color sections of the magazine. In the small ads in the back part, occasionally there was a girl pictured who had black hair. (*Seventeen* had not changed when, in 1968, my daughter started reading it. Blondes were still in the great majority.) Despite the magazine's neglect of my "type", I faithfully followed their instructions. Somehow I managed not only to survive but to become obsessed. I became overly concerned about my hair, my posture, make-up (which I had to "sneak on" once I left the house. Papa forbade make-up), and clothes. I sewed most of those myself, making my own patterns, just as Mama had taught me. I was not aware that one could actually buy patterns, until my friend Gerry Jamiolkowski told me about them.

Dolls were no longer of interest to me, and boys became even more important than before. In fact, they were suddenly the most important concern of all. Irrevocable forces of nature were at work; that part of nature that brings on adolescence. I was vaguely aware that subtle changes were taking place, transforming my body and my hormones. I was a pre-adolescent female in the first throes of puberty and on my way down the long road to maturity. The one conclusive thing that clinched it occurred that August.

It was a hot, humid day and I was riding my bike over the bumpy and pebble-strewn Jenkinstown road, returning from a visit with my friend, Lucille Miller. Pedaling up a hill made me sweat profusely and my bicycle seat, especially, felt extremely wet. It was an unusually hot day so it did not seem strange that I should be sweating so much that even my thighs felt sweaty. I could feel the moisture seeping down my leg. When the wetness did not evaporate once I hit flat ground and was no longer straining, and since I had never before perspired in that way, I became curious. Pulling off the road and stopping, I got off my bike and looked down to where

I felt moist. You can imagine my horror when I saw blood oozing out and trickling down my inner thighs from somewhere inside my blood-stained shorts!

For a moment, I stood petrified with fear! Searching my memory, I tried to recall if I had hit a bump somewhere and that it had somehow caused the bleeding. No, I was sure I had not! Frightened, I jumped back on my bike and pedaled home as fast as I could. I flew like the wind and even pumped the bike all the way up the hill of the driveway! (I normally had to jump off and walk the bike up.) At the front porch, I came to a screeching halt. Driveway pebbles scattered as I braked. Jumping off, I let the bike fall where I had stopped, the rear wheel still spinning. Taking the stairs two at a time, I ran up, entered the hallway, and started yelling, *"Mama, Mama, oh Mama mia, mi strupiavu, mi strupiavu!"* (Mama, Mama, oh Mother of mine, I hurt myself, I hurt myself!) Hearing the fear in my voice, my mother rushed out of the kitchen, drying her hands on her apron, her face white with anxiety.

"Che ti su'chithi? Che cos' a fatto? A dolori? Fami vididi uni ti strupiasti." (What happened? What did you do? Do you have pain? Let me see where you hurt yourself.)

While standing there I suddenly was aware of where the blood was *actually* coming from. I stood very still and looked down. I was so ashamed. Mortified, I watched my mother's reaction as I slowly crooked my knee to one side so that my upper thigh was visible. I stared at it warily then looked at Mama with apprehension as she watch a thin stream of blood course slowly, very slowly down my leg. The worried look suddenly left her face and she started to laugh. A high gleeful sound, a laugh filled with joy and delight. Indignant, I straightened my leg and scowled at her.

"Mama, Mama, what'sa matter with you? Maa? Are you crazy or som'th'n? I'm bleeding, cant'cha see I'm bleeding and from what I don't even know and you're laughing at me. What is it? How come you're laughing?"

Mama then reached out, pulled me very close, and hugged me hard. I was suddenly aware that it had been a long time since Mama had taken me into her ample arms in this way.

It was a delicious feeling to be held with such love and affection. Mama held me tightly and stroked my hair as she put her cheek close to mine. Then she kissed the top of my head and sighed a soft, long sigh.

Holding me at arms length, she looked deep into my eyes. We both stared intently at one another for a long moment. My mother's light reddish brown eyes locked into mine, those dark, almost black, brown eyes I had inherited from my father.

"Ah, figlia mia, si cresceiuta, ora si cresceiuta!" (Ah, daughter of mine, you are grown, now you are grown!) She kissed me gently on both cheeks. Taking my hand, she led me into the bathroom. In Sicilian she said, "First, take off those bloody clothes and wash yourself. Meanwhile, I'll get some clean rags and make you something to use until we get to the store to buy you some Kotex. You are now a young lady and what has happened to you is what happens to all women when they reach a certain age. You are no longer a little girl. Now you are a woman. This will happen every month. It will last sometimes two, sometimes three days, and sometimes even for a week. It depends on you and what kind of body you have. So, now, clean up, and I'll be right back. Don't worry, this will not kill you. It's really just a pain in the neck, but we all live through it."

With that my mother turned and left the bathroom, closing the door firmly behind her. As I stood there, still in shock over what had just occurred, strange feelings engulfed me. I shook my head in consternation and disbelief. I couldn't believe all this "stuff" was really happening. I thought to myself "Good God. Here I thought it was the end of the world when the war began! Then Caroline left and now look at this! Look at what's happening now. An' there's no Caroline to share it with and to ask questions of." So many came to mind. I knew that Mama either could not or would not answer them because what had just happened involved that "taboo" part of my body. I was certain it was futile to even ask.

As I got undressed and then washed, I realized that what had just occurred was a real turning point in my life. Now I was truly no longer anybody's "baby" sister. I also knew that things would never again be as they were before.

While I did my chores and walked around the farm that day, I was constantly aware of the discomfort of the thickly folded, torn piece of bedsheet cloth between my legs. Certain that it made a huge bulge that was visible in the crotch of my slacks, I was convinced that it was discernable to everyone who saw me. All the boarder ladies smiled broadly and made warm, clucking and "ahh" sounds when I passed by. Some giggled and waved.

That night, when I removed Papa's shoes, his eyes were warm and had a soft look about them. He smiled at me gently. I knew then that even he knew and knowing that everybody knew, made me feel both proud and uncomfortable at the same time. There was an awareness, and sorrow mixed with joy, that finally I was leaving childhood behind. It came as a surprise that it took no real effort on my part. I was simply joining the many women who had traveled the path now before me.

Yes, I was of Sicilian extraction and had grown up as such, learning the ancient ways. But I was also an American, living in modern America, facts, too, that had shaped my growth and would continue to do so. That evening, poised on the brink of a new and different stage of life, I went to fetch Papa his slippers. As I carried them back to him, I wondered what other changes were in store for me. There were to be very, very many. Looking back now, I can see that not only did I grow up Sicilian and female, I actually survived it.

Mama's Sicilian Recipes

Frankies "Garlic Balls" (meatballs, polpette) & Sauce

To each pound of ground beef (may be mixed with pork and veal) add:
    one cup plain breadcrumbs
    1/2 cup chopped parsley (preferably Italian)
    two eggs
    1/2 cup grated cheese: romano or pecorino
    five large cloves garlic, sliced thin
    two to three tablespoons water
    about 1 tsp, or to taste:
    1/4 tsp black pepper
    1/4 tsp sugar
    pinch of basil

Mix thoroughly, squeezing through fingers and combining ingredients well by hand. Shape by *gently* rolling a small handful of mixture between palms. Do NOT press or squeeze together or meatballs will be hard. Use as much or as little of the mixture to achieve the size meatball desired. Use your own judgement.

These meatballs make a wonderful spagetti sauce if you do the following:
    pour approximately 1/8 inch olive oil in large skillet (10") heat gently for a few minutes and then add;
        6 cloves of freshly sliced garlic
        two medium sized onions, finely sliced
    saute until wilted and light tan in color (use medium heat)
        Pour into large, 6 qt. pot (NOT aluminum), simmer it. Meanwhile, add oil to skillet and heat, brown meatballs, as many at a time as fit. When pale golden on two sides, add to 6 qt. pot, add two large cans crushed tomatoes and two small cans Hunts, or whatever, tomato sauce. Stir in:
        1/2 tsp basil (or 1 tsp fresh basil, chopped)
        pinch of oregano, crushed with fingers as added
        1/4 tsp sugar
        1 tsp salt,(or to taste)
        a few flakes of red or black pepper (to taste)
Stir gently and let simmer for 3/4s to 1 1/2 hour. Serve over favorite pasta, cooked al dente and sprinkle with grated cheese, your favorite kind. I like pecorino. This should be enough for 2 lbs pasta, of any kind.

Mama's Lentil Soup

Beware this soup. Once you serve it, *everyone* will want the recipe. It is simple, inexpensive, delicious and nutritious. Make it early on a Saturday morning, let it simmer for a few hours and it will reward you as a wonderful lunch. Especially if accompanied by a loaf of hot Italian bread and your favorite wine, of any color.

Fill a 6 qt. pot (not aluminum, unless its Calphalon) within three inches of the top with water.
    set on range and turn on heat.
Peel four large cloves garlic, trim off stem end,
    add to water, whole, do not cut or slice

Sort and rinse one bag of lentils (they are pretty well processed today, so eliminate the sorting part unless you are fussy)
    add lentils to gently boiling water, lower to simmer.
Meanwhile:
    Carefully wash a 1 1/2 to 2 1/2 head of escarole, separating the leaves and rinsing it two or three times. Discard black or discolored leaves. When clean of silt,
        cut into two inch chunks
When lentils have simmered for two hours,
Add:
    cleaned, cut escarole to simmering pot
    add enough salt to cover your palm (about two tablespoons otherwise.)
    Let simmer gently for 1/2 hour

    add 1 1/2 cups mixed pastas,
    elbows
    spaghetti in 2" pieces
    orzo
    vermicelli in 2" pieces or whatever leftover small pastas you might have on hand.

When pasta is cooked to your taste, soft or al dente, turn off heat. Drizzle 1 to 2 tablespoons good olive oil into soup. With side of a spoon, crush floating garlic heads against side of pot. Stir the whole thing together and serve hot, warm or cold, with or without bread. Grated cheese adds another dimension.

Cuderunni

These can be addictive. Have them for breakfast once, and you will want to make them everyday for the next week. At least that is what my friends, who have tried them, have told me. They are light and airy, but probably sinful in calories and fat.

Use the following reciepe for basic dough or, do what I do. Go to the frozen sections in your favorite market and buy any frozen white bread or pizza dough. Better yet, go to your favorite bakery and buy one lb. of fresh bread dough. You can freeze it. Take it out the night before you plan to use it. By morning it should be twice its size and ready to use. Store unused portion in the fridge.

Set 10" frypan on range and set heat to medium/low

Remove dough from wrapper;
    cut pieces approximately 2" x 3"
    holding dough between finger, squeeze and gently pull to make flat oblong shapes about 3" x 4".
Oil should be hot before frying these "cakes"
    if heated while you shape dough, after the first cake is shaped, oil should be hot enough. You may have to experiment, the first one is like your first pancake (and some say your first child).
    Test by putting one cuderruni in, if it sizzles its OK
Fry three pieces of dough, or whatever number fits uncrowded until golden on one side and puffy on top. Turn over with tongs and press down immediatly if it starts to puff up unevenly. Hold just a moment, then let go. After both sides have browned evenly (once on each side), drain on paper towel. Sprinkle plain or cinnamon, granulated sugar (lightly) on surfaces and serve.

These make a delightful and satisfying breakfast. They can be split and filled with jam or honey. They could probably be used in place of bread. Use your imagination and enjoy.

Should you relish these recipes, look for my next book, which should be one on ancient and authentic Sicilian recipes. The lentil soup recipe is definitely ancient.

To order a copy of this book, please fill out order form and send a check or money order for total (do not send cash). Be sure to print. Make check payable to: Penzato Enterprises, and mail to:

Penzato Enterprises
Box 582
Highland, N.Y. 12528

------------------- cut on dotted line --------------------

Please send _____ copy(s) of "Growing Up Sicilian and Female"

@ $14.95 copy to:

Name _____

Address _____

_____

State _____ Zip _____

(Please print, this is your mailing label)

Number ordered: _____ X $14.95 .... $_____

Postage and handling .... $2.50 first, $2.00 each addtl. $_____

Taxes where applicable .... $_____

TOTAL .... $_____

Please allow 4 to 6 weeks for delivery. Order will be shipped immediately.

To order a copy of this book, please fill out order form and send a check or money order for total (do not send cash). Be sure to print. Make check payable to: Penzato Enterprises, and mail to:

Penzato Enterprises
Box 582
Highland, N.Y. 12528

-------------------- cut on dotted line --------------------

Please send _____ copy(s) of "Growing Up Sicilian and Female"

@ $14.95 copy to:

Name _____

Address _____

_____

State _____ Zip _____

(Please print, this is your mailing label)

Number ordered: _____ X $14.95 .... $_____

Postage and handling .... $2.50 first, $2.00 each addtl. $_____

Taxes where applicable .... $_____

TOTAL .... $_____

Please allow 4 to 6 weeks for delivery. Order will be shipped immediately.